Praise for
Unbalanced Influence

"*Hammett supports his case for effective leadership with sound research as well as with clear, practical advice on what senior executives can do not only to live with paradox, but also to harness it to their advantage and that of their firm. I strongly recommend this book to anyone who aspires to a senior leadership role.*"

—**JOHN ALEXANDER**, PRESIDENT,
CENTER FOR CREATIVE LEADERSHIP

"*Hammett's wonderful concoction of data, insights, and wisdom results in a delightful stew that is delicious and nutritious and will make you feel ambitious! It will give you the nutrients you need to grab the next rung on your effective leadership ladder, and it is my bet that you'll enjoy the meal!*"

—**DENNIS QUAINTANCE**, CEO,
QUAINTANCE-WEAVER RESTAURANTS AND HOTELS

"*A fresh look at how executive leadership can influence the productivity, sustainability, and well-being of organizations through an effective use of power. Hammett's skillful and articulate rendering provides essential insights for balancing successful leadership credibility while strategically expanding a leader's sphere of influence.*"

—**JIM HENDERSON**, NATIONALLY RECOGNIZED LEADER
IN THE DEFENSE INDUSTRY

"If you want to improve your leadership effectiveness and create a healthy organization, this book is a must read. Whether you are a senior leader or just beginning to develop as a leader, you will find real value in the principles Hammett presents."

—**BRUCE E. WINSTON,** PHD, DEAN, SCHOOL OF GLOBAL
LEADERSHIP & ENTREPRENEURSHIP, REGENT UNIVERSITY

UNBALANCED
INFLUENCE

UNBALANCED
INFLUENCE

Recognizing and Resolving the
—— Impact of Myth and Paradox ——
in Executive Performance

PETE HAMMETT

DAVIES-BLACK PUBLISHING
MOUNTAIN VIEW, CALIFORNIA

Published by Davies-Black Publishing, a division of CPP, Inc., 1055 Joaquin Road, 2nd Floor, Mountain View, CA 94043; 800-624-1765.

Special discounts on bulk quantities of Davies-Black books are available to corporations, professional associations, and other organizations. For details, contact the Director of Marketing and Sales at Davies-Black Publishing: 650-691-9123; fax 650-623-9271.

Visit the Davies-Black Publishing Web site at www.daviesblack.com.

Printed in the United States of America.

11 10 09 08 07   10 9 8 7 6 5 4 3 2 1

Library of Congress Cataloging-in-Publication Data
Hammett, Pete
    Unbalanced influence : recognizing and resolving the impact of myth and paradox in executive performance / Pete Hammett. — 1st ed.
        p. cm.
    Includes bibliographical references.
    ISBN 978-0-89106-218-9 (hard cover)
    1. Executives. 2. Executive ability. 3. Leadership. I. Title.
    HD38.2.H347 2007
    658.4—dc22

2007007433

FIRST EDITION
First printing 2007

To my dad, John, and father-in-law, Cliff—
two men who taught me the importance of
asking questions and listening to the answers.
You continue to be a source of strength,
learning, and support.

Contents

Preface

It has been suggested that we live in the "Era of Execution," where strategies and organizations are measured solely by their ability to perform (Neilson, Pasternack, and Mendes 2003, 1). This plays out on a regular basis, as board and market intolerance for underperformance force turnover and downgrade valuations (Hay Group 2003, 1). This Era of Execution allots no points for original thought; it ascribes no credit for the effort committed. The drive to achieve bottom-line results and improve time-to-market has yielded a maniacal focus on hitting numbers and meeting Wall Street expectations. The pressure on executives to produce quick results is reflected in the many high-profile missteps from senior executives at companies such as Enron, Tyco, WorldCom, and others. But are profit and contribution margins the only things that distinguish the effective from the ineffective executive?

In connection with these issues, a number of better questions come to mind:

- Is an effective executive's decision-making process values based or results oriented?

- Can an effective executive be grounded in day-to-day business objectives while simultaneously focusing on future opportunities?

- Can effective executive leadership be measured through hitting performance metrics? Or does performance need to encompass a greater good to be truly effective?

- And—most intriguing—what influence does an executive really exert over an organization's effectiveness (or are executives simply along for the ride)?

Based on extensive observation, I believe that multiple influencers shape people's behavior and perceptions in their struggle to be effective leaders. And these influencers often seem unbalanced—encumbered with countless paradoxes or misguided myths. Even more problematic is that for many executives, the perception of what constitutes effective leadership has been shaped by a relatively narrow sphere of influence— that is, the way executives choose to lead and the benchmarks they use for defining effective leadership are shaped by a limited, often conflicting set of influencers. With a better awareness of these influencers, it becomes possible to bring balance to the way leadership scholars and practicing leaders alike define (and perhaps shape) effective executive leadership.

THINGS TO KEEP IN MIND

In the search for answers to the questions listed above, several other questions become relevant: Who are executive leaders? What are influences? And what is the definition of effectiveness?

Who Are Executive Leaders?

Over the course of its thirty-five-year history, the Center for Creative Leadership® (CCL®) has had remarkable access to countless executive leaders throughout the world. The body of knowledge derived from this access to executive leaders serves as a grounding point for framing questions and observations for this book.

The group regarded as senior executives for my purposes here includes what is often referred to as the "C-level": the "chief" titles, including CEO, CFO, CIO, COO, and the rest, and also the corporate or division presidents. The data reported here are drawn from insights CCL has gained over the past several years working with executives attending its Leadership at the Peak programs. Specifically, the database comprises input on more than seventy C-level executives as well as feedback on the performance of these senior executives from more than seven hundred bosses, peers, and subordinates. Specific sources for this body of knowledge include an analysis of the empirical data embedded in CCL's data repositories on C-level executives, collected by instruments such as the *Campbell™ Organizational Survey* (COS®) and the *Campbell™ Leadership Index* (CLI®),* as well as the MBTI®, FIRO-B®, and CCL *Executive Dimensions* assessments, which together provide an overview of the personality preferences, interpersonal interactions, personal characteristics, and leadership competencies of executive leaders.

What Are Influences?

It is also helpful to understand how "influence" is defined in this book. To begin with, consider the way Yukl chooses to define leadership (2002, 7; emphasis added): "Leadership is the process of *influencing* others to understand and agree about what needs to be done and how it can be done effectively, and the process of *facilitating* individual and collective efforts to *accomplish* the shared objective."

I highlight three key words in this definition to draw attention to my approach to effective executive leadership. *Facilitation* speaks plainly to "getting things done" and can be measured in work effort, while *accomplishment* suggests tangible results coming from the effort.

Influencing, on the other hand, is somewhat soft; it connotes *how* executives go about directing others in the engagement of a shared

*CLI and COS are registered trademarks and Campbell is a trademark of David P. Campbell, PhD.

objective. Within this definition of leadership, Yukl further highlights several key processes where leaders attempt to exert influence such as setting strategy, motivation, talent development, and stakeholder management. So while it may be easy to envision how executives will influence others in achieving a shared objective, the critical question to be addressed is what inputs and processes influence executives as they attempt to lead their organizations? For example, what sources of data will an executive consider (or ignore) when making a decision? What motivates an executive to put in time on one activity or initiative at the expense of another? Who does the executive look to for advice (or ignore)—and why? Most important, how do executives balance these multiple influencers—those inputs and processes that impact how they lead?

Answering this question begins with considering leadership, and particularly executive leadership, as a multi-dimensional phenomenon that makes it necessary to "analyze leaders' relations to their contexts and to the outcomes in light of a configuration of influences" (Meyer, Tsui, and Hinings 1993, 1189). In simpler terms, a great many factors come into play as executives seek to lead their organizations—and it is not only necessary to grasp these factors but also to consider how they interact in concert or context with one another.

Illustrations for this point come from data collected by CCL in its work with C-level executives. The collection makes it possible to distill several key influencers that shape how executives approach their leadership positions, along with both paradoxes and myths that often cloud or confuse how executives engage others in accomplishing critical objectives. These paradoxes often reflect a struggle for executives as they seek to balance competing demands and pressures. More problematic, however, are the embedded myths that encumber executives with a misconception of the actions and methods they should employ as they seek to move their organizations forward. On the following page are summaries of the myths and paradoxes presented in this book.

What Is Effectiveness?

Finally, it is worth taking a moment to put a stake in the ground and specify a definition of leadership effectiveness. The perception of what

MYTHS	
Power, Influence, and the Myth of Effective Leadership	While power and influence are tools for leading, the way these tools are used colors our perceptions regarding the nature of effective leadership.
Myth of Effective Decision Making	To counteract the traditional top-down executive mandates, senior executives need to create an environment that not only encourages multiple scenarios and alternative solutions but also acknowledges that the only bad decision is the one not made.
Intuition, Analytics, and the Myth of "Elegant Reasoning"	Compelling strategies are those that emerge through both intuitive thought (elegant reasoning) and careful analytical consideration in discerning the best path to follow.
PARADOXES	
Values, Ethics, and the Performance Paradox	The performance paradox confronts executives as they weigh two distinct ROI calculations: return on investment and risk of incarceration.
Creativity, Innovation, and the Operational Excellence Paradox	For an innovative organization to thrive competitively it must build infrastructure and processes to facilitate delivery of goods and services at a compelling value. However, the resulting operational processes are often what constrain the creative energies that lead to the organization's success.
Gifted Leadership's Paradox of Developing Future Leaders	Senior executives gifted in leadership may be unable to develop leaders under them. This may lead to a challenge in developing an organization's next generation of leaders.
The Paradox of Balance in Work and Life	Executives are drawn toward areas where they have the most visible and immediate rewards—specifically work—and shy away from areas whose rewards may be more long-term in materializing (such as family life). How executives identify and respond to this imbalance is critical to their own lives and to their organizations.

defines *effective* leadership is as broad and varying as that of leadership itself. Clearly there is a distinction between leadership effectiveness and organizational effectiveness. Organizational effectiveness is concerned with the assessment of multiple stakeholder groups such as owners, stockholders, customers, and employees—and is evaluated by the extent to which stated outcomes are achieved (market share, stock price, and the like; Daft 2004, 23, 66). However, in the context of C-level executives, is it really feasible to separate organization and leadership effectiveness? In other words, if the organization is effective, doesn't it follow that the executives running the organization are effective leaders?

Once again, Yukl speaks to the topic of leadership effectiveness: "The selection of appropriate criteria depends on the objectives and values of the person making the evaluation" (2002, 7). In other words, effectiveness is often in the eyes of the beholder.

To counter this problem, Yukl recommends outlining multiple effectiveness criteria and examining the impact of the leader on each criterion over time. Anthony Rucci, VP and chief administrative officer of Cardinal Health, helps focus our attention on these multiple criteria by highlighting three common traits of effective senior executives (Silzer 2002, 25):

- **Passion.** They have personal passion for their work—so much passion that if they hit the lottery, they'd keep doing what they're doing now.

- **Performance.** They are very competitive and absolutely hate to lose. They hold themselves and others to very high standards.

- **Principle.** They live by the mantra that what is accomplished is nothing without consideration for how it is accomplished.

In thinking through these insights, I've come to regard *executive leadership effectiveness* as the ability of executives to balance the influencers outlined in the list of myths and paradoxes while achieving a measure of success associated with the typical organizational effectiveness metrics (ROE, shareholder value, and the rest). In a real sense, Hackman and Johnson's definition of team effectiveness (2000, 262) can apply equally to executive leadership effectiveness: "The realization of organizational outcomes [consumables/services] that meet the quality standards of its market while ensuring that the long-term sustainability of the organization is enhanced and the general well-being of the organization's workforce is ensured." With a little embellishment, this also defines effective executive leadership as comprising three equal components: *producing desired results, ensuring long-term sustainability,* and *enhancing the well-being of the workforce.*

FORMAT OF THE BOOK

Each chapter deals with one myth or paradox from the list presented earlier, along with the associated influencers, and adheres to the following general plan:

- After a brief introduction to the main topic, the chapter summarizes views of relevant research to add clarity and insight to applicable issues and challenges.

- Next it outlines the insights CCL has gained in working with C-level executives, reviewing assessment data regarding the personality preferences, interpersonal interactions, personal characteristics, and leadership competencies these executive leaders display.

- Observations related to executive influencers then bring real-life examples and outstanding questions to the foreground.

- The "Call to Action" section highlights key points of the research and data reviewed in the preceding sections and suggests what executives can do to become more effective in the specific competency.

- Finally, I offer my own "Personal Reflection" and insights.

INSIGHT FROM ASKING QUESTIONS

While suggested calls to action and points to consider pepper the pages of this book, the driving goal is to to be both insightful and inciting. Readers are encouraged to reflect on the rich data gathered by CCL and the wide range of experiences it has had in working with executives. Further, readers are challenged to consider and answer tough questions—prompting them to ask even more in-depth questions. This cycle of asking questions and listening to answers, leading to more questions, is captured beautifully in Halcolm's epistemological parable of the three students (Patton 1990, 277–278) paraphrased below:

> Wanting to broaden the education and experience of his students Halcolm chose three of his best pupils and sent them on a journey across the province to observe villagers at the various markets. Upon their return, Halcolm asked them what they had learned.
>
> The first student observed the similarity in each market he visited—villagers came, bought, socialized, and left. Thus, the student proclaimed, "All things are ultimately the same from place to place."
>
> The second student likewise noted similar activities in the various markets and had gleaned that life is all about coming and going in search of the basics of life—no more, no less.
>
> The last student was very reserved. "My mind is full of questions," he said humbly. "I wonder where the villagers came from and what are they thinking and feeling. Why did they come to a particular village, and who did they leave behind and who and why someone may have come with them. In the end I am more filled with questions and I'm unsure of what I have learned."
>
> Halcolm smiled at the last student and said, "You have learned the most of all—the value of asking questions and listening to what people say."

This is the goal of *Unbalanced Influence*—to make observations, to ask questions, and to listen to the answers, and in so doing perhaps find more compelling questions that will help us further our learning and understanding of the influencers, unbalanced as they may be, that shape executives' perception of effective leadership and in the end help leaders attain better balance.

Acknowledgments

There's an episode of *Everybody Loves Raymond* where after receiving a prestigious award for his work, Ray proceeds to acknowledge those people who had been most influential in his life. True to form, Ray forgets one of the most important people in his life—his wife. This, of course, is great comedy—if you're watching it unfold for someone else. It is paralyzing when it's your turn to acknowledge those whose influence has been invaluable to you. I've also been witness to more than one post-project review where the fear of forgetting to acknowledge *all* the key contributors has influenced a leader to opt for not acknowledging *any* contributors.

So now I have the challenge of wrestling with the fear of omission as I strive to recount all those who provided invaluable support, insight, and guidance on this work. And while I'm not as clever, funny, or witty as Ray Barone, no doubt I'll suffer the same fate—forgetting someone of extreme importance. Nevertheless, here goes . . .

This work clearly would not have been possible were it not for the support, encouragement, and guidance of my peers and colleagues at the Center for Creative Leadership (CCL). Perhaps one of the greatest strengths of CCL is its ability to facilitate the convergence around the science and practice of leadership. In practical terms, how this science/practice dynamic plays out is quite remarkable, as the Center constantly balances and encourages the tension between assertions supported by research and applicability supported by workable actions that apply in a leader's day-to-day life. So my role at CCL is that of a "practicing leader"—that is, my day job actually involves leading others, about fifty others in fact, in the work of CCL's contact center and back-office operations. In that I'm neither a researcher by training nor faculty by trade, you might think that I'd receive some quarter from the researchers and faculty at CCL who provided feedback on this book. But in reality, as a practitioner, my ideas and notions receive the same scrutiny and challenge as those of anyone else. And if I were to list all the people at CCL who have helped shape my thinking around *Unbalanced Influence,* I'd have to attach the CCL employee directory. Hardly a day goes by at CCL that some conversation (or argument) doesn't ensue around a critical leadership concept.

Still, I do want to single out a few CCL'ers who've pushed me to advance the ideas outlined in this book. Specifically, Drs. Ellen Van Velsor and Gina Hernez-Broome provided a wealth of insight and feedback as they sat on my dissertation committee, enduring a number of debates and revisions. Likewise, Michael Campbell was a lifesaver in helping to gather the various psychometric data on C-level executives attending CCL's program. And then there are my friends at CCL who've allowed me the airtime and space to bounce ideas around and offered their unique perspectives. This group includes Sara King, Sylvester Taylor, Roger Conway, and Cile Johnson. I have also found remarkable insights from multiple conversations with Drs. Rich Hughes and Kate Beatty, whose work on building strategic leaders opened my eyes to the myth of "elegant reasoning." This is true also for Stan Gryskiewicz and David Horth, whose work and research on the topic of creativity continue to fascinate me. And clearly this book would have been impossible were it not for the support from Martin Wilcox and Kelly Lombardino, whose understanding of the publication process provided invaluable guidance during the editing process.

Then there is Lil Kelly, CCL's EVP for global leadership development. Here is a story I've not shared until now. Prior to coming on board as an employee, I was providing technology consulting to CCL. During this time I had the opportunity to sit in on a debriefing for CCL's planned entry into Asia via Singapore. The question was asked as to why CCL wanted to move into Asia. A number of well-reasoned responses emerged, such as Asia's potential market and CCL's aspirations to expand globally. While Lil acknowledged these as positive goals, in her mind there were two overriding motivators that influenced why CCL would build a presence in Asia. First, CCL clearly has something to share with Asian leaders on the understanding, practice, and development of leadership. However, more important for Lil was that there were insights on leading in Asia that CCL needed to learn, and the only way we would learn them would be to go to Asia. It was at that moment I decided I wanted to find a way to work for CCL.

Tom Hanks tells the story that, during the making of *Philadelphia*, he learned so much from watching Denzel Washington that it continues to influence his approach to acting to this day. I share this sentiment in relation to Dave Altman, CCL's SVP of research and innovation. Dave has an uncanny ability to encourage and challenge almost in the same sentence. I continue to learn a great deal about the practice of leadership by watching Dave motivate and encourage CCL to live up to its middle name (Creative).

During the final phase of my doctoral work and the genesis of this book, I had the opportunity to report directly to CCL's president, John Alexander. A journalist and newspaper editor by trade, John was a finalist in 1979 for the Pulitzer prize in editorial writing. So I was a bit nervous approaching John about my idea to publish this book. But John proved to be a great source of encouragement, and I will always appreciate his support in this effort.

It would be a major misstep on my part not to mention the talented people I've had the privilege of leading the past four years at CCL: the

Client & Assessments Services Group. I heard Lou Holtz comment that when he was offered the head coaching position at Notre Dame he was told by the school, "We can make you the coach—but the team will make you their leader." The forty-five-plus members of the Client Services team have graciously allowed me to be their leader. They have endured my many, many stories and have kindly tolerated my foibles. I especially want to mention the Client Services Management team, whose members have been remarkably patient as I tested out my various leadership theories on them; and my Senior Leadership team—Sylvia Burgess, Tina Cockman, and Shannon Cranford—who often came to my aid to bring reason and reality to my many other wild ideas.

Outside CCL I received invaluable support from our friends at CPP, Inc., specifically Nancy Schaubhut, who was extremely helpful in running the group MBTI® and FIRO-B® reports. And perhaps one of the people most responsible for this book being published by Davies-Black is Amy Ferris. Amy is one of the best relationship managers I've encountered. I first approached Amy for help at CPP in producing the group C-level reports. During this conversation I casually mentioned to Amy that I was hopeful the insights from this data would evolve into a publication. Amy immediately asked if I had a publisher in mind, and at that time a specific publisher hadn't even crossed my mind. Within two days Amy had me on the phone with Davies-Black Publishing, and the rest is history. Which brings me to Connie Kallback at Davies-Black. Connie was a godsend for me on this work. She guided me through the many revisions and offered incredible critique on the work. The strength of the work, including its layout, readability, and impact, is a direct result of Connie's fine-tuning.

I also want to acknowledge the support of our friends at Pearson Performance Solutions, and in particular Dr. Joe Orban and Dawn Allen, who ran multiple group reports of the CLI® and COS® data. The partnership between Pearson and CCL over the years has been extremely valuable and continues to grow to this day.

I owe a tremendous debt of gratitude to faculty and staff at Regent University. Over the course of the three and a half years I was immersed in the strategic leader doctoral program, I learned so much from professors such as Corne Bekker, Jacque King, and Tedd Simmons. And I doubt I will ever forget Dr. Bruce Winston's many admonishments, including "No opinions until your third year"; "Make your point in 200 words or less"; and "Give me a paper I can learn from!" I also formed lifelong friendships with peers such as Jim Henderson at Raytheon and Col. Cynthia Islin and Luann Brodbeck at Pilkington, who continue to challenge and shape how I view leadership.

If Jim Collins were to ask me for examples of what he calls Level 5 leaders, leaders whose humility and compassion constantly place others ahead of themselves, I would point him to Paul Bonitatibus and Dennis Quaintance. Paul is senior EVP of Capital One (formerly Hibernia Bank) in Louisiana, and he lives and works in New Orleans. I've had the opportunity to observe Paul's leadership pre- and post-Katrina. Paul has many passions in his life: his family, coworkers, New Orleans, and Notre Dame. With all the trappings that might ordinarily go to someone's head, Paul is perhaps one of the most unassuming senior leaders I have met. I had the opportunity to partner with him in training a group of MBA students at Notre Dame on leadership. With all the demands on Paul's time, the fact that he'd freely give his time to up-and-coming leaders was remarkable. Not to mention that Paul personally introduced me to Lou Holtz.

Dennis Quaintance is a principal partner and owner of several widely successful hotels and restaurants in North Carolina. I once heard a group of CCL clients as they were deciding what restaurant to frequent. They were staying in Dennis's hotel, and as they ran through the list of restaurant options, someone noted that one particular restaurant was owned by the same person who owned the hotel where they were staying. The decision was made—any restaurant run by the same person running their hotel had to be great. Dennis doesn't just have a passion for his customers; I truly believe if he could, he'd have each and every customer to his home for coffee. Dennis tells a great story that reflects this personal connection he has with customers. Dennis was walking through one of his restaurants when a long-time customer, an elderly woman, grabbed him by the arm and told him that the rice she was served was the worse she had ever eaten. He calmly shared with her that what she had received wasn't rice but *riso,* which is more like pasta. The woman paused and took another bite, then pleasingly looked at him and said, "Dennis, this is the best pasta I've ever had."

Finally, as you will see in the book, I draw on several experiences I had while working at American Express and ILC Dover (manufacturer of the shuttle space suits). As with CCL, there are so many people at Amex and ILC that I'd want to acknowledge, but there's simply not enough space. So allow me simply to thank the many colleagues and friends who've over the years allowed me to lead and to learn, to laugh and cry, and best of all, to share countless incredible experiences.

And lest I pull a "Ray Barone," I absolutely can't forget my greatest source of encouragement and support, my wife, Debbie. Debbie has patiently endured four years of doctoral studies that entailed several residencies at Regent University, many trips away from home, countless sleepless nights, and an unending barrage of "Hey, did you know…" observations from me whenever I came across a new insight or learning. Debbie is one of the most brilliant and insightful people I know and is well suited to both challenging and supporting me at the same time. She is proof-positive that a good wife is indeed a gift from God.

It has been said that providence is the hand of God in the glove of history. As I consider how the steps of my life have been ordered, I'm awestruck to have been afforded the opportunities that have come my way. To be certain, not every opportunity has been "wonderful" nor has every experience been one I'd want to repeat. However, the grace and mercy of God have given me a most precious perspective—distinguishing the difference between being successful and being faithful. Regardless of the level of success that providence may afford me, my prayer is that I be faithful to the charge I've been given.

About the Author

Pete Hammett is director of the Client and Assessment Services Group at the Center for Creative Leadership® (CCL®) and has more than twenty years' experience in areas such as operations, technology, client relationship management/sales, and business process reengineering. He holds a doctorate degree in strategic leadership from Regent University, an MA degree in business administration from Wilmington College, and a BS degree in computer science from Wesley College. While at CCL Hammett has published numerous articles in journals such as *Executive Excellence, Chief Learning Officer,* and *Regent's Leadership Advance.* Earlier in his career, he published articles in technical trade journals and presented on topics relating to the space shuttle program.

Prior to joining CCL, Pete held a variety of key positions at American Express, including technology leader/VP technology, where he was in charge of business process automation and strategic planning for several point-of-arrival technology platforms. While at Amex, he also served as director of new product development and participated in building the systems, relationship management, and business operations framework required to support Amex's entry into the co-branding and affinity marketplace. In this role he also oversaw the delivery of several new products for Amex including the Optima True Grace card and advised on the European-Accor co-branding card.

Pete's professional experience prior to joining American Express includes a distinguished career in the aerospace and defense industry with accomplishments that include the design and implementation of the software application responsible for allocating space suit components to shuttle flight crews.

PART I

Myths
of Effective Executive Leadership

— MYTH —

A usually traditional story of ostensibly historical events that serves to unfold part of the world view of a people or explain a practice, belief, or natural phenomenon; a popular belief or tradition that has grown up around something or someone; especially one embodying the ideals and institutions of a society or segment of society; **an unfounded or false notion.** *(Merriam-Webster, emphasis added)*

— LEADERSHIP MYTH —

Embedded view that encumbers leaders with a misconception of the actions and methods they should engage as they seek to move their organizations forward.

Power, Influence, and the Myth of Effective Leadership

Leadership is a myth! Or more specifically, *effective leadership* is a myth. As provocative as this statement may seem, the truth is that some people choose to exercise power and wield influence to accomplish their objectives, rather than lead. Some might argue that as long as there's forward momentum toward achieving desired objectives, then indeed leadership has occurred. This feels right when we define leadership as setting direction, creating alignment, and maintaining commitment (McCauley and Van Velsor 2003, 18). Clearly a leader can set direction, build alignment, and secure commitment by leveraging power and influence. But while power and influence are tools for leading, how these tools are used colors our perceptions regarding effective leadership.

At CCL people tell the story of a senior manager at a manufacturing plant who was attending a leadership development program. As the class discussed the reasons people wanted to become better leaders, a general consensus arose that it was "to improve performance of the organization and its workforce." However, the plant manager disagreed with this premise. He maintained that he was more than capable of improving the performance of his plant by simply controlling the incentives he extended (promotions and pay) and the security he offered (demotions or firing). In fact, he had achieved notable success in his plant using these tactics of reward and coercion. However, he was looking for more than a carrot-and-stick approach to leadership.

Well-known research on social influence highlights two critical principles of reward power and coercion power. *Reward power* comes from a person's ability to administer positive recognition as a result of demonstrating or achieving desired behaviors or results. *Coercive power* is the converse and focuses on the person's ability to administer punitive measures for poor performance (Kramer and Neale 1998, 183; Yukl 2002, 146–149). However, research has shown that use of this type of power and influence "is very costly and inefficient for organizations to manage . . . because [organizations must] expend resources to provide material rewards or pay the cost of surveillance to detect rule-breaking behavior" (Kramer and Neale 1998, 252). In bottom-line terms, while using power and influence in a rewarding and coercive manner can in fact achieve short-term results, this approach to leadership is not only inefficient, it will not last in the long term.

Returning to the plant manager, it's clear that he recognized two underlying problems with the reward-and-coercion approach. First, he did not believe it was sustainable—at some point rewards and coercion would cease to generate increasing results. Second, he wanted to sleep better at night. In other words, the plant manager wanted to stop making people do what was needed and start *leading* his employees in moving the plant forward. I use this story to highlight my working definition of *effective leadership:*

> *The realization of organizational outcomes (consumables and services) that meet the quality standards of the market while enhancing the long-term sustainability of the organization and ensuring the general well-being of the organization's workforce.*

In other words, results that aren't sustainable or are achieved at the expense of the well-being of the workforce cannot be attributed to effective leadership. While power and influence can certainly get things done, the results will not last in the long run, and the health of the organization's workforce will diminish. Consider the fast-moving executive who uses power and influence to achieve quick results and springboards to the next higher position—leaving a successor to deal with the sustainability issues.

Executives face a challenge as they move up the chain of command and their power and influence increase. Their legitimate power stems from the prescribed authority of the position along with the power to grant rewards and administer coercion. These are part of the relevant and expert power derived from attainment of a high-level position. Within this dynamic, executives find they are more and more isolated from critical sources of input and feedback. Kaplan, Draft, and Kofodimos make this point in *Beyond Ambition* (1991, 31):

> The organization does executives a disservice if it sets them too far apart in rank, privilege and location. This is because structure and physical setting exert a profound influence on patterns of interaction. Yet just when the need to build and maintain a network of contacts becomes critically important, executives are placed in settings that militate against this networking function.

However, as a leader's power and influence increase, the motivation to *influence action* rather than *exert power* wanes. So senior executives often find it easier to simply direct subordinates' activity rather than influence them to take action. Compliance is easier to achieve than commitment. A senior military officer told me that once she made a certain rank, the military removed the bone in her brain that compelled her to explain the rationale behind the orders she gave to others.

The net effect is that as senior executives move up the corporate ladder, their sphere of influence is reshaped. *Outwardly* they become more engaged, causing others to take action more readily, while *inwardly* their influence becomes more constricted, with fewer inputs and insights available to them as they attempt to lead their organizations. Again, Kaplan and his colleagues highlight this point, suggesting that when executives do interact with people from outside their small sphere of influence, the trappings of power ensure that "subordinates will feel too uncomfortable to deliver critical messages" (1991, 32). Senior executives may be seen as unable to draw on external insight or adapt to unforeseen conditions, so they eventually develop tunnel vision from locking on to an initiative that is ineffective or, worse, damaging to the organization.

Executive leaders need to understand and regularly calibrate their *sphere of influence;* that is, to be aware of how their actions and decisions affect those around them, as well as understand the external factors that directly and indirectly influence the way they lead.

VIEWS ON POWER, INFLUENCE, AND EFFECTIVE LEADERSHIP

Three topics are key to the consideration of effective leadership: the dark side of power and influence (organizational politics), the blind side (the illusion of influence), and the space between power and influence where leadership occurs.

The Dark Side

While research investigating the relationship between power and influence is somewhat limited, we do know that the amount of power you have shapes the way in which you interact with people. So, subtle as it is, there is a distinction between power and influence. Power is the capacity to direct people's attitudes and behavior toward a desired outcome, and is generally contingent on one's level or position in an organization (Yukl 2002, 170). Conversely, influence is the ability to direct attitudes and behavior based on one's personal status, charisma, and the real or perceived implication of quid pro quo. A practical example of the misuse and misunderstood application of power and influence plays out in organizational politics—or "the dark side of the Force" of power and influence.

Most people might characterize organizational politics as an unhealthy activity—that if senior management would simply have the common good (or common sense) in mind, the organization would be able to break through the politics and make better, timelier decisions.

However, Daft draws a distinction between political behavior (using power to get things done—good or bad) and *organizational politics:* attempts to acquire, develop, and use power and other resources to obtain preferred outcomes where there is uncertainty or disagreement around choices (2004, 504). In other words, higher up in the organization, decisions are less black-and-white, and political maneuvers are often more necessary to get things done.

One manifestation of organizational politics is apparent in "political alignments—[those] micro-institutions that generate coordinated efforts to influence organizational strategy, policy and practices" (Kramer and Neale 1998, 67). Organizational politics may simply be the way things get done, but rather than limiting such activities to the unsanctioned or nonrational domains, some senior executives use power, power perception, and power deployment as the key resource to obtain their objectives. In some organizations with unrestrained internal politics, these political alignments are the corporate version of street gangs—a bit more sophisticated and less overtly violent, but just as ruthless and self-serving. Bacharach may have sensed a similar comparison; he refines his definition of organizational politics further to encompass "political action as purposive behavioral moves and countermoves to influence the perceptions of others and thus, at least indirectly, to influence organizational policies, strategies and practices" (quoted in Kramer and Neale 1998, 69). This may be why so many employees see organizational politics in a negative light—they perceive executives as engaged in backroom dealings, bargaining toward their own gain or aspiring to prolong the status quo.

Organizational politics aside, in the end the question isn't whether leaders will use power and influence to accomplish their goals, but whether they will use these tools wisely in an effective manner. So how should a leader engage power and influence effectively?

The Blind Side

While organizational politics provide an outward look at executives' spheres of influence, looking inward requires wrestling with executives' illusion of influence. Pfeffer and Cialdini shape our understanding regarding the illusion of influence by suggesting that unrealistic (or better, *unbalanced*) perceptions are created when executives selectively process and interpret information in ways that promote or cater to their own personal bias (cited in Kramer and Neale 1998, 3). This aspect of an illusion of influence can be seen in an executive self-enhancement—where executives choose to see themselves as more intelligent, skilled, ethical, honest, persistent, and original than their counterparts and even consider themselves to be better leaders. This even plays out as some senior executives believe that those who agree with their decisions are unquestionably more intelligent that those who challenge them (Kramer and Neale 1998, 4). This may be why some senior executives appear to surround themselves with people who think and believe the way they do, thus adding to the constriction of their spheres of influence.

So then, the "illusion of influence [is] the belief that one has influence over a behavior or outcome even when one does not or at a minimum overestimating one's degree of influence and control in a particular setting or situation." Pfeffer and Cialdini point to Langer's research that demonstrated how people were more inclined to believe that they had some level of influence over those events (even events of chance) where they have more invested (time, resources, sweat equity). Gamblers shooting craps, for example, tend to believe they actually control the outcome of the dice. From the executive perspective, Pfeffer and Cialdini challenge us to simply look at any number of annual reports. When the results are positive, senior executives take credit, and when things are down, senior executives point to uncontrollable external factors. We see this in politics, where incoming presidents are credited with (or blamed for) economic turns that in fact were most likely in motion long before the candidate even declared an intention to run for office.

The antithesis of this illusion of influence is seen in Collins's depiction of Level 5 leaders (2005, 145):

> The emphasis on luck turns out to be part of a broader pattern that we have come to call "the window and the mirror." Level 5 leaders, inherently humble, look out the window to apportion credit—even undue credit—to factors outside themselves. If they can't find a specific person or event to give credit to, they credit good luck. At the same time, they

look in the mirror to assign responsibility, never citing bad luck or external factors when things go poorly. Conversely, the comparison executives frequently looked out the window for factors to blame but preened in the mirror to credit themselves when things went well.

Leadership: The Space Between

There is a space between power and influence—between the dark side and the blind side—and that is where effective leadership occurs. While it can be difficult to find examples of this type of effective leadership, it is easy to find examples of ineffectiveness. One example that springs to mind is the government's response to Hurricane Katrina. Katrina was perhaps the most planned for, simulated, and anticipated natural disaster in the history of the United States. And yet local, state, and federal agencies performed miserably in their leadership. Instead of leading, those who had the capacity to take action opted to exert power or influence rather than lead. This is not just visible in the way local, state, and federal officials responded to the crisis, it is most evident in the slow, inept recovery of the devastated areas.

Without question the impact of Katrina revealed significant tension in the Gulf Coast states. This tension arose out of a confluence of two critical factors: the interdependence of those affected on their communities and government to provide assistance, and the diversity within the communities themselves. Kotter points out that within communities (work or social) that have both a strong interdependence (people must depend on one another to achieve their goals) and high diversity (differing values, assumptions, beliefs, and perceptions) conflict and tension will be inevitable (1985, 17–18).

So while *interdependence* forces people to work together, the *diversity* associated with the group makes finding consensus for action nearly impossible. In this vacuum of needing to take action but not readily finding solutions for what to do, two possible outcomes occur: inaction and self-centered use of power and influence to the benefit of a select few. And with Katrina we saw both paralyzing inaction and inefficient use of power and influence that addressed only a narrow slice of the residents and businesses caught up in the disaster.

It is during times of crisis that leading effectively can be problematic because of the often competing goals and priorities. In a crisis, finding solutions everyone can accept becomes both time-consuming and frustrating, and people tend to stop leading toward common ground and look to find solutions that serve narrow interests. As leadership falls by the wayside, it is replaced by power and influence exerted through what Kotter terms "parochial political processes and destructive power struggles" (1985, 31–32).

The federal government's report on Katrina, "A Failure of Initiative," includes the observation that despite the massive power and influence of the government agencies responding to the Gulf Coast states, the lack of clear communications regarding what support was needed and where resulted in paralysis and inaction: "Leadership requires decisions to be made even when based on flawed and incomplete information. Too often during the immediate response to Katrina, sparse or conflicting information was used as an excuse for inaction rather than an imperative to step in and fill an obvious void" (Select Bipartisan Committee 2005, 441).

But the same events also showed elements of effective leadership. Filling the void between power and influence was the 82nd Airborne, which within seven hours of receiving the call to respond to the disaster had forces on the ground in New Orleans. While the 82nd also encountered significant problems with clear communications as to where assistance was needed most, the values inherent in its leadership enabled commanders to make decisions and take action quickly. Admittedly many of these early actions, while well meant, were less than efficient. However, as the situational awareness became clearer, the actions of the 82nd became more efficient. Did the 82nd use power and influence in responding to Katrina? Without question. But even when faced with the same lack of information and overwhelming needs that paralyzed the civil authorities, its personnel were able to fill the space between power and influence and lead effectively. How effectively? So much so that when recovery operations were concluding, the mayor of New Orleans said, "Everyone else can go home, but the 82nd needs to stay."

HOW SENIOR EXECUTIVES APPROACH POWER, INFLUENCE, AND LEADERSHIP

At this point, it is helpful to look at specific characteristics of senior executive leadership styles. As noted in the preface, CCL has collected data on more than seventy C-level executives who have attended its Leadership at the Peak development program over the past several years. The data provide insight into such executives' personality preferences, how they relate interpersonally, and the manner in which they lead their organizations, lead others, and lead themselves. In addition, other available data reflect senior executives' leadership characteristics personally and organizationally. This makes it possible to begin to form a picture of those leadership competencies where senior executives demonstrate proficiency and how these strengths may impact a senior executive's sphere of influence.

Personality Preferences of Senior Executives

The CCL data on C-level executives yield some intriguing insights. First, the *Myers-Briggs Type Indicator*® (MBTI®) assessment is a fascinating resource. It provides insight into your preference or disposition in four areas (Hirsh and Kummerow 1998, 1):

- You draw energy from being with other people (you prefer Extraversion) or from being on your own (you prefer Introversion).

- Your perceptions are more fact-based (you prefer Sensing) or are drawn from associations (you prefer Intuition).

- Your decision making is based on structured, organized information (you prefer Thinking) or comes from your heart and values (you prefer Feeling).

- Your life reflects a planned, well-ordered style (you prefer Judging) or you're more spontaneous and flexible (you prefer Perceiving).

Figure 1.1 (CPP 2005) diagrams these four pairs of MBTI personality preferences. Your preferences as described here combine to form your

E (Extraversion) means that you probably relate more easily to the outer world of people and things than to the inner world of ideas.	**I (Introversion)** means that you probably relate more easily to the inner world of ideas than to the outer world of people and things.
S (Sensing) means that you probably would rather work with known facts than look for possibilities and relationships.	**N (Intuition)** means that you probably would rather look for possibilities and relationships than work with known facts.
T (Thinking) means that you probably base your judgments more on impersonal analysis and logic than on personal values.	**F (Feeling)** means that you probably base your judgments more on personal values than on impersonal analysis and logic.
J (Judging) means that you probably like a planned, decided, orderly way of life better than a flexible, spontaneous way.	**P (Perceiving)** means that you probably like a flexible, spontaneous way of life better than a planned, decided, orderly way.

Figure 1.1 • MBTI® Personality Preferences

MBTI personality type. If, for example, you have a preference for Introversion (designated I), Intuition (N), Feeling (F), and Perceiving (P), your personality type is indicated as INFP. The four pairs of preferences yield sixteen distinct types.

In considering how these personality preferences play out, it is important to understand that a preference is just that—a tendency or bias toward a particular way of acting. As Peter Myers and Katharine Myers point out, "there is no right or wrong" associated with any particular preference (CPP 2005, 8). For example, some people are right-handed, others left-handed, but these days society does not regard one as better than the other. While it is possible to learn to write with either hand, you have a preference for one over the other. The hand you use for writing is the one that feels natural and comfortable. Likewise, your disposition toward a certain manner or personality pattern is based on several factors including your environment, skills, and attitudes, and the people surrounding you. Therefore, "each type represents a valuable and reasonable way to be, [reflecting] its own potential strengths, as well as its likely blind spots" (Myers 1998, 8).

It is also important to note that, while we tend to rely more on one preference or the other in each pair shown in Figure 1.1, everyone can and does use all eight of the preferences to some extent.

The distribution of personality types found among the C-level executives in CCL's research sample is shown in Figure 1.2, from which several observations emerge:

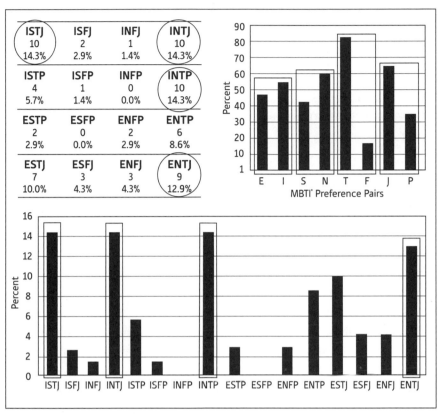

Figure 1.2 • C-Level Executives' Personality Type Preferences

- Four MBTI types appear to occur more often than the others in this sample: ISTJ (preference for Introversion, Sensing, Thinking, and Judging), INTJ (preference for Introversion, Intuition, Thinking, and Judging), INTP (preference for Introversion, Intuition, Thinking, and Perceiving), and ENTJ (preference for Extraversion, Intuition, Thinking, and Judging). Within these four types is a strong grouping of senior executives who prefer Intuition and Thinking (NT) as well as Judging (J)—suggesting a strong preference toward rational thinking and concern with knowledge and competence (Isachsen and Berebs 1991, 59).

- Although some personality types occurred more frequently than others, the senior executives in our sample represented fourteen of the sixteen types. While this sample population did not include any INFPs or ESFPs, the sample size would not support concluding that people with these personality types would not make effective senior executives. In other words, senior executives come in all personality shapes and sizes.

- While there is some distinction in the Extraversion–Introversion pairing (46 percent Extravert and 54 percent Introvert), more significant distinctions appear in the other three pairings:

  - Sensing (42 percent) and Intuition (58 percent)

  - Thinking (82 percent) and Feeling (18 percent)

  - Judging (64 percent) and Perceiving (36 percent)

Another approach in analyzing the personality preferences for C-level executives is to focus on those activities that appear most frequently. So while a slight distinction can be made between senior executives who are Extraverted or Introverted, the sample includes much higher occurrences of executives who have a preference for Intuition, Thinking, and Judging. As a result, the observations, assertions, and calls to action I present in this book are framed against the backdrop of the four most frequently occurring personality types. Please keep in mind that this is a generalization of senior executives' personality types that provides a convenient frame for understanding how senior executives approach their leadership positions. If your MBTI type is not among this group, you will find added value in reviewing the specific characteristics and dimensions of your type.

Myers helps us visualize the specifics of these personality preferences as follows (1998, 9–10):

- **Intuition** (how you prefer to take in information). "People who prefer Intuition like to take in information by seeing the big picture, focusing on the relationships and connections between facts. They want to grasp patterns and are especially attuned to seeing new possibilities."

- **Thinking** (how you make decisions). "People who prefer to use Thinking in decision making like to look at the logical consequences of a choice or action. They want to mentally remove themselves from the situation to examine the pros and cons objectively. They are energized by critiquing and analyzing to identify what's wrong with something so they can solve the problem. Their goal is to find a standard or principle that will apply in all similar situations."

- **Judging** (how you deal with the outer world). "People who prefer to use their Judging process in the outer world like to live in a planned, orderly way, seeking to regulate and manage their lives. They want to make decisions, come to closure, and move on. Their lives tend to be structured and organized and they like to have things settled. Sticking to a plan and schedule is very important to them, and they are energized by getting things done."

Finally, it may be helpful to review the specific leadership styles associated with the four predominant personality types found in the CCL sample of senior executives (see Table 1.1; Isachsen and Berebs 1991, 97, 100, 101, 103; Hirsh and Kummerow 1998, 10, 22, 23, 25).

How Senior Executives Relate Interpersonally

Data are also available on the way C-level executives relate interpersonally with others. The *Fundamental Interpersonal Relations Orientation–Behavior*™ (FIRO-B®) assessment provides insight into behavior in the following areas (Waterman and Rogers 2004, 1):

- How you come across to others, and why this may not be the way you see yourself or the impression your might want to make

- How and why conflict develops between well-meaning people

- How to understand your own needs and how to manage them as you interact with others

The FIRO-B model identifies three areas of interpersonal needs, focusing on Inclusion, Control, and Affection (Schnell and Hammer 1993, 3). Waterman and Rogers (2004, 2) characterize them as follows:

LEADERSHIP STYLE	LEADERSHIP METHODS	CONTRIBUTIONS TO ORGANIZATION
ISTJs (Introversion, Sensing, Thinking, Judging)		
Might be titled "Inspectors," no-nonsense leaders who work quietly to get the job done and are responsible and trustworthy. They like organization and structure and embrace challenges. They are frustrated with emotional situations and people who don't adhere to the rules. They can create conflict by being overly focused on getting the job done and have a tendency to roll over people in achieving desired tasks.	• Use experience and knowledge of the facts to make decisions • Build on reliable, stable, and consistent performance • Respect traditional, hierarchical approaches • Reward those who follow the rules while getting the job done • Pay attention to immediate and practical organizational needs	• Get things done steadily and on schedule • Concentrate on details and are careful about managing them • Have things at the right place at the right time • Can be counted on to honor commitments and follow through • Work comfortably within organizational structure
INTJs (Introversion, Intuition, Thinking, Judging)		
Might be titled "Strategists," leaders who are high-achieving innovators whose extremely tight focus allows them to realize significant results. They enjoy tackling problems and flourish in environments that provide freedom and autonomy. They are frustrated by being told what to do or losing focus because of other people's needs or opinions. They create conflict because they are unyielding to others' insight.	• Drive themselves and others to attain the organization's goals • Act strongly and forcefully in the field of ideas • Can be tough-minded with self and others • Conceptualize, create, and build new models • Are willing to relentlessly reorganize whole systems when necessary	• Provide theoretical insights and design skills • Organize ideas into action plans • Work to remove obstacles to goal attainment • Have strong ideas of what the organization can be • Push everyone to understand the system as a whole with complex interaction among parts

Table 1.1 • Leadership Styles of Senior Executives with Predominant Personality Types

LEADERSHIP STYLE	LEADERSHIP METHODS	CONTRIBUTIONS TO ORGANIZATION
INTPs (Introversion, Intuition, Thinking, Perceiving)		
Might be titled "Definers," leaders who possess strong logical thinking and enjoy theoretical and scientific topics. They enjoy variety in their work and need regular positive feedback and validation for their achievements. They become irritated with what they perceive as unintelligent demands and they create tension by not paying attention to details and following through on tasks.	• Lead through conceptual analysis of problems and goals • Apply logical systems thinking • Want to lead other independent types while seeking autonomy for themselves • Relate to people based on expertise rather than on position • Seek to interact at an intellectual rather than an emotional level	• Design logical and complex systems • Demonstrate expertise in tackling intricate problems • Add short- and long-range intellectual insight • Apply logic, analysis, and critical thinking to issues • Concentrate on core issues
ENTJs (Extraversion, Intuition, Thinking, Judging)		
Might be titled "Field Marshals"; these leaders are frank and decisive, good at thinking on their feet, and are perceived as natural leaders. They enjoy mental challenges and greatly respect clever ideas. They become frustrated when others are not as adept at problem solving as they are and they create tension by coming off as arrogant, overly confident, and impersonal.	• Plan theoretical systems to meet organizational needs • Encourage independence in others • Apply logic and find models for change • Use compelling reasons for what they want to do • Act as catalysts between people and systems	• View limitations as challenges to be overcome • Provide new ways to do things • Bring a conceptual framework to problems • Take initiative and spur others on • Enjoy complex challenges that address future needs

- **Inclusion:** the degree of attention, contact, and recognition between you and groups—small or large

- **Control:** the amount of influence and responsibility you desire and how much influence and responsibility you'd like others to exert— again as either one-to-one relationships or in groups

- **Affection:** how close and warm (personable) you are toward others and how personable you'd like others to be toward you

Additionally, within each interpersonal need of Inclusion, Control, and Affection, the FIRO-B assessment further defines two dimensions of Expressed Behavior (how much you prefer to initiate the behavior) and Wanted Behavior (how much you prefer to receive the behavior toward you (Schnell and Hammer 1993, 4). The components of the FIRO-B assessment are summarized in Figure 1.3 (CPP 2005).

Figure 1.4 presents a modal view, showing the patterns that occur most frequently in the FIRO-B data from CCL's C-level executives. The modal FIRO-B data suggest several interesting observations about the way C-level executives relate interpersonally. For example, although engaging with others is a source of satisfaction for most people, for senior executives the satisfaction varies greatly depending on who is involved and the context of the engagement. Additionally, close personal relationships at work can become frustrating, and senior executives perceive these relationships as potentially interfering with their jobs. Therefore senior executives work better in small groups with regular contacts or perhaps even alone, and while their work performance depends on input from others, they do not rely on others for decision making. Figure 1.5 provides further insight into the way senior executives work in teams (CPP 2005).

A review of the FIRO-B data leads to four distinct observations about how senior executives relate interpersonally (CPP 2005):

- Senior executives are likely to focus on establishing trust relationships, exchanging personal reactions and opinions, getting close to people, and building loyalty.

The FIRO-B tool provides information about three fundamental dimensions of interpersonal needs:

INCLUSION

is about recognition, belonging, participation, contact with others, and how you relate to groups

CONTROL

concerns influence, leadership, responsibility, and decision making

AFFECTION

is about closeness, warmth, sensitivity, openness, and how you relate to others

The FIRO-B assessment also indicates your preferences in regard to two distinct aspects of each of these needs areas:

EXPRESSED BEHAVIOR

• How much do you prefer to initiate the behavior?

• How do you actually behave with respect to the three fundamental interpersonal needs?

• What is your comfort level engaging in the behaviors associated with the three needs?

WANTED BEHAVIOR

• How much do you prefer others to take the initiative?

• How much do you want to be on the receiving end of those behaviors?

• What is your comfort level when others direct their behaviors associated with the three needs to you?

Figure 1.3 • FIRO-B® Components

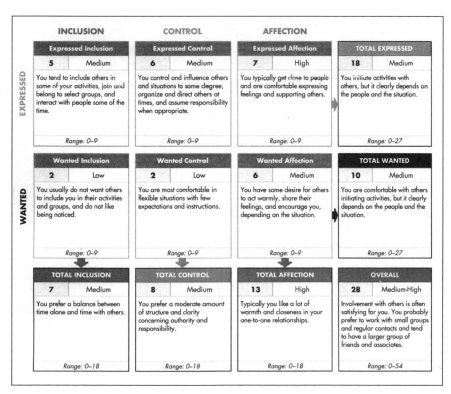

Figure 1.4 • Modal View of C-Level Executives' FIRO-B® Data

How You Work in a Team

Your FIRO-B scores can shed some light on how you are likely to respond to the opportunities and pressures of working in a team.

el 6 / wl 0

Your expressed and wanted needs for Inclusion suggest that you enjoy teams in which

☑ there are many opportunities (but no pressure from others) to
☐ there are many opportunities to
☐ there is no pressure to
☐ there are many opportunities for others (but no pressure on you directly) to

- state an opinion and join in the discussion
- share information and take an interest in the activities of others
- maintain a high profile on the team

- acknowledge the unique strengths of individuals on the team
- recognize people's contributions and accomplishments
- produce highly visible results

eC 0 / wC 3

Your expressed and wanted needs for Control suggest that you enjoy teams in which

☐ there are many opportunities (but no pressure from others) to
☐ there are many opportunities to
☑ there is no pressure to
☐ there are many opportunities for others (but no pressure on you directly) to

- create structured roles and rules
- clearly define the goals and activities of the team
- take action and show progress immediately

- establish formal agendas
- make final decisions rather than advise or recommend
- assign specific areas of accountability
- directly influence others

eA 5 / wA 5

Your expressed and wanted needs for Affection suggest that you enjoy teams in which

☐ there are many opportunities (but no pressure from others) to
☑ there are many opportunities to
☐ there is no pressure to
☐ there are many opportunities for others (but no pressure on you directly) to

- develop a team consensus
- encourage and support individual efforts
- offer personal guidance
- build rapport with team members early on

- give individual reactions and opinions
- work intensely for many hours at a time
- have frequent contact with other team members
- develop interdependencies for information collecting and action

Figure 1.5 • Typical C-Level Executive Teamwork Report

- Senior executives are probably less interested in fitting in, making new connections, becoming known, and getting involved with many people on a project than they are in satisfying their need for Control.

- Senior executives are very flexible, changing the roles they play over time and across different circumstances. Depending on the situation, senior executives can take on the role of clarifier, or act as a director, and at other times play the role of encourager.

- Senior executives are more apt to engage power and influence by developing strong personal loyalties, networks, and commitments. Senior executives will likewise look to expand their base of influence by adhering to important personal and organizational values and by showing how they serve others.

HOW SENIOR EXECUTIVES LEAD THE ORGANIZATION, OTHERS, AND THEMSELVES

In May 2000 CCL introduced *Executive Dimensions,* an assessment specifically designed for presidents, chief executive officers, chief operating officers, chief information officers, executive vice presidents, and other senior executives to address leadership issues at the top levels of an organization. *Executive Dimensions* is a 360-degree assessment—that is, it collects feedback from executives and their peers, direct reports, and bosses to better understand executives' effectiveness in leading the organization, leading others, and leading themselves. Key to the assessment is the ability to capture those leadership competencies that are deemed most critical for success while concurrently identifying areas where the executive demonstrates the greatest strengths as well as areas that show room for possible improvement.

Within the *Executive Dimensions* taxonomy (leading the organization, leading others, and leading yourself), leadership competencies turn out to be grouped as shown in Table 1.2.

Drawing on the data collected from the sample of C-level executives, it is possible to uncover interesting patterns between those leadership competencies they rate as important and where they see their strengths. Meanwhile, observer data from *Executive Dimensions* reflect nearly seven hundred bosses, peers, and direct reports and identify what they see as important leadership competencies and where they perceive the senior executives' demonstrated strengths. This comparison is presented in Table 1.3, which reflects importance and strength of the top five leadership competencies as rated by C-level executives and their observers as a group.

LEADERSHIP CATEGORY	LEADERSHIP COMPETENCY
Leading the Business	• Sound Judgment • Strategic Planning • Results Orientation • Leading Change • Global Awareness • Business Perspective
Leading Others	• Inspiring Commitment • Forging Synergy • Developing and Empowering • Leveraging Differences • Communicating Effectively • Interpersonal Savvy
Leading Yourself (Leading by Example)	• Courage • Executive Image • Learning from Experiences • Credibility

Table 1.2 • *Executive Dimensions* Leadership Competencies

Note: Appendix A outlines each leadership competency measured by *Executive Dimensions* and the behaviors that would be observed for the competency.

Table 1.4 provides further refinement by looking specifically at input from bosses and direct reports of C-level executives.

It's useful to slice these data one more time and compare those leadership competencies that executives regard as strengths or as important (or both) alongside summaries from all observers, bosses, and direct reports. (Refer to Appendix B for a detailed report by all observers for *Executive Dimensions.*)

Table 1.5 reveals some fascinating data. Senior executives rate as most important three competencies related to leading the business (Sound Judgment, Results Orientation, and Strategic Planning), one related to leading others (Communicating Effectively), and one to leading by example (Credibility). However, these senior executives rate themselves as having strength in only three of these competencies

EXECUTIVE SELF-RATED IMPORTANCE	EXECUTIVE SELF-RATED STRENGTH	ALL OBSERVERS RATED IMPORTANCE	ALL OBSERVERS RATED STRENGTH
Sound Judgment	Credibility	Sound Judgment	Credibility
Credibility	Sound Judgment	Credibility	Executive Image
Results Orientation	Leveraging Differences	Strategic Planning	Courage
Strategic Planning	Results Orientation	Results Orientation	Results Orientation
Communicating Effectively	Courage	Leading Change	Communicating Effectively; Leveraging Differences

Table 1.3 • Senior Executive and Observer Ratings of Leadership Competency Importance and Strength

Note: These are simply the top five rated competencies as identified by executives and observers. Absence of a competency does not indicate it is either unimportant or missing from the executive's skills inventory. These tables reflect relative ranking of competencies as compared to the whole.

BOSS RATED IMPORTANCE	BOSS RATED STRENGTH	DIRECT REPORTS RATED IMPORTANCE	DIRECT REPORTS RATED STRENGTH
Sound Judgment	Credibility	Sound Judgment	Credibility
Credibility	Executive Image	Strategic Planning	Executive Image
Results Orientation	Results Orientation	Credibility	Courage
Communicating Effectively	Courage	Leading Change	Results Orientation
Strategic Planning	Sound Judgment	Results Orientation	Communicating Effectively

Table 1.4 • Boss and Direct Report Ratings of Leadership Competency Importance and Strength

LEADERSHIP COMPETENCY	C-LEVEL EXECUTIVES	ALL OBSERVERS	BOSSES	DIRECT REPORTS
Credibility	I & S	I & S	I & S	I & S
Sound Judgment	I & S	I & S	I & S	I
Results Orientation	I & S	I & S	I & S	I & S
Strategic Planning	I	I	I	I
Leading Change		I		I
Communicating Effectively	I	I	I	S
Courage	S	S	S	S
Executive Image	S	S	S	S

⬛ Competency is both important (I) and a strength (S)

◻ Competency is a strength (S)

☐ Competency is important (I) but not identified as a top strength (S)

Table 1.5 • Summary of Competency Importance and Strength Ratings

(Credibility, Sound Judgment, and Results Orientation). Observers likewise identified Credibility, Sound Judgment, Strategic Planning, and Results Orientation as important, but they differed from the senior executives by also identifying Leading Change as one of the top competencies.

Meanwhile, although everyone identified Sound Judgment as important, direct reports did not note this as a top demonstrated strength of executives. This area involves the following behaviors (CCL 2000, *Executive Dimensions Development Planning Guide*):

Sound Judgment

- Sees underlying concepts and patterns in complex situations
- Gives appropriate weight to the concerns of key stakeholders
- Readily grasps the crux of an issue despite having ambiguous information
- Makes effective decisions in a timely manner

- Accurately differentiates between important and unimportant issues

- Develops solutions that address underlying problems effectively

It is interesting to compare this area to that of Strategic Planning, which everyone regards as an important competency but no one, including the executives themselves, identifies as a strength. Following are the behaviors associated with Strategic Planning.

Strategic Planning

- Regularly updates plan to reflect changing circumstances

- Translates his or her vision into realistic business strategies

- Weighs concerns of relevant business functions when developing plans

- Articulates wise long-term objectives and strategies

- Develops plans that balance long-term goals with immediate organizational needs

- Develops plans that contain contingencies for future changes

- Successfully integrates strategic and tactical planning

Agreement is unanimous that Results Orientation is both important and a strength. Direct reports also identified leading change as a demonstrated strength of executives. While similar in context, the Results Orientation and Leading Change competencies show subtle distinctions, as shown below.

Results Orientation

- Assigns clear accountability for important objectives

- Pushes the organization to address the concerns of key stakeholders

- Clearly conveys objectives, deadlines, and expectations

- Holds self accountable for meeting commitments

- Aligns organizational resources to accomplish key objectives

- Acts with a sense of urgency

Leading Change

- Correctly judges which creative ideas will pay off
- Supports activities that position the business for the future
- Pushes the organization to adopt new initiatives
- Offers novel ideas and perspectives
- Fosters a climate of experimentation

Everyone but direct reports identified Communicating Effectively as a top important competency, suggesting a premium on the senior executives' ability to express ideas fluently and eloquently, convey ideas through lively examples and images, and encourage direct and open discussions about important issues.

Everyone also agreed that both Courage and Executive Image are demonstrated executive strengths. Here again the two competencies show strong similarities.

Courage

- Takes the lead on unpopular though necessary actions
- Acts decisively to tackle difficult problems
- Perseveres in the face of problems and difficulties
- Confronts conflicts promptly, so problems do not escalate
- Has the courage to confront others when necessary

Executive Image

- Communicates confidence and steadiness during difficult times
- Projects confidence and poise
- Adapts readily to new situations
- Commands attention and respect
- Accepts setbacks with grace

Another competency on which senior executives and all the rest agreed was Credibility, as everyone identified this competency as both important and a strength for executives. Following are the behaviors associated with Credibility.

Credibility

- Uses ethical considerations to guide decisions
- Through words and deeds encourages honesty throughout the organization
- Speaks candidly about tough issues facing the company
- Tells the truth, not just what important constituents want to hear
- Can be trusted to maintain confidentiality
- Places ethical behavior above personal gain
- Follows through on promises
- Acts in accordance with his or her stated values

Personal Characteristics and Leadership Success of Senior Executives

The *Campbell Leadership Index,* which measures those "personal characteristics that are related to an individual's leadership success," provides additional data (Nilsen and Campbell 1998, 3). As with *Executive Dimensions,* the *Campbell Leadership Index* is a 360-degree assessment, collecting input from senior executives as well as bosses, direct reports, peers, and others. The personal characteristics measured by the *Leadership Index* are divided into five broad orientations, with several specific leadership scales tied to each. Table 1.6 provides an overview of these categories (3–4).

Several of the *Leadership Index* personal characteristics make a difference when it comes to effective executive leadership. Other *Leadership Index* characteristics will prove relevant in the context of topics such as decision making, creativity, and balance.

PERSONAL CHARACTERISTICS	SCALE
Leadership *The act of being out in front, making new and creative things happen*	Ambition Daring Dynamic Enterprising Experienced Farsighted Original Persuasive
Energy *A recognition of the physical demands required of leaders [such as] long hours, stressful days, difficult decisions, wearying travel and public appearances*	(No scales are defined with the Energy orientation.)
Affability *An acknowledgment that leaders need to foster teamwork and cooperation and make people feel valued*	Affectionate Considerate Empowering Entertaining Friendly
Dependability *Being credible and able to allocate organizational resources and manage details*	Credible Organized Productive Thrifty
Resilience *The ability to show optimism, mental durability, and emotional balance*	Calm Flexible Optimistic Trusting

Table 1.6 • *Campbell™ Leadership Index* Personal Characteristics
of Leadership Success and Scales

Figure 1.6 reflects senior executives' self and observer (bosses, peers, direct reports) ratings for each personal characteristic. For example, for the Ambitious scale, executives and observers were asked to rate on a scale ranging from "Never" to "Always" issues such as "Likes to take on challenges and win" and "Has a burning, overwhelming passion to succeed." Responses to these questions are tallied and given a percent favorable rating for the scale, with scale ratings rolling up to the specific orientation (Leadership, Dependability, and so on). The following insight is from the *Campbell Leadership Index* guide (CCL 2004):

> [*Campbell Leadership Index*] results are reported in a standard score format, that is, with a bell shaped distribution where the mean is 50, and a standard deviation is 10. Thus a score of 50 is considered typical or normal, a score of 40 is considered very low and a score of 60 is considered very high. Sixty-eight percent of the individuals in the database score between 40 and 60 [and] nearly all of the scores fall between 25 and 75.

Figure 1.6 shows, for example, that the Ambitious scale has the same standard rating from senior executives and from observers of 59. The overall ratings were very close together, with 58 for executives and 56 for observers. Again, ratings of 60 and above are considered very high, and ratings below 40, very low (Pearson 2005a).

In reviewing Figure 1.6 a few observations quickly come to mind. First, all the scores fall at or above the midline 50 level, indicating relatively high ratings. This is not surprising given that "scores near 50 are typical of people holding leadership positions" (Nilsen and Campbell 1998, 28). We also see little distinction between the scores of senior executives and others, as all seem in agreement on how they perceive senior executives' performance on each characteristic. What is noteworthy is how those characteristics associated with Leadership and Dependability fall into the higher end of the scores (55–60), while the characteristics relating to Affability and Resilience are in the 50–55 range.

It may be helpful to reflect on interpretations of the higher ratings associated with the Leadership scale. Senior executives had scores at or near the 60 standard rating in the Ambitious, Dynamic, Experienced, and Persuasive scales. According to Nilsen and Campbell, the following interpretations are mainly applicable to individuals with very high scores (above 60 percent favorable) for these scales (1998, 6–27).

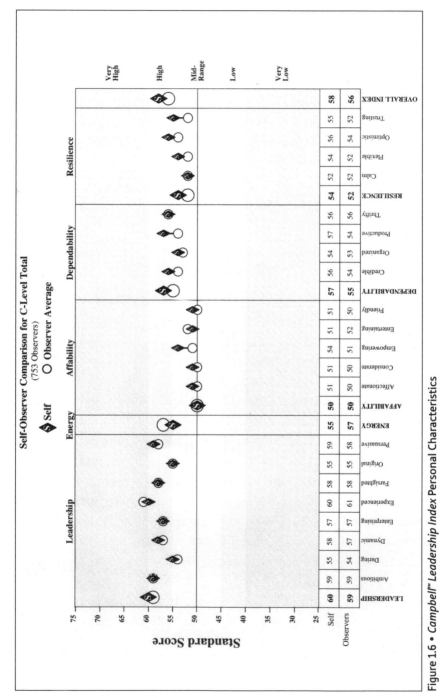

Figure 1.6 • *Campbell™ Leadership Index* Personal Characteristics

Ambitious. "People with *high* Observer scores on the Ambitious Scale reflect a sense of drive, of urgency, of an expressed desire for forward progress. High ratings belong to those who want to make things happen and who have the strength, motivation, and passion to do so."

Dynamic. "People with *high* Observer scores on the Dynamic Scale display enthusiasm, even passion, about their work. They are engaged in activities that they find compelling, and their excitement and dedication are inspiring to others. They appear confident, enthusiastic, and full of life. They are often described as born leaders."

Experienced. "People with *high* Observer scores on the Experienced Scale know their industry well, and they are comfortable with its technical jargon. They typically have cultivated a wide range of useful contacts. Others tend to turn to them for a broad perspective. They continue to grow and see new opportunities and challenges in their industries rather than stagnate in their positions."

Persuasive. "People with *high* Observer scores on the Persuasive Scale tend to be articulate and influential. They can generate public acceptance of their ideas. They have achieved a certain amount of power through their abilities to convince others of the desirability of their proposals."

However, it is possible to refine the review of the *Campbell Leadership Index* data on senior executives a bit more by breaking out how observers in each category ranked their perception of senior executive performance. Figure 1.7 shows the *Leadership Index* scores isolated by each review group: senior executives (self-ratings), superiors, peers, subordinates (direct reports), and others. For most C-level executives, superiors would include the president or CEO, while for those who are presidents and CEOs, superiors most likely are board chairs. Others may include individuals outside the organization, business associates, or even spouses.

With regard to the specific scales within the Leadership orientation of the *Campbell Leadership Index,* it's once again useful to focus on higher-rated items: Ambitious, Dynamic, Experienced, and Persuasive. (Later chapters provide closer looks at the Leadership scales of Ambitious, Dynamic, Daring, Enterprising, Farsighted, and Original.)

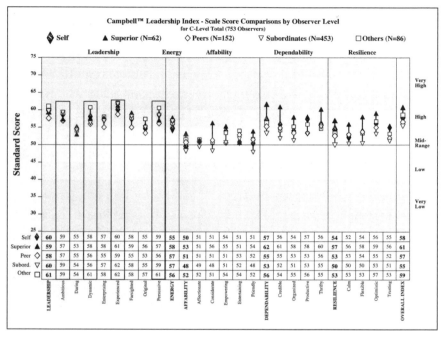

Campbell™ Leadership Index - Scale Score Comparisons by Observer Level
for C-Level Total (753 Observers)

◈ Self   ▲ Superior (N=62)   ◇ Peers (N=152)   ▽ Subordinates (N=453)   □ Others (N=86)

	LEADERSHIP	Ambitious	Daring	Dynamic	Enterprising	Experienced	Farsighted	Original	Persuasive	ENERGY	AFFABILITY	Affectionate	Considerate	Empowering	Entertaining	Friendly	DEPENDABILITY	Credible	Organized	Productive	Thrifty	RESILIENCE	Calm	Flexible	Optimistic	Trusting	OVERALL INDEX
Self ◈	60	59	55	58	57	60	58	55	59	55	50	51	51	54	51	51	57	56	54	57	56	54	52	54	56	55	58
Superior ▲	59	57	53	58	58	61	59	56	57	58	53	51	56	55	51	54	62	61	58	58	60	57	56	58	59	56	61
Peer ◇	58	57	55	56	55	59	55	53	56	57	51	51	51	51	53	52	55	55	53	53	56	53	53	54	55	52	57
Subord. ▽	60	59	54	56	57	62	58	55	59	55	48	49	48	51	52	48	53	52	51	53	55	50	50	53	51	55	55
Other □	61	59	54	61	58	62	58	57	61	56	52	52	51	54	54	52	56	54	55	56	55	53	53	53	57	53	59

Standard Score: 75, 70, 65, 60, 55, 50, 45, 40, 35, 30, 25 — Very High, High, Mid-Range, Low, Very Low

Figure 1.7 • *Campbell™ Leadership Index* Report with Observer Breakout

---

Experienced Scale

39. Experienced - Has seen and done a great deal.

	Nev	Sel	Occ	Som	Usu	Alw	%Fav
You			1	15	34	23	
All Obs	12	15	84	347	295		85
Superior		1	5	26	30		90
Peer	2	4	23	70	53		81
Subord	10	9	45	215	174		86
Other		1	11	36	38		86

67. Naive - Foolishly simple and unsophisticated.

	Nev	Sel	Occ	Som	Usu	Alw	%Fav
You	33	36	2	3			
All Obs	481	207	30	25	4	4	92
Superior	46	13	2	1			95
Peer	88	46	9	7	2		88
Subord	296	120	17	14	2	3	92
Other	51	28	2	3		1	93

82. Savvy - Experienced and well-informed.

	Nev	Sel	Occ	Som	Usu	Alw	%Fav
You			1	18	48	7	
All Obs	5	26	86	429	206		84
Superior		4	6	36	16		84
Peer	1	4	24	93	30		81
Subord	3	16	46	254	134		86
Other	1	2	10	46	26		85

88. Sheltered - Has little experience in dealing with the world.

	Nev	Sel	Occ	Som	Usu	Alw	%Fav
You	35	35	3	1			
All Obs	413	259	35	34	4	1	90
Superior	38	19	2	3			92
Peer	76	56	7	9	2		87
Subord	250	160	20	18	2		91
Other	49	24	6	4			88

99. Well-connected - Knows people who can make important things happen.

	Nev	Sel	Occ	Som	Usu	Alw	%Fav
You			5	27	33	9	
All Obs	1	20	38	122	333	235	76
Superior		1	6	18	26	11	60
Peer		7	10	28	66	41	70
Subord	1	10	18	65	203	153	79
Other		2	4	11	38	30	80

Persuasive Scale

17. Convincing - Capable of influencing others.

	Nev	Sel	Occ	Som	Usu	Alw	%Fav
You			13	48	13		
All Obs	8	33	124	434	153		78
Superior	1	3	9	41	8		79
Peer	1	9	33	85	24		72
Subord	6	17	73	249	107		79
Other		4	9	59	14		85

45. Fluent - Persuasive and articulate with words.

	Nev	Sel	Occ	Som	Usu	Alw	%Fav
You		1	26	38	9		
All Obs	20	35	116	353	229		77
Superior	1	3	11	34	13		76
Peer	6	6	27	77	36		74
Subord	11	25	68	201	148		77
Other	2	1	10	41	32		85

72. Persuasive - Can influence others toward a plan of action.

	Nev	Sel	Occ	Som	Usu	Alw	%Fav
You			14	46	14		
All Obs	1	6	41	115	422	168	78
Superior	3	1	8	41	9		81
Peer			11	31	87	23	72
Subord	1	3	27	64	243	115	79
Other		2	12	51	21		84

Figure 1.8 • *Campbell™ Leadership Index* Questions on Experienced and Persuasive Scales

Figure 1.8 reflects the item-level questions that constitute the Experienced and Persuasive scales. Note that "Percent Favorable" reflects observers' answers that class as favorable. For positive statements such as "Open and honest when dealing with others," favorable responses would be "Always" or "Usually." For negative statements such as "Naïve—Foolishly simple and unsophisticated," favorable responses would be "Never" or "Seldom."

Favorable percentages on the Persuasive scale are in line with what we might expect from senior executives, reflecting a positive perception regarding the executive's ability to convince and influence others toward a plan of action. However, reviewing the questions for Experienced reveals high favorable percentages for nearly all questions—except the one on "Well-connected," which reveals a noticeable perception gap between superiors and subordinates. While it is not possible to draw definitive conclusions for why this perception gap exists, an explanation for this difference may be that superiors and subordinates assess a senior executive's connectedness relative to their own. That is, subordinates may assume that the nature of the position of a senior executive will expose the executive to more important and better-connected people than the subordinate may know. The converse might likewise play out—in that superiors may perceive that the nature of their position gives them greater connections than those of the executives they are reviewing.

Organizational Data for Senior Executives

The final assessment data source reviewed here is the *Campbell Organizational Survey* (COS). The *Organizational Survey* is designed to collect and analyze information regarding employees' "opinions and attitudes toward various aspects of organizational life such as supervision, promotional opportunities, organizational ethics, co-workers and support for innovation" (Campbell and Hyne 1995, 1). A particular strength of the *Campbell Organizational Survey* is that its standardized scales enable comparisons between specific work groups, such as executive leaders (1995, 2).

As with the *Campbell Leadership Index,* the *Organizational Survey* reflects insight in standard ratings from senior executives and observers (see Figure 1.9; Pearson 2005b). Thus ratings in the 50–60 range are considered high. In reviewing the *Organizational Survey,* several observations immediately surface. First, nearly all ratings fall into the high range for both senior executives and observers. However, the two sets of ratings show notable distinctions. For example, within the scale of Work Itself, the senior executives' rating is 58, while the others' ratings come to 54. While both ratings are high, this is clearly a difference—not only on the Work Itself scale, but also in that with nearly each *Organizational Survey* scale the senior executives' scores are higher. Campbell and Hyne refer to this pattern as the "Hierarchy Effect"—the universal tendency for those of higher rank (or of higher status) to provide more favorable ratings than their subordinates (1995, 32, 98). Note that for this survey, observers classed as subordinates are not necessarily direct reports of the C-level executive. Depending on how broadly the COS survey was administered within the organization, subordinates may actually be several layers beneath the senior executive.

As with the *Leadership Index,* a number of scales in the *Campbell Organizational Survey* will be considered in the light of other topics such as ethics and creativity. However, three scales are helpful to review in the context of effective executive leadership, particularly as it plays out at the organizational level: Supervision, Top Leadership, and Feedback.

The Supervision scale "includes statements about whether the supervisor is willing to listen to the subordinate's opinions, to provide feedback and to help the subordinate grow and develop" (Campbell and Hyne 1995, 12)—or, in other words, how well employees and tasks are managed in the company. While the ratings in Supervision are within the mid-range of the *Organizational Survey* scale (50–55), the difference between ratings (52 versus 54) may reflect a disconnect between how lower-level employees and senior executives see the company being managed. Figure 1.10 shows this same pattern of a perception gap more clearly in responses to three specific questions within the Supervision scale. Again, while the data don't permit firm diagnoses for these perception gaps, these factors could be possible causes:

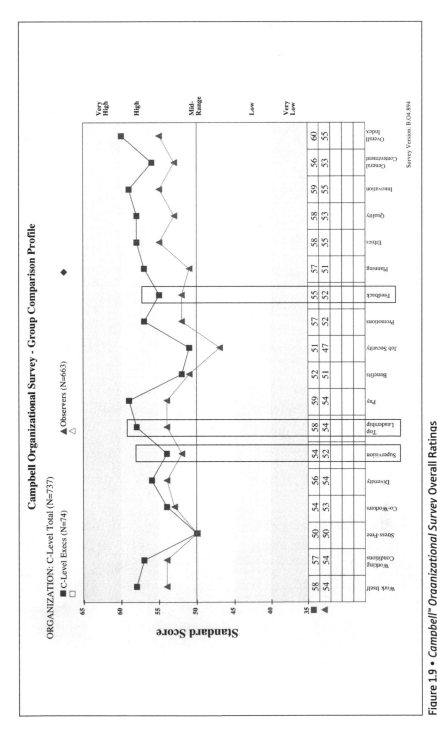

Figure 1.9 • *Campbell™ Organizational Survey* Overall Ratings

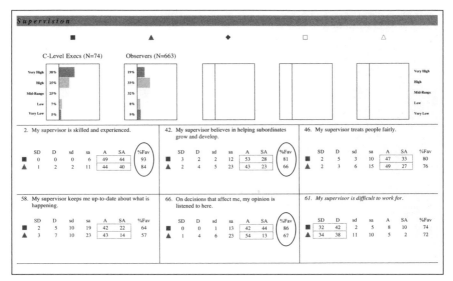

Figure 1.10 • *Campbell™ Organizational Survey* **Supervision Scale Questions**
Note: "Percent Favorable" reflects answers that indicate approval. For positive statements favorable responses would be "Always" or "Usually" and for negative statements favorable responses would be "Never" or "Seldom."

- Senior executives may feel ownership for placing supervisors in leadership positions and therefore assess Supervision performance high as a reflection of their own ability to identify talent.

- Senior executives clearly have their input heard by supervisors and may infer that supervisors are listening equally attentively to their subordinates.

The Top Leadership scale in the *Campbell Organizational Survey* is an indication of how senior leaders are perceived; that is, if they are seen as competent, dynamic, and having a vision of where the company is going. In general this scale rates opinions regarding "how well the organization is being led" (Campbell and Hyne 1995, 13). The ratings for the Top Leadership scale fall closer to the high mark with senior executives (58)—somewhat higher than with others (54). So from the point of view of "leading the organization," the scale of Top Leadership reflects a highly favorable rating, while the scale of Supervision (which is more reflective of managing people and tasks) is at the mid-level favorable rating, suggesting higher perception for how the organization is led com-

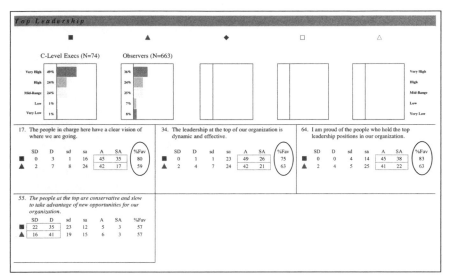

Figure 1.11 • *Campbell™ Organizational Survey* Top Leadership Scale Questions

pared to how the organization is managed (supervised). However, reflecting on the item-level questions for the Top Leadership scale reveals several interesting perception gaps between senior executives and the others (see Figure 1.11).

With regard to having a vision, leading effectively, and overall pride in top leadership, it is clear that senior executives have a rosier view than that of the rest—with differences ranging from twelve to twenty percentage points. As noted earlier, this perception gap can be attributed to the Hierarchy Effect, where those at the top have a more favorable perception than those further removed from the executive ranks.

The last scale in the *Organizational Survey* to consider here is Feedback—the communication channels, appraisal process, and overall dissemination of information within the workplace. In this scale senior executives provided a standard 55 rating, while the others provided a standard 52 rating. Again, what is of keen interest in the Feedback scale is the difference in responses, as reflected in Figure 1.12.

Several observations can be made on the item-level questions on the Feedback scale. First, in general the scores are still favorable but lower, ranging in the mid-fifties. Also, while no one provided very high ratings, the same perception gap between senior executives and others appears

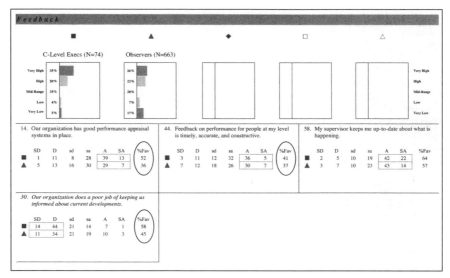

Figure 1.12 • *Campbell™ Organizational Survey* Feedback Scale Questions

on questions relating to performance appraisals and performance feedback. This perception gap is also reflected in the questions on corporate
communications.

What is interesting in the data on the Feedback scale, in addition to
the perception gap between senior executives and observers, is that neither group sees feedback as an organizational strength. So while executives rate Feedback higher than observers do, they still see Feedback on
performance and organizational communications as marginal at best.

SUMMARY OF DATA

So what can be gleaned from all the data collected on C-level executives?
Senior executives are driven to contribute to their organization's success
by seeking structure and designing strategies toward broad goals. They
also like to deal directly with problems that are causing confusion and
inefficiency, and their leadership style is one that provides long-range
plans, engages tough decisions when necessary, and embraces complex
problems. And senior executives are most comfortable when they are
running as much of the organization as possible.

Consequently, C-level executives will approach their leadership positions with the following mind-set (Waterman and Rogers 2004, 3–32), as they:

- Demonstrate a somewhat moderate need for interpersonal contact and interaction that suggests they are "choosy about how, when and where [they] associate with others—and [are] cautious about how [they] use or share authority"

- Prefer a limited amount of warmth and are more focused on the task than on the relationship

- Are inclined to take the initiative

- Gravitate toward structure and order

- Work well in areas that come naturally and where they can increase their expertise and shore up their self-assurance

- Exhibit the ability to moderate their behavior based on the situation—reflecting strong social intelligence skills

Senior executives demonstrate leadership behaviors such as "sound judgment" when they are able to see concepts and patterns in complex situations and readily grasping issues despite having ambiguous data. These key strengths also emerge in senior executives' proclivity to demonstrate leadership dimensions such as these:

- **Business Acumen.** Understand how strategies and tactics work in the marketplace.

- **Customer Orientation.** Know who the customers are, how they are motivated, and the competitive threats to their loyalty.

- **Results Orientation.** Focus on getting the job done, without confusing activity with accomplishment.

- **Strategic Thinking.** Look ahead to see trends in the market, industry, and environment.

- **Innovation.** Look for new approaches and view setbacks as opportunity to learn.

- **Integrity.** Make decisions against an uncompromising set of values and standards.

- **Interpersonal Maturity.** Have care and concern for others and take a collaborative approach to bringing out the best in others.

These insights highlight just a few of the leadership characteristics associated with the assessments reviewed thus far. The comments in this section are drawn from several development guides including Lombardo and Eichinger's *FYI—For Your Improvement;* Waterman and Rogers' *Introduction to the FIRO-B® Instrument;* Hirsh and Kummerow's *Introduction to Type® in Organizations;* Nilsen and Campbell's *CLI Planning Guide;* CCL's *Executive Dimensions Planning Guide,* and CPP's *FIRO-B® and MBTI® Form K Modal Profiles.* This summary forms a backdrop and reference point for the relevant research on the topic of power, influence, and effective leadership.

OBSERVATIONS ON
HOW SENIOR EXECUTIVES LEAD

Reflecting on the data and research reviewed thus far, two questions come to mind:

- How much real influence do senior executives have on the overall performance of the organization?

- "It's lonely at the top," they say. If this is so, how much is attributable to the leadership style of the executive and how much to the inherent distance associated with senior positions?

How Much Real Influence Do Executives Have?

Countless books on leadership recount the way great leaders have defined, reinvented, or saved their company. Yet Henry Mintzberg reminds us that people we once praised as brilliant leaders we soon criticize as ineffective. With this in mind Mintzberg admonishes us that "organizations that need to be turned around by [great] leaders will soon turn back again" (1996, 64). So, he continues, while a visionary leader can build a great company, once the organization has achieved momentum, what's needed is a leader who is competent, devoted, knows what's happening, and is in tune with the spirit and heart of the organization. The question to be asked now is, How much influence does an executive leader really have on an organization? This question came home to me just as I was leaving American Express.

I had been with Amex for eleven years and had risen to a senior position in the organization. We had just completed a very successful project that brought several of us involved with the effort into the limelight. As typically happens after such an initiative, a few of us associated with the effort were courted away by other companies—first my boss, then his boss, and then me. My boss went to a very large manufacturer, and his boss went to a world-renowned service provider—both with higher-level positions and much more money. I kept in touch with them, even taking opportunities to drop in and visit as my travel permitted. I was taken aback as I soon realized how difficult it was proving for them to lead effectively—that is, to get things done in their new companies. At Amex all my boss (and his boss) had had to do was think a thought or wish an idea and people would turn on a dime. But in their new organizations their influence was greatly diminished—even though they had higher-level positions. They couldn't just direct activity to get it done—they had to marshal support and buy-in, and they had to win over their direct reports to the value of a particular initiative and why they needed to jump on board. In the end one of the ex-Amex senior executives left his new company and the other learned how to adapt to a culture where very little got done.

Why Is It Lonely at the Top?

From working with senior executives, CCL staff have come to understand some fascinating perspectives. One such perspective is that the higher up an executive goes in the organization the more rarified the atmosphere—and consequently the less interaction with others inside the organization. The result is that senior executives are less likely to have access to unbiased input on how the company is performing or, for that matter, how well they themselves are doing as leaders. To some extent it's easy to see how this plays out naturally for a typical C-level executive based on the personality data reviewed thus far—these senior executives have a preference for being very selective regarding the people they work with closely and perhaps even more exclusive regarding those they socialize with.

This may provide some insight as to why senior executives who come to a new organization will soon tap prior associates from other organizations to join them. These old cronies are comfortable working partners for the senior executives and provide a sense of stability, loyalty, and assurance. But the question to ask is whether this tendency of senior executives to build and stick to a close-knit grouping of confidants overly constricts their sphere of influence. Even a tight-knit group of Nobel chemists, while brilliant in their specific fields, will generally see the world as compounds of elements and chemical reactions. It may take the addition of a few math people, a machinist, a baker, and a banker to solve complex problems.

CALL TO ACTION

The final question to consider with regard to power, influence, and effective leadership is what Lee and Pinney refer to as the "Now what?"—putting what's been learned into action (2002, 3). It is a good idea to consider the caution these authors provide: the time lag between changing behavior and seeing results can be interminable for people used to quick action and faster outcomes—and it can be problematic to stay with the program (7). In this "Now what?" phase it is helpful to look for markers along the way that can provide some level of progress of your efforts and keep you on track.

Calibrating Your Sphere of Influence

The data and research reported in this chapter highlight some of the implications that can result if your sphere of influence is too narrow:

- Inability to adapt to unforeseen conditions
- Danger of groupthink

- Tunnel vision from locking on to an initiative that is ineffective or damaging to the organization
- Inaccurate assessment—overstatement or underestimate of your impact on others

To address these potential issues, senior executives must develop the ability to regularly calibrate their sphere of influence—that is, to take stock of the *how, who,* and *what* that come into play as they lead their organizations. This calibration occurs as a result of consciously reflecting on those factors that influence how you lead. This includes taking stock of your leadership style and preferences and making sure you're not overrelying on a particular strength or bias.

Likewise, it is critical for senior executives to evaluate how much influence they are exerting on those around them. Consider how many tough questions people ask when you suggest a particular course of action. Are people interested in understanding the rationale for decisions you make or do they simply want to know how high to jump? If you find that your sphere of influence is out of balance, the following actions may prove helpful to recalibrate to a healthy position.

Finding and Listening to Other Voices. The assessment data reported here show that when making decisions, C-level executives will often ignore their own feelings, let alone the feelings of others (Hirsh and Kummerow 1998, 25). I recall working for a bank president who for the life of him could not understand why his employees would get worked up over the size and furnishings of their offices. I asked him if these things mattered to him—noting of course that he already had the biggest and best-decorated office in the bank. "Not at all," he replied. "I'm never in the office anyway and I could work out of my briefcase in the middle of the Operations floor." "This is why you don't understand your employees' concern with offices," I replied. "Since it's not a concern for you, you think it shouldn't concern others."

If you find that your actions are having unintended impacts on others, it may be helpful to find a voice that speaks to the feelings of others and bring this voice into your sphere of influence. Although the ability to tap into others' feelings is something you might develop over time, in the short run it's useful to include in your inner circle someone who has this insight—and make sure you check in with this person on a regular basis.

Additionally, if you are finding that people are for the most part buying into your decisions unquestioningly, then by all means quickly find someone who is comfortable (and formidable) enough to present an opposing point of view. I had the privilege of co-leading the launch of a major new credit card at Amex. My co-leader was extremely bright and brought a customer service perspective to the table. My background at that time was primarily technology and operations. Needless to say, it was like oil and water; we clashed on nearly every issue. But in the end we learned several valuable lessons:

- The actions resulting from our bumping heads were always better than what either of us would have come up with on our own.

- We each gained a perspective we had not previously held.

- Because of the energy it took to get to consensus, we learned to recognize actions where we could acquiesce to one position or the other and separate them from actions we really needed to hash out.

Engaging in Stretching Exercises. You may find that you're often taking action too quickly or that you've become so fixated on a prescribed plan that you are surprised and unable to respond when unforeseen events unfold. If this is happening on a regular basis, one technique that may help you slow down and work though your action plans is to engage in "stretching exercises"—thoughtfully and considerately debating, challenging, and assessing the course of action you've developed. Bill Marriott Jr. tells of how his father regularly put him through stretching exercises—making him explain, defend, and rationalize why he was in favor of a particular action. Whether the elder Marriott was in favor of the action or not, he served as a sparring partner for his son. The most memorable experience occurred when Marriott Jr. wanted to get into the hospitality business—something Marriott Sr. was at best lukewarm toward. Yet after several stretching exercises both men were convinced of the merits of the venture, and the rest, as they say, is history.

Key to engaging in stretching exercises is finding a worthy sparring partner. This is difficult for senior executives because, as noted earlier, the higher up in the organization you go, the less likely you are to find people willing to disagree with you. However, having someone or some group of people regularly challenge your thinking and presumptions can be a powerful asset in engaging thoughtful, well-planned actions.

Understanding the Power of Self-Awareness. One of the most powerful interventions in CCL programs occurs when executives come face-to-face with feedback from peers, bosses, and direct reports. This self-awareness enables leaders to honestly assess their strengths and weaknesses and allows them to understand when they should draw on their experience and when they should seek experiences from others. Two senior fellows at CCL draw attention to the power of self-awareness:

> But self-awareness also means that people must understand why they are the way they are; what traits, learned preferences, experiences, or situational factors have shaped their profile of strengths and weaknesses. Self-awareness means understanding the impact their strengths and weaknesses have on others, on their effectiveness in various roles in life and on reaching their goal." (McCauley and Van Velsor 2003, 13)

The power of self-awareness is threefold:

- Understanding what got you to the dance (where your strengths are)
  - Allowing you to maintain and grow this strength, while being careful not to overuse or come to rely too heavily on a particular strength
- Awareness of your weaknesses
  - Not using a weakness as a crutch (for example, avoiding statements like, "Forgive me for talking too much, but you know I'm a strong extrovert")
  - Working on developing this skill
  - Seeking out others who have this as a strength as the situation warrants
- Awareness of how you interact with others (the impact of your sphere of influence)

- Determining how you affect the behavior and actions of others

- Being aware of what impact others' actions and behaviors have on you

PERSONAL REFLECTION: HOW'D I GET HERE?

Warren Bennis tells the story of how he became a university president. He wanted to see if his ideas for leadership had legs and would work in the real world, so he set out to become a university president. He left MIT (where he had tenure and a corner office), did four years as provost at SUNY in Buffalo, and then took the position of president at the University of Cincinnati. During a gathering at Harvard a colleague caught Bennis off-guard by asking him directly, "So, Warren, do you like being a university president?" Bennis's immediate response was, "I don't know." After spending time thinking about the question, he realized that, in fact, his passion was not in being a university president—the answer was no, so he stopped (Bennis 2004, 3–4).

So ask yourself, *How did I get here?* Like Bennis, did you set out to get that corner office, that senior executive position, or did you fall into the job? Were you in the right place at the right time? Then ask yourself, *Is this my calling?* (Not, *How am I doing?*) The trappings of success may mask the real issue, which is whether you're doing what you were created to do. Just because you're good at something, that doesn't mean you're called to do it. If you could go back ten, fifteen, twenty years, would you still take the path that led you to the executive ranks?

Keep in mind that to some organizations you are a commodity—something to manage, invest in, and shape to grow in a certain direction. "High potentials" are nurtured by organizations to assume higher levels of responsibility *within* the company—to the company's benefit. But if this is not what you're called to do, despite a handsome salary, you may find you're unfulfilled.

2

The Myth of
Effective Decision Making

In *Whatever It Takes,* McCall and Kaplan lay out the classic four-step decision-making process:

- Clearly define and state the problem to be addressed

- Conduct an exhaustive search for information and contextual details regarding the problem

- Generate numerous alternatives, ideas, and solutions

- Make a careful, calculated, and deliberate choice among alternatives

Senior executives are known for being remarkably adept at achieving results—then raising the bar higher. In these accomplishments senior executives make countless decisions every day. But herein lies the myth in decision making: *that a problem, crisis, or opportunity can in fact be resolved with a well-timed, well-considered decision.*

Most problems or crises are not solved, they're merely contained (McCall and Kaplan 1990, xvii). Likewise, most opportunities are not captured with a well-executed decision—they are temporarily secured. This myth about decision making stems in part from the fact that many decision-making processes don't consider all possible options, just those options that are in bounds. Thus, contrary to the myth that senior executives call the shots, these executives rarely have much latitude in their strategic decision making because they must continually navigate boundaries such as working capital, market pressures, board bias, and so on.

In reality, most so-called decisions are streams of choices that are anything but discrete events—rather, each separate decision combines as a force multiplier that in the end can sweep an executive down an unintended path. McCall and Kaplan draw this distinction, suggesting that "decision makers in an organization are floating in the stream, jostled capriciously by problems popping up, and finding anchors through action at a given time and a given place" (1990, 5). This is a terrific analogy to grab onto: decisions are merely anchors that give you a momentary respite to catch your breath, get your bearings, and ready yourself to navigate the next wave of decisions. In fact, the only difference between a strategic decision and a more tactical one is the amount of time an anchor might hold you in place before the next wave of choices comes along.

The effectiveness of decision making is then composed in equal parts of how you approach problem solving and how your organization is structured to facilitate making decisions. Consider why it is that some organizations are able to address complex issues in a timely manner, while other organizations struggle with even the simplest decisions. Are there characteristics in an organization's structure that empower people to make more timely decisions? Is an organization's strategy so compelling that it inspires employees to action? The answer may lie in understanding the linkage between an organization's structure, its strategy, and the executive processes it uses in approaching challenging problems. Research on influencers in the decision-making process can help further this understanding.

VIEWS ON DECISION MAKING

The volume of material and research on the topic of decision making is astounding. However, a few areas may shed light on two critical influencers in the decision-making process: how senior executives reflect inwardly and externally when making decisions, and what organizational structures support or inhibit the decision-making process. First, however, take a moment for a closer look at some of the myths typically associated with effective decision making.

Decision-Making Myths

Donaldson and Lorsch highlight a number of myths surrounding decision making that stand in contrast to the reality facing senior executives (1983, 7–9) as seen in Table 2.1.

To this last point Donaldson and Lorsch expand on the dilemma that occurs when executives' belief systems overly influence their decision making:

> Central to each belief system is management's vision of the company's distinctive competitive advantage. In its managers' minds, this vision defines what the company's economic, human, and technical resources can—and cannot—accomplish: the kinds of economic activity the firm should undertake and how this activity is to be conducted. In essence, therefore, it shapes the strategic means they select. Moreover, by leading management to select specific product markets and competitive environments, the belief system is ultimately responsible for the particular parameters of the demand side of the funds-flow equation and the financial goals systems. Thus management's subjective beliefs about individual competence and comparative advantage lie behind the objective realities of the firm's economic and financial environment. (1983, 80)

Understandably, senior executives will develop preconceived notions of where the organization's strengths lie, how the firm stacks up against the competition, what its customers want, and so on. However, these beliefs can cause executives to isolate themselves from critical external

MYTH	REALITY
Senior executives have free rein to make the decisions they feel are needed.	Senior executives are confronted with multiple constraints in their decision making: • Board directives and preferences • Availability of funding and capital • Competition • Personal biases
Executives move between companies often, and thus corporate leadership (governance and decision making) is impaired by a transitory leadership.	In many companies the core executives leading the firm are long-tenure employees who deeply associate their success with the well-being of the organization. (Notwithstanding Cappelli and Hamori's 2005 research suggesting that many of today's senior executives do jump from company to company, a fair number of core executive decision makers have been with their organization for some time.)
The overall goal of senior executives is to strengthen shareholder value.	The primary goal of senior executives is the survival of the organization they are highly invested in—which translates into increasing and ensuring corporate wealth and well-being—not necessarily shareholder wealth.
Decision making at the executive level is a rational process that considers multiple factors in a logical manner.	Many decisions are based on forecasts and projections that are for the most part no more than educated guesses. Thus executive decision making typically reflects non-rational considerations that have been filtered by the senior executive's own belief system.

Table 2.1 • Decision-Making Myths and Realities

perspectives. Even when an organization's senior executives work as a collective team, their group thinking can create a consensus filter that blocks consideration of external views. As Senge and Joni point out, "Many people hold the idea that when leaders and teams engage in collective inquiry [group decision making], members' isolation will de facto be reduced. True and not true. In many cases the better people get at wading into the hardest inquiry, the more it raises the level of isolation" (2005, 8). Signs of this isolation can range from overconfidence all the way to overinflated, out-of-control egos.

Blinded by Their Own Light

A paradox encumbers senior executives as they move up the corporate ladder. The drive for results begins to fuel a desire—perhaps even a passion—to achieve stellar performance. After a while executives may begin to believe that there is very little they can't accomplish if they simply put their mind to the task at hand. To a degree, it is this very self-confidence that propels executives forward in their careers. However, if left unchecked, an imbalance can occur whereby senior executives build a false sense of self-confidence for work that they themselves produce, and develop lack of confidence in the work of others. This plays out as doubt that anyone other than themselves is capable of making sound decisions. Eventually they tend to maintain a stranglehold on a failing strategy despite signs and advice to change course. Thus, as Pfeffer asserts, "there is persistence with flawed decisions not simply as a way of justifying one's previous commitments but also because, given the level of involvement in the decision making process, the decision maker does not accurately perceive the outcomes and therefore never really apprehends the true extent of the problem or failure" (quoted in Kramer and Neale 1998, 13). So even when external observers clearly see the danger in continuing with a course of action, executives who have fallen into this pattern see themselves as steadfastly sticking to their guns. Noted executive adviser David Nadler recounts a real-life example of just such a condition (2005, 71):

I faced that situation in the late 1990s while consulting to the CEO of a major technology firm. In a frank conversation with my client, I explained my concern that the company's flashy results masked pervasive, potentially disastrous organizational rot. I cited unsound business strategies, questionable methods for booking sales, and deteriorating morale among the firm's key people. At my persistent urging, the CEO reluctantly appointed a top-level committee of very bright people to investigate my complaints.

Several months later, they came back with findings even worse than I had expected. As the committee presented its report, I saw the CEO's eyes glaze over. He didn't buy it, or he didn't want to buy it. Weeks passed, and he did nothing. Eventually, I had to accept that he would never act. This CEO was steering his company toward a crisis, and I was powerless to stop it. So I told him how I felt: that I was no longer having any impact and it was time to end our relationship. He readily agreed. All the problems uncovered by his task force persisted. Within a year, the company's results cratered, and the CEO was fired.

The root cause for such failures is executives' overinflated ego—their perception that they have all the right answers or that without them, the organization is lost. In contrast, Jim Collins offers a counter to the egocentric executive by describing what he terms "Level 5" leaders; those who build "enduring greatness through a paradoxical combination of personal humility plus professional will" (2005, 140). From the personality and leadership characteristic data discussed thus far, one theme that has emerged is a senior executive's professional will—that is, the desire and perseverance to achieve results. What has not emerged, however, is the *humility* of the most effective executives. In fact, most researchers don't even attempt to measure humility as a leadership competency, and humility is a leadership quality that is often mistaken for weakness or lack of confidence. However, there is no purer strength or assuredness than that found in genuine humility. Most leaders would not be comfortable being characterized as humble—nor would many leaders recognize humility as a key factor in realizing their success. Rather, most leaders point to their ability to successfully maneuver within the corporate infrastructure or their ability to be resourceful and get things done. Here again Collins highlights this point by suggesting "the great irony is that the animus [will or spirit] and personal ambition that often drives peo-

PERSONAL HUMILITY	PROFESSIONAL WILL
Demonstrates a compelling modesty, shunning public adulation; never boastful.	Creates superb results, a clear catalyst in the transition from good to great.
Acts with quiet, calm determination; relies principally on inspired standards (and not inspiring charisma) to motivate.	Demonstrates an unwavering resolve to do whatever must be done to produce the best long-term results, no matter how difficult.
Channels ambition into the company, not the self; sets up successors for even more greatness in the next generation.	Sets the standard of building an enduring great company.
Looks in the mirror, not out the window, to apportion responsibility for poor results, never blaming other people, external factors, or bad luck.	Looks out the window, not in the mirror, to apportion credit for the success of the company—to other people.

Table 2.2 • Level 5 Leaders' Balance of Personal Humility and Professional Will

ple to become a Level 4 [effective] leader stands at odds with the humility required to raise to Level 5" (145). To further illustrate this point Collins (142) compares the balance that Level 5 leaders strike between personal humility and professional will, as seen in Table 2.2.

Coaches, Advisers, and Third Opinions

Senior executives today have several options available to them for expanding their sphere of influence by bringing in external perspectives through formal coaching, trusted advisers, and third opinions. To be sure, there is a resurgence today of formal coaching for executives. Formal coaching is a collaborative practice intended to assess and understand a leader's developmental opportunities, to "challenge current constraints while exploring new possibilities and to ensure accountability and support for reaching goals and sustaining development" (McCauley and Van Velsor 2003, 116). In the end the primary goal in coaching is leader development, which all parties hope will translate into increased and improved individual and organizational performance (150).

In contrast to a coach, an adviser to a senior executive is someone who can bridge the gap between the isolation of top-level positions and the realities that senior executives face each day. Here again Nadler (2005, 70) points to the challenges that come with the role of the senior executives, who:

- Rarely receive unbiased information

- Receive hard truths only after they've have been filtered or watered down

- Become a lightning rod for internal and external criticism

- Often have the final word on critical business decisions

It is helpful then for senior executives to develop a "close, long-term relationship with a trusted adviser" who can provide open and honest insight and reflection. But as Nadler points out, the role of adviser is difficult to define and more difficult to fill (72–77). Advisers to senior executives struggle with balancing their loyalty to the senior executive and their commitment to the executive's organization. Advisers become privy to endless streams of information—so much information that discerning what and how to communicate upward to the senior executive is a particular challenge. Advisers must be wary not to be drawn toward an inclination to provide their own perspective and opinions regarding the performance or potential of specific employees in the organization. Also, advisers can become so involved with the senior executive that they form a surrogate relationship with the organization, becoming too impassioned and taken with the trappings of power access and privilege. Finally, advisers need to beware of becoming so personally connected with the senior executive that they lose their ability to provide objective counsel and insight.

According to Senge and Joni, executives' spheres of influence have three layers. The first layer is the executive's own self-refection, ideas, and thoughts. The second is the subject matter experts who have an interest in the outcome of any given decision (direct reports, others within the organization, board members, perhaps key stakeholders such as partners and investors). The last (or third opinion) layer consists of outside voices that are not aligned organizationally with the executive nor vested personally or directly in the outcome of the decision. In this regard third opinions are even further removed from the day-to-day activity than advisers and thereby can provide insight with no intent to expand their interest beyond that of being a sounding board. So while a coach will focus specifically on the executive's leadership development and the adviser will split the focus between the executive and the organization, third-opinion providers focus on individual business demands within specific contexts and within specific levels of complexity of the business (2005, 3–8).

Execution, Organizational DNA, and Decision Rights

The drive to achieve bottom-line results and improve time-to-market has yielded a maniacal focus on how organizations can "break through their performance barriers" through "ruthless execution." While the term *ruthless execution* might imply "results at all costs," this isn't necessarily the case. For example, Hartman, Sifonis, and Kador suggest that in its basic form "ruthless execution" is simply about taking quick, decisive action (2002, 2)—in other words, to:

- Assess the problem

- Frame the issue within the constructs of available resources

- Define and analyze trade-offs and

- MAKE A DECISION AND GO! (Bennett 2003, 1)

So why do firms like Booz Allen Hamilton regularly recount case studies of organizations with brilliant strategies that are unable to execute against clearly defined action plans (Booz Allen Hamilton 2002, 1)? To help answer this question, it is helpful to examine an organization's structure under the lens of its DNA and focus on the specific decision-making process.

Just as individuals have unique characteristics, companies have distinct traits of their own. From this comparison, the analogy of organizational DNA has been used to "codify the idiosyncratic characteristics of the company" into four base components (Neilson, Pasternack, and Mendes 2003, 3–4):

- Structure (the boxes and lines of a hierarchy)

- Motivators (reward and recognition)

- Information (metrics used to identify and measure activity)

- Decision rights (the specific decision-making authority assigned)

While the interaction of each base component is critical to the functioning of an organization, it is within the area of decision rights and specifically the decision-making process that some of the barriers that interfere with an organization's ability to achieve its goals become clear. To help in developing this understanding, it is useful to start by reviewing the way executives approach decision making.

SENIOR EXECUTIVES AND DECISION MAKING

The personality data for the population of C-level executives under discussion provide some interesting insight into the executive approach to decision making.

Personality Types and Relating Interpersonally

Four predominant personality types—ISTJ, INTJ, INTP, ENTJ, reflected in Table 2.3—show how our sample of senior executives make decisions and solve problems (Myers 1998, 14, 18, 23, 25; Hirsh and Kummerow 1998, 10, 11, 22, 25).

Schnell's work highlights how executives' interpersonal styles can affect the way they engage with teams and decision making (Schnell and Hammer 1993, 16–25). Specifically, executives are likely to exhibit the following tendencies:

LEADERSHIP CHARACTERISTICS	APPROACH TO DECISION MAKING
ISTJs (Introversion, Sensing, Thinking, Judging)	
Are clear and steadfast in their opinions because they have arrived at them by carefully and thoroughly applying logical criteria based on their experience and knowledge.	Want to be thoroughly grounded in the facts that are analyzed in a logical framework.
INTJs (Introversion, Intuition, Thinking, Judging)	
Are excellent long-range planners and often rise to positions of leadership. They are independent, trusting their own perceptions and judgments over those of others.	Want to use their internal vision for strategies, systems, and structures that they have objectively determined.
INTPs (Introversion, Intuition, Thinking, Perceiving)	
Quickly see inconsistencies and illogicality and enjoy taking apart and reworking ideas. They naturally build complex theoretical systems to explain the realities they see.	Want to use their internal logic to structure problems and solutions while attending to the facts and specifics.
ENTJs (Extraversion, Intuition, Thinking, Judging)	
Typically are excellent solvers of organizational problems as they are keenly aware of the intricate connections within organizations and are action oriented.	Want to logically analyze and control situations based on an internal understanding of what could be.

Table 2.3 • Senior Executives' Leadership Characteristics and Approaches to Decision Making

- Will approach working in a team as a dependent function—"it depends on what's at stake and what the potential rewards are"
- Will be more focused on time and actually making a decision than on the decision-making process—perhaps resulting in
  - Cutting off group dialogue too quickly
  - Imposing undue pressure to act
- May be quick to set limits on what can and cannot be considered in the decision (for example, acknowledging that they may not know what the answer is, but they certainly know what's it's not)
- Will engage in team decision making by leading with authority— which will be problematic if
  - Team members do not get along
  - Team members have a high level of independent thinking
  - Many defined problems and solutions arise and are untested

Insights on Three Dimensions of Decision Making

Three leadership characteristics within the *Executive Dimensions* assessment are particularly interesting in the context of how executives engage decision making: how they lead their business through sound judgment; how they lead others in forging synergy; and how they lead themselves through personal courage. It's useful to review each of these leadership characteristics more closely.

Sound Judgment. Table 2.4 outlines the behaviors associated with leading the organization through Sound Judgment as well as how executives, bosses, and direct reports rated the senior executives' perceived competence in these behaviors.

Recall from Chapter 1 that while executives, bosses, and direct reports identified Sound Judgment as one of the more important competencies, only direct reports failed to rate this as one of the top strengths for executives. Table 2.4 shows the overall competency rating on Sound

SOUND JUDGMENT	EXECUTIVES	BOSSES	DIRECT REPORTS
Sees underlying concepts and patterns in complex situations	3.89	3.61	3.62
Gives appropriate weight to the concerns of key stakeholders	3.40	3.56	3.41
Readily grasps the crux of an issue despite having ambiguous information	3.82	3.59	3.60
Makes effective decisions in a timely manner	3.65	3.58	3.46
Accurately differentiates between important and unimportant issues	3.71	3.73	3.50
Develops solutions that effectively address underlying problems	3.53	3.48	3.30
Average	3.67	3.59	3.48

Table 2.4 • *Executive Dimensions* Sound Judgment Scale

Judgment in the mid-3s (ratings are 1–5, with 5 being the highest), which is a good rating, and what can be expected for high-performing executives.

It is interesting to note that senior executives rate their performance toward the high end of the scale in the areas of seeing patterns in complex situations, grasping the crux of an issue despite ambiguous information, and differentiating between important and unimportant issues. For the most part bosses and direct reports likewise rate these behaviors higher. However, everyone seems to agree that the executives' ability to weigh the concern of key stakeholders is not as strong a behavior. Finally, bosses and particularly direct reports perceive senior executives' performance in addressing underlying problems as one of the lesser-rated behaviors—which may perhaps reflect that while senior executives are adept at solving problems, they may not get to the root cause as effectively.

FORGING SYNERGY	EXECUTIVES	BOSSES	DIRECT REPORTS
Focuses others' energy on common goals, priorities, and problems	3.49	3.66	3.34
Helps subordinates resolve their conflicts constructively	3.30	3.35	2.97
Seeks common ground in an effort to resolve conflicts	3.46	3.52	3.20
Works harmoniously with key stakeholders	3.40	3.69	3.61
Identifies and removes barriers to effective teamwork	3.14	3.32	3.05
Maintains smooth, effective working relationships	3.44	3.62	3.40
Average	3.37	3.53	3.26

Table 2.5 • *Executive Dimensions* Forging Synergy Scale

Forging Synergy. Table 2.5 outlines the behaviors associated with leading others in Forging Synergy, and how executives, bosses, and direct reports rated the senior executives' perceived competence in these behaviors.

Again, recall from Chapter 1 that executives, bosses, and direct reports did not identify Forging Synergy as highly important or as a top strength. This is reflected in the overall ratings of low 3s shown in Table 2.5. So as it relates to getting things done, fostering collaboration (Forging Synergy) is not a behavior senior executives draw upon most readily. This is most evident in the ratings for behaviors around resolving conflict and removing barriers to effective teamwork. Thus senior executives may be more inclined to achieve results and less focused on how the results are achieved. This approach may lead to diminished sustainability for the organization as the overall well-being of the workforce—one of the three key components of effective leadership, as pointed out in the preface—will be undercut.

COURAGE	EXECUTIVES	BOSSES	DIRECT REPORTS
Takes the lead on unpopular though necessary actions	3.61	3.45	3.49
Acts decisively to tackle difficult problems	3.75	3.76	3.56
Perseveres in the face of problems and difficulties	4.16	4.08	3.92
Confronts conflicts promptly, so problems do not escalate	3.26	3.42	3.26
Has the courage to confront others when necessary	3.57	3.79	3.8
Average	3.67	3.70	3.61

Table 2.6 • *Executive Dimensions* Courage Scale

Courage. Table 2.6 outlines the behaviors associated with leading others through Courage as well as how executives, bosses, and direct reports rated the senior executives' perceived competence in these behaviors.

As noted in Chapter 1, there was unanimous consent that Courage is a strength demonstrated by senior executives, which is clearly played out in the ratings for executives' behavior to act decisively and persevere against difficult problems. Noteworthy are the lower ratings for executives' behavior to deal with issues before they become problems ("confronts conflicts promptly")—perhaps suggesting that while senior executives are great at killing problems, they aren't so adept at preventing issues from turning into problems.

Insights on Personal Characteristics and Leadership Success

Several characteristics addressed in the *Campbell Leadership Index*— consideration, productivity, calmness, optimism, and flexibility—may

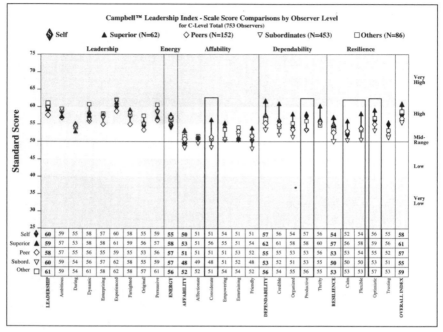

Figure 2.1 • *Campbell™ Leadership Index* **Scales Relating to Decision Making**

prove productive in a continuing review of the way C-level executives approach decision making. Figure 2.1 highlights these characteristics in the *Leadership Index* profile.

You can gain some fascinating insight by looking a bit more closely at the individual item-level questions raised for each leadership characteristic. For example, Figure 2.2 shows that senior executives score high from all observers (superiors, peers, and subordinates) on the questions of dependable, productive, and efficient (the opposite of wasteful). And excellent scores relating to timeliness were drawn out on the questions of effectiveness and procrastination. However, scores on the question of prudence, which is framed in the context of planning for the unexpected, are rather lower, a point that also bears on the issue of flexibility.

While the overall scores on the Optimistic scale indicate that senior executives in general have confidence in their abilities (and their people) to successfully deal with difficult challenges, the item-level questions in

Productive Scale

24. Dependable - Performs as promised.

	Nev	Sel	Occ	Som	Usu	Alw	%Fav
You	1		3		56	14	
All Obs	3	6	25	79	421	218	85
Superior		2	3	32	25		92
Peer	1	1	8	11	90	41	86
Subord	2	5	12	58	257	118	83
Other			3	7	42	34	88

31. Effective - Gets projects done well and on time.

	Nev	Sel	Occ	Som	Usu	Alw	%Fav
You				3	58	13	
All Obs	2	10	40	109	436	156	79
Superior		1	8	36	17		85
Peer		1	11	20	92	28	79
Subord	2	8	24	69	263	87	77
Other		1	4	12	45	24	80

74. Procrastinating - Can't get necessary tasks done on time.

	Nev	Sel	Occ	Som	Usu	Alw	%Fav
You	17	36	9	10	2		
All Obs	244	326	72	75	26	8	76
Superior	26	21	6	9			76
Peer	45	72	13	13	8	1	77
Subord	141	194	46	47	17	6	74
Other	32	39	7	6	1		83

75. Productive - Gets a lot done.

	Nev	Sel	Occ	Som	Usu	Alw	%Fav
You				8	50	16	
All Obs	2	11	32	93	394	220	82
Superior			1	6	36	19	89
Peer		2	12	20	82	36	78
Subord	1	7	18	60	232	134	81
Other	1	2	1	7	44	31	87

76. Prudent - Plans for the unexpected.

	Nev	Sel	Occ	Som	Usu	Alw	%Fav
You		3	4	13	50	4	
All Obs	5	36	62	189	386	73	61
Superior		1	1	16	34	10	71
Peer	1	6	15	39	80	11	60
Subord	3	24	43	111	229	42	60
Other	1	5	3	23	43	10	62

97. Wasteful - Uses time, money, or other resources foolishly.

	Nev	Sel	Occ	Som	Usu	Alw	%Fav
You	31	38	4	1			
All Obs	398	274	33	32	11	1	90
Superior	42	17		2	1		95
Peer	82	58	4	6	2		92
Subord	228	168	27	19	7	1	88
Other	46	31	2	5	1		91

Figure 2.2 • *Campbell™ Leadership Index* Productive Scale Questions

Note: "Percent Favorable" reflects answers that indicate approval. For positive statements favorable responses would be "Always" or "Usually" and for negative statements favorable responses would be "Never" or "Seldom."

the Optimistic scale provide additional insight. Figure 2.3 reveals a bit of a dichotomy in the responses. For example, senior executives received high scores on the questions regarding disposition and resilience. However senior executives received lower scores on questions relating to mood, temperament, and seeing the best in people and situations. While definitive conclusions can't be drawn from these data, a few speculations are tempting:

- The optimism of senior executives may be highly situational—that is, when things are going well senior executives are buoyant, but this can change if conditions worsen.

- Even though senior executives' temperament may turn sour with a setback, they are very resilient personally—able to bounce back quickly. This may be a result from or be an effect of their self-confidence.

- It may be possible that senior executives' high level of self-confidence influences the way they perceive others and situations—perhaps suggesting that at times they may see the glass as half-empty rather than half-full.

Optimistic Scale

25. Discouraged – Feels gloomy and unhappy.

	Nev	Sel	Occ	Som	Usu	Alw	%Fav
You	29	35	3	7			
All Obs	391	289	32	37	2	1	90
Superior	30	26	3	3			90
Peer	77	59	7	7	1	1	89
Subord	239	171	18	24			91
Other	45	33	4	3	1		91

66. Moody - Shows sudden changes of emotion.

	Nev	Sel	Occ	Som	Usu	Alw	%Fav
You	5	45	14	9	1		
All Obs	164	345	71	123	40	10	68
Superior	25	23	6	8			77
Peer	33	75	15	21	6	2	71
Subord	83	208	43	81	30	8	64
Other	23	39	7	13	4		72

68. Optimistic - Sees the best in people and situations.

	Nev	Sel	Occ	Som	Usu	Alw	%Fav
You			10	52	12		
All Obs	26	50	177	394	103		66
Superior		3	12	40	7		76
Peer	5	7	38	79	22		67
Subord	19	39	109	224	60		63
Other	2	1	18	51	14		76

78. Resilient - Recovers quickly from failures or adversity.

	Nev	Sel	Occ	Som	Usu	Alw	%Fav
You			1	4	55	14	
All Obs	3	20	89	490	147		85
Superior		1	5	39	17		90
Peer		2	28	94	26		80
Subord	2	13	53	298	85		85
Other	1	4	3	59	19		91

93. Temperamental - Moody, irritable, and overly sensitive.

	Nev	Sel	Occ	Som	Usu	Alw	%Fav
You	12	48	11	2	1		
All Obs	246	323	65	83	30	3	76
Superior	37	14	8	3			82
Peer	48	75	10	14	5		81
Subord	130	193	44	56	25	3	72
Other	31	41	3	10			85

98. Well-adjusted - Handles personal and emotional problems well.

	Nev	Sel	Occ	Som	Usu	Alw	%Fav
You		1	5	57	11		
All Obs	1	13	36	90	403	203	81
Superior			2	5	32	23	89
Peer		2	5	23	81	41	80
Subord	1	8	26	54	242	116	80
Other		1	5	8	48	23	84

Figure 2.3 • Campbell™ Leadership Index Optimistic Scale Questions

Calm Scale

8. Calm - Unhurried, unruffled.

	Nev	Sel	Occ	Som	Usu	Alw	%Fav
You	7	9	10	44	4		
All Obs	6	74	84	157	344	87	57
Superior	4	4	15	28	11		63
Peer	9	20	36	66	20		57
Subord	6	52	53	91	204	47	55
Other		9	7	15	46	9	64

29. Easy-going - Has a calm and unhurried manner.

	Nev	Sel	Occ	Som	Usu	Alw	%Fav
You	2	10	11	23	28		
All Obs	25	88	108	153	294	84	50
Superior	1	5	3	12	31	9	66
Peer	1	5	20	35	58	23	53
Subord	20	56	77	87	170	43	47
Other	3	12	8	19	35	9	51

87. Serene - Calm and unruffled.

	Nev	Sel	Occ	Som	Usu	Alw	%Fav
You	1	5	8	21	38	1	
All Obs	16	60	93	176	341	63	54
Superior	1	13	17	40	63	18	53
Peer	15	38	64	102	203	28	51
Subord		7	7	20	41	10	60

Flexible Scale

2. Adaptable - Easily adjusts to changing conditions.

	Nev	Sel	Occ	Som	Usu	Alw	%Fav
You	1	6	50	17			
All Obs	7	29	152	418	143		75
Superior		5	46	11			92
Peer	4	39	76	31			71
Subord	7	22	88	248	86		74
Other	3	20	48	15			73

44. Flexible - Handles change and ambiguity well.

	Nev	Sel	Occ	Som	Usu	Alw	%Fav
You	1	8	52	13			
All Obs	21	60	173	382	116		66
Superior		4	13	34	11		73
Peer	1	12	40	76	23		65
Subord	19	37	98	230	68		66
Other	1	7	22	42	14		65

51. Headstrong - Difficult to reason with, opinionated.

	Nev	Sel	Occ	Som	Usu	Alw	%Fav
You		2	16	26	4		
All Obs	84	216	96	221	101	32	40
Superior	16	16	9	17	4		52
Peer	23	43	26	43	10	6	44
Subord	39	121	57	134	79	23	35
Other	6	36	4	27	8	3	50

90. Stubborn - Fixed in purpose or opinion; is difficult to change.

	Nev	Sel	Occ	Som	Usu	Alw	%Fav
You	9	22	17	22	4		
All Obs	99	218	125	190	101	18	42
Superior	23	15	7	12	5		61
Peer	22	45	31	38	15	1	44
Subord	41	129	78	118	72	14	38
Other	13	29	9	22	9	3	49

Figure 2.4 • Campbell™ Leadership Index Calm and Flexible Scales Questions

Considerate Scale

16. Considerate - Thoughtful of the needs and feelings of others.

	Nev	Sel	Occ	Som	Usu	Alw	%Fav
You	2	3	18	41	10		
All Obs	5	48	75	156	359	106	62
Superior	3	5	3	36	15		82
Peer	1	9	10	26	89	15	69
Subord	4	33	53	104	198	59	57
Other		7	23	36	17		62

18. Cooperative - Willing to work with the ideas of others.

	Nev	Sel	Occ	Som	Usu	Alw	%Fav
You		2	13	51	8		
All Obs	1	12	35	162	415	128	72
Superior		1	1	5	41	14	89
Peer			8	32	89	23	74
Subord	1	11	18	109	244	70	69
Other			8	16	41	21	72

53. Helpful - Ready and willing to give a hand to others.

	Nev	Sel	Occ	Som	Usu	Alw	%Fav
You			7	52	15		
All Obs	1	13	39	123	397	178	77
Superior			6	31	24		89
Peer		2	3	20	95	32	84
Subord	1	9	32	81	235	94	73
Other		1	4	16	36	28	75

58. Insensitive - Unaware of the feelings of others.

	Nev	Sel	Occ	Som	Usu	Alw	%Fav
You	15	31	12	13	3		
All Obs	165	263	107	143	61	6	57
Superior	24	15	10	10	3		63
Peer	39	55	21	22	12		63
Subord	78	162	67	96	39	6	54
Other	24	31	9	15	7		64

81. Sarcastic - Makes cutting remarks belittling others.

	Nev	Sel	Occ	Som	Usu	Alw	%Fav
You	15	36	9	11	3		
All Obs	265	269	74	109	28	6	71
Superior	30	19	7	5			79
Peer	58	54	14	20	4	2	74
Subord	148	168	43	71	19	4	70
Other	29	28	10	13	5	1	66

85. Self-centered - Concerned primarily with own interests and goals.

	Nev	Sel	Occ	Som	Usu	Alw	%Fav
You	19	35	9	2			
All Obs	218	263	91	94	63	23	64
Superior	30	23	4	2	2	1	85
Peer	45	55	18	19	11	4	66
Subord	121	152	61	59	44	15	60
Other	22	33	8	14	6	3	64

86. Sensitive - Highly aware of the feelings of others.

	Nev	Sel	Occ	Som	Usu	Alw	%Fav
You		3	12	14	39	6	
All Obs	5	88	120	175	282	80	48
Superior		2	7	10	34	9	69
Peer	1	14	24	41	56	15	47
Subord	4	62	77	109	157	43	44
Other		10	12	15	35	13	56

Figure 2.5 • Campbell™ Leadership Index Considerate Scale Questions

Looking closely at the questions on the Calm and Flexible scales (Figure 2.4) provides additional insight that might help explain the variation in mood and temperament that is occasionally observed in senior executives. For example, the Calm characteristic includes lower scores on questions relating to hurriedness and being ruffled. Reasons for these lower scores may be found in the item-level Flexible questions, particularly those relating to the ability to adapt to change and deal with ambiguity—which are also lower scores for senior executives. One note to make here is the higher score from superiors (92 percent favorable) on the question of senior executives' adaptability—which stands in stark contrast to the mid-70s percent favorable ratings from other observers. This is just one of several characteristics where superiors see senior executive performance quite differently from other observers.

As it relates to decision making, two questions in the Flexible characteristic are interesting—senior executives' proclivity to be both headstrong and stubborn. In these questions all observers provided significantly lower scores. Going back to the research on how executives approach decision making, these data lend support to the notion that at times, executives can become enthralled with their own ideas and decisions—even when others see these ideas as clear mistakes. This then brings up the last leadership characteristic that bears on decision making—Considerate.

Figure 2.5 details the questions used to draw out an understanding of a senior executive's Considerate characteristic. There are two observations to consider from these data. First, the standard scores fall within the mid-range of the *Leadership Index*—that is, around the 50 mark—which is generally on the lower side of the scores for senior executives.

The second observation is the perception gap between superiors and all other observers. This gap appeared initially in the Adaptability question, and it is pervasive in the questions on consideration. One possible suggestion for this gap (albeit somewhat sardonic) is that senior executives have either more capability or more motivation to manage up than they have to lead down.

Considering the *Leadership Index* as a whole, Table 2.7 shows the significance of high and low scores in these leadership characteristics.

Insights on Decision Making and Organizational Effectiveness

While the reported personality and leadership characteristics show that senior executives are able to make quick decisions, the next question to consider is twofold: How effective are those decisions, and how well is the decision-making process engaged throughout the organization?

Data from the *Campbell Organizational Survey* (COS) can help us to understand the quality of executive decision making as it relates to organizational effectiveness. The Quality scale of the *Organizational Survey* focuses on the following factors:

> the perceived attention paid to quality in the organization, the degree of managerial support for producing high-quality products or services, and various pressures such as quotas or time constraints that impede quality performance. High scores are found in organizations where there is a pervasive emphasis on excellence; low scores are often associated with other problems in the organization such as poor planning or poor supervision. (Campbell and Hyne 1995, 17)

Figure 2.6 (p. 68) outlines the questions on Quality posed by the *Organizational Survey*. High scores appear on the questions regarding organizational commitment and the importance placed on quality, and the score is also high for the message top management communicates on quality. However, there appears to be a perceived willingness on the part of organizational managers to bypass quality objectives to meet budgets or quotas. And another disturbing perception gap opens between senior executive and observer scores on two questions relating to the engagement of continuous process improvement practices—as senior executives perceive these items significantly higher than observers do.

From the *Organizational Survey* scores on Quality it seems likely that the effect of the senior executives' decision making as well as the organizational support for making quality decisions is well perceived. However, given the perception gap on the questions of continuous process improvements, the actual level of quality that is delivered and its sustainability are both in doubt.

LEADERSHIP CHARACTERISTIC	STANDARD RATING			
	Sr. Executives	Superiors	Peers	Subordinates
Productive *High Scores:* Gets things done on time and on budget. Solves problems as promised. *Low Scores:* Has difficulty focusing on needed work or hitting targets—procrastinator.	57	58	53	53
Considerate *High Scores:* Sensitive to people's needs and feelings; concerned with group harmony. *Low Scores:* Perceived as self-centered, competitive, crude and arrogant.	51	56	51	48
Calm *High Scores:* Unhurried, shows grace under fire. *Low Scores:* Tends to overreact and tense up under pressure.	52	56	53	50
Flexible *High Scores:* Handles change well; good at adapting. *Low Scores:* Strong-headed; difficult to reason with.	54	58	54	50
Optimistic *High Scores:* Confident outlook, good at dealing with uncertainty. *Low Scores:* Seen as moody, pessimistic, and preoccupied with own problems.	54	58	54	50

Table 2.7 • *Campbell™ Leadership Index* Characteristics Relating to Decision Making

Note: Campbell Leadership Index results are reported in a standard score format, that is, with a bell-shaped distribution where the mean is 50 and a standard deviation is 10. Thus a score of 50 is considered typical or normal, a score of 40 is considered very low, and a score of 60 is considered very high. Sixty-eight percent of the individuals in the database score between 40 and 60, and nearly all scores fall between 25 and 75.

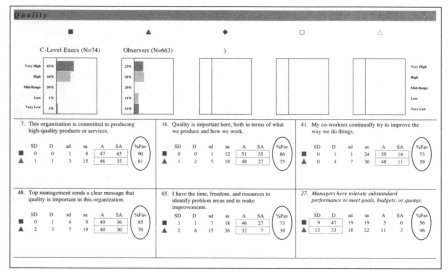

Figure 2.6 • *Campbell™ Organizational Survey* Quality Scale Questions

Note: "Percent Favorable" reflects answers that indicate approval. For positive statements favorable responses would be "Always" or "Usually" and for negative statements favorable responses would be "Never" or "Seldom."

Summary of Data

From the data, it seems likely that senior executives enjoy tackling difficult problems and are inclined to address issues in a structured, well-organized manner. Clearly making things happen and driving for results is a strength for executives. However, within this strength are implications for how an executive interacts with others that must not be overlooked. Most notable is that senior executives may be so focused on getting the task done that they tend to look past people's feelings and their individual accomplishments. Additionally, in their drive to move quickly, senior executives may be unable to anticipate or react to unforeseen circumstances. Most important, senior executives may not take time to celebrate their success (or the success of others) because they're too busy and focused on moving to the next big project or problem.

OBSERVATIONS ON
EXECUTIVE DECISION MAKING

When I was working for a large bank, each year we would have an annual golf outing for senior management and bank associates. During one outing my team was playing behind four of the bank's senior executives. At one point, from where my team stood on the tee-box, we could see the group of bank execs ahead standing over their golf balls—picking out various clubs as they struggled to decide what shot to hit. In frustration one of my playing partners mumbled aloud: "We'll be here all day. We have four VPs in front of us. They couldn't make a quick decision if their lives depended on it." This story reminds me of the misperceptions that can be communicated not in the decisions themselves but in the process of making the decisions. Three key examples come to mind: been-there-done-that, asking the choir to pick the song, and January 28, 1986, a bad day for spaceflight.

We Already Tried It—It Didn't Work

I wish I had a nickel for every time I've heard an executive counter a suggestion for a new approach to solving a problem with the comment, "We tried that once—it didn't work." One of the greatest inhibitors to senior executives' decision making is that they become stuck in what they've done (or tried) before.

A great example of this occurred when I was leading a team tasked with developing a new system for replacing credit cards at Amex. We had decided we would use a technology platform that was somewhat new for the company. While a number of other organizations had successfully deployed mission-critical applications using the new platform, Amex's experience with the new technology had produced very costly missteps. So costly that the people responsible for defining technology standards for the organization had all but outlawed any more attempts to deploy applications with the "unproven" architecture.

Needless to say, senior executives at Amex were highly reluctant to consider our proposal to once again try to deploy a mission-critical application with the same platform that had already been the cause of delays and budget overruns. But I had a few things going on my side that helped us break free of the tried-that-didn't-work bottleneck. First, I had just come off a very successful initiative overseeing the technology and operations support for launching Amex's co-branding products. So in a sense I had earned the right to push the envelope a bit. Second, I reported to a senior executive who was willing to let us build a proof-of-concept model to demonstrate we could make the application work. Finally, I had the lessons learned from those who tried before as well as the successful applications already running elsewhere to use as a model. In the end, we broke free of the tried-that-didn't-work mind-set and launched the first successful application with the new platform.

Soliciting the Choir for Song Selections

Another decision-making challenge for senior executives is their tendency to seek advice from people who think the way they do. If executives have highly talented teams surrounding them, and they all think alike and have the same experiences, odds are good they will all come to the same conclusions. Likewise, senior executives can become comfortable soliciting input from sources that they know and understand. For example, it should have been no surprise that Winston Churchill would be a strong supporter for using the atomic bomb to end the war with Japan. In Churchill's mind, "There was never a moment's discussion as to whether the atomic bomb should be used or not. To avert a vast, indefinite butchery, to bring the war to an end, to give peace to the world, to lay healing hands upon its tortured peoples by a manifestation of overwhelming power at the cost of a few explosions, seemed, after all our toils and perils, a miracle of deliverance" (McCall and Kaplan 1990, 3).

You can likewise see evidence of how Churchill's thinking was shaped by considering his comments in his May 28, 1940, address to the House of Commons following the capitulation of King Leopold: "I have only to add that nothing which may have happened in this battle can in any way relieve us of our duty to defend the world cause to which we have vowed ourselves; nor should it destroy our confidence in our power to make our way, as on former occasions in our history, through disaster and through grief to the ultimate defeat of our enemies" (Churchill 1941, 286).

As an ally, Truman regarded it as important to confer with Churchill on the U.S. decision to use the atomic bomb. However, had Truman limited his decision making to just input from Churchill, the outcome would have been a foregone conclusion. In fact there were many, many voices weighing in on Truman's decision whether or not to use the atomic bomb against Japan. But many of these voices were from the same choir and had similar mind-sets. Not surprisingly, the generals advising Truman were in favor of using the bomb to quicken an end to the war. And while some voices were not in favor of using the atomic bomb, their attempt to raise concerns was ineffective. This is highlighted in a 1960 *U.S. News and World Report* interview with Leo Szilard, a physicist who was one of several scientists advising Truman on the bomb. Dr. Szilard recalled that he and many of his colleagues were opposed to using the bomb against Japan, but in the end they were unsuccessful in presenting an effective argument ("President Truman Did Not Understand" 1960).

Clearly there is much more I could say regarding the process and influences surrounding one of the most significant decisions of modern times. But the point that draws my attention is how Truman himself wrestled with the most grave of decisions—noting in his diary on July 25, 1945: "We have discovered the most terrible bomb in the history of the world. It may be the fire destruction prophesied in the Euphrates Valley Era, after Noah and his fabulous Ark" (Truman 1945).

While there was and continues to be much debate since that fateful day in 1945, what stands out in my mind are the voices weighing in on the decision who were essentially members of the choir. They were all connected directly with the war, in its prosecution, administration, or collateral support. How could any other decision come from this collection of voices? Indeed, how could other voices have been added to the decision, given the secrecy and gravity associated with using the atomic bomb? Perhaps the most insightful observation and question to consider in reviewing the decision Truman faced, particularly in light of the decisions political leaders face in the war on global terrorism, centers not on the decision to use the bomb but on which targets the bomb would be deployed. Accounts from Truman's diary and his address to the public on August 9th (announcing the bombing of Hiroshima) suggest that Truman believed the United States had targeted purely military assets. How would Truman's decision have been affected had he fully understood the civilian composition of Hiroshima and Nagasaki?

Perhaps the lessons from Truman's decision as well as those we live with today point most clearly to the need to ensure that those around the table influencing the decision making are as diverse and varied as possible and to ensure the choir doesn't have sole discretion as to which songs will be sung.

One Bad Day

On January 28, 1986, NASA launched STS-51L—space shuttle *Challenger*. On board were Mike Smith, the pilot; Dick Scobee, the commander; Ron McNair, Ellison S. Onizuka, and Judy Resnik, mission specialists; Greg Jarvis, payload specialist; and Sharon Christa McAuliffe, the first teacher in space.

I was working in the aerospace and defense industry when the *Challenger* was lost, and had written the software that allocated space suit components to astronauts. On January 28th I was in my office at the ILC plant in Frederica, Delaware, where the shuttle space suits were manufactured. By the time this mission came around, launching shuttles had become routine. The shuttle program was in full swing, and we were in full-up production mode. Just to give you a sense of the original scope of the program, the software application I developed to allocate space suit components was built to accommodate shuttle launches occurring every nine days. It was a heady time. I had the opportunity to meet the first two space shuttle astronauts, John Young and Robert Crippen, and even met America's first female astronaut, Sally Ride.

But like many of my peers at the plant, I had stopped watching the shuttle launches. So I was sitting at my desk when I heard loud screams coming from upstairs. I thought a field mouse had gotten inside (our plant was in the country). Then someone came running into my office saying the shuttle had exploded. But I didn't believe it. Perhaps a booster had malfunctioned or an engine had flared out, but surely the shuttle could have aborted and returned to Kennedy. Or maybe the shuttle went into the Atlantic and we had a water rescue under way. It wasn't until I was able to see the video of the flight that I knew—we had lost *Challenger*.

I was with a small group who were at our plant near Johnson Space Flight Center the day after *Challenger* was lost. It was surreal—some of our employees were watching the children of the lost astronauts while their spouses flew to Kennedy. Months later I was at the Morton-Thiokol plant in Huntsville where the O-rings were made. At this point we knew we had experienced a burn-through on the rings. A more solemn place you could not find. In the midst of all this was the unending question, "How did this happen?"

Reams of reports outline the technical, mechanical, and leadership problems that led to the loss of *Challenger*. However, in all the accounts of the decision making that led up to the launch on January 28th I've not heard mention of two interesting facts: STS-51 was the first mission with a teacher in space, and the media attention that came with putting a teacher in space was enormous.

Clearly we had significant design flaws and indeed warnings went unheard. But in my mind another critical influencer entered into the mix with the added media attention from having a teacher in space. The cameras were on, people were watching, and there was pressure to make it happen—to show results. I can't help wonder how this pressure built as the launch was delayed from the day before—first from a stubborn hatch that wouldn't close, then because of poor weather (NASA 1986). I've heard the accounts from the engineers who were saying something wasn't right, and no one listened. I've always wondered if their voices were drowned out by the clicking of the cameras anxiously waiting to see our first teacher sent into space. Whenever I feel hurried to make a decision I think back to that bad day in 1986 and ask, "Why do I have to make this decision now?"

CALL TO ACTION

The myth in decision making is that a problem, crisis, or opportunity can really be resolved with one well-timed decision when, in truth, problems are rarely solved, they're merely contained. As I note at the beginning of the chapter, senior executives attempt to navigate the endless streams of choices that come their way, and decisions serve as temporary anchors that permit a momentary respite so they can catch their breath, get their bearings, and ready themselves to navigate the next wave of decisions. To aid in this navigation senior executives might consider three helpful holding grounds for their anchors: constructing structural influences to decision making, learning to ask questions and listen to the answers, and deflating their egos.

Operating at the Edge of Chaos

Although much has been made of the importance of aligning structure and strategy, it is in the context of decision making that effective approaches for enabling creativity, resolving conflict, and driving toward more effective and timely decisions can be found. Key to establishing a more effective decision-making process is fostering an environment that encourages alternative if not radical solutions to address complex problems while allowing freedom to conservatively discover both good and not-so-good ideas. Beinhocker has suggested that most of us "operate at the edge of chaos"—a place somewhere between the stasis of business as usual and the hectic pace of "What have you done for me lately?" (1997, 35).

Structure and strategy are enablers to effective decision making, but without an appreciation for how people lead and follow during challenging times, the best-laid plans may become little more than a laminated poster at headquarters or a plaque on an employee's wall (Bennett et al.

2003, 3). This is supported by Eisenhardt's research, which suggests that "adaptive processes" to decision making are superior, more effective, and more timely than traditional "forecasts and plans" (Galbraith 2000, 199). Considering this adaptive decision-making process in the context of organizational structure and strategy benefits from several observations:

- Establishing an effective organizational structure is dependent on understanding the actions and activities (decisions) required to achieve desired results (Bennett et al. 2003, 4).

- When scope is clouded (and strategies are unclear), direction to and from decision makers will be equally unclear, resulting in a risk-avoidance environment (Hay Group 2003, 11).

- To counteract the traditional decision-making process associated with top-down executive mandates, organizations need to create an environment that not only encourages multiple scenarios and alternative solutions but acknowledges that the only bad decision is the one not made (Galbraith 2000, 200).

Asking Questions, Listening to Answers

Recall Halcolm's parable of the three students, which I recounted in the preface. The third student looked beyond the surface of events and wound up more puzzled than informed.

He said, "My mind is full of questions. I wonder where the villagers came from and what are they thinking. . . . In the end I am more filled with questions and I'm unsure of what I have learned." To which Halcolm smiled and said, "You have learned the most of all—the value of asking questions and listening to what people say" (Patton 1990, 278). Halcolm's parable often plays out in real life. For example, consider these observations by Charan, Drotter, and Noel in *The Leadership Pipeline* (2001, 123–124):

> The best CEOs come to value asking questions and listening to a broad spectrum of people. This is almost counterintuitive value, given the power that comes with the CEO position and the ego that's required to obtain it. In fact, a significant percentage of chief executives have risen from one leadership level to the next based on their strong, aggressive

style and their ability to wield power. Power, however, becomes dysfunctional when enterprise managers don't exercise restraint. Although CEOs possess ultimate position power, true leaders at this level don't rely exclusively on position power to get things done. They recognize that influence can get things done with energy and innovation rather than just with grudging compliance. Influential enterprise managers share their vision with a variety of people in order to capture their interest and motivate them to perform.

To help ask better questions and reflect more thoughtfully on the answers, senior executives would do well to develop "a network of informed, trusted and truly impartial advisers who can provide a sounding board for the kinds of decisions executives make" (Senge and Joni 2005, 1). In this network of advisers, senior executives will want to find insight from people who have no personal stake in the outcome other than their reputation as a thoughtful adviser. They will also want to find people who are able to connect and relate to the executive's world. An adviser who is too academic, or too entrenched in an ivory tower, will be unable to fully comprehend the issues and stresses the executive faces. Prospective advisers will find a great example of the importance of connecting with the world under study in the movie *Jaws*.

> As Quint, the boat's captain [actor Robert Shaw] and researcher Matt Hooper [actor Richard Dreyfuss] sat around swapping stories, each proudly displayed the scars he'd received from various dangers of ocean life. In this exchange, there is an immediate connection between the two men. While they come from different worlds—one, an academic ocean scholar, the other, a tough-as-nails fisherman—they understand one another; and there was credibility. How many leadership researchers [or advisers] are able to show their scars from living in the worlds they study [and advise on]? (Hammett 2005b)

Why is it so important for senior executives to develop a network of informed, trusted advisers? Here again Bennis offers insight: "Wise leaders know that their power will isolate them and [they take] action to guard against that isolation, both before and after decision making." To help in this, Bennis offers an additional piece of advice, urging "leaders to engage in decision-making postmortems to revisit the reasoning behind a decision" (2004, 4). The decision-making postmortem goes deeper than a normal after-action review. Here Bennis is suggesting that leaders seek to understand why they were influenced to act or respond in a particular way. What external influencers came into play to move them toward or away from a course of action? This is critical for senior executives: "When leaders lack self-awareness their decision making is compromised." If you are unaware of what drives you, including your biases and predispositions, you are more likely to mishandle information. Therefore, Bennis maintains, "a lack of self-knowledge is the most common, everyday source of leadership failures" (4).

Letting Go of Your Ego

Finally, returning to Charan and his colleagues, I see one more note worth considering that helps lay the foundation for this call to action.

> The dictatorial, ego-driven CEO tends not to ask many questions or listen to the answers. He values his own opinion above all others, and as a result tunes out ideas and perspectives that clash with his own. While most new CEOs don't fit the dictatorial prototype, many do not fully value listening to multiple perspectives. Too often, a new CEO relies on one trusted adviser rather than soliciting a broad range of opinions and ideas." (Charan, Drotter, and Noel 2001, 124)

Senior executives need to find it within themselves to let go of their egos. This is extremely difficult at the top of an organization because self-determination and self-confidence (which translates into a strong ego) have typically been a major factor in reaching that level. However, one of the critical outcomes from Collins's good-to-great research has been the identification of humility as an essential characteristic of those leading great companies. The challenge for senior executives to let go of their egos is further complicated by the continual affirmation they receive to keep doing what they've done. Collins highlights this problem:

> [As] boards of directors frequently operate under the false belief that a larger-than-life, egocentric leader is required to make a company great, you can quickly see why Level 5 [humble] leaders rarely appear at the top of our institutions. We keep putting people in positions of power who lack the seed to become a Level 5 leader, and that is one major reason why there are so few companies that make a sustained and verifiable shift from good to great." (2005, 145)

The question we must ask is how do we find, develop, and nurture leaders who are committed to achieving results—and at the same time are willing to "subjugate their own needs to the greater ambition of something larger and more lasting than themselves" (Collins 2005, 145)? Consider the following example offered by Henry and Richard Blackaby (2001, 60):

> Napoleon Bonaparte was constantly involved in warfare as he led the French Empire in its attempt to conquer Europe. In defeat, Napoleon surmised, "If I had succeeded, I should have been the greatest man known to history." There is no doubt that Napoleon made a name for himself in history, but it's questionable whether his soldiers would have willingly sacrificed their lives on the battlefields of Europe had they known the primary cause was to secure their emperor's fame. Today, many are called upon to make sacrifices and to give their best efforts on behalf of their organizations, but they do so with nagging doubts that their personal sacrifices are for no more noble purpose than furthering their leader's career.

If it's difficult for senior executives to let go of their personal ambitions for the good of a greater cause, how on earth can they let go of ego when they are confronted with differing opinions from their peers—other senior executives who most likely are vying for that higher rung on the corporate ladder?

I don't believe the question "Can we develop humble leaders?" has any easy answers. I don't believe that people are either born with the ability to be humble or not. I do believe senior executives can be inspired to lead humbly. Perhaps this begins with a few basic questions: Who do I work for—do I work for the company, its customers, the employees, the mission? What lasting contribution do I want to make—do I want to be remembered for the revenue I produced or the impact I made? What leader do I want to be most compared to—what leader do I most admire, and how can I imitate that leader's leadership qualities?

PERSONAL REFLECTION: THE GIFT OF A SPOUSE

One of the most important sources of honest, helpful insight I have found over the years has been my wife. She is uniquely adept at keeping me balanced—not letting any overinflated title or job assignment go to my head while at the same time being able to lift my heart when things are going south in a big way. Personally I am amazed at how many executives I've spoken with who do not rely on their spouses for insight and feedback. They say, "I don't want to bring my problems home to my spouse," or "I don't think my spouse would be able to comprehend the complexity of my work." But this is exactly why your spouse is so well suited to be a source of insight.

If you can forgive the gender-biased analogy, let me share a great story that helps make this point:

> A very successful executive and his wife decided to attend the wife's high school reunion. Driving into town they stopped at a local gas station. The service manager politely attended to their car and quickly recognized the wife as his old high school sweetheart. After spending a little time catching up they agreed to visit more at the reunion. Pulling away the husband commented, "Good thing you married me or you'd be married to a gas station manager." Without missing a beat the wife replied, "My darling—had I married him he'd be the successful executive and you'd be a gas station manager."

Amen!

3

Intuition, Analytics, and the Myth of "Elegant Reasoning"

It was reported that the French jurist Saleilles would regularly render judgments based on his instincts and then afterwards back up his decision with qualified legal precedent and case work (Greenleaf 2002, 151). Sometimes textbooks on strategic thinking and planning convey a sense that those who are successful at setting the strategy for their organizations have a great deal in common with Saleilles. It is not unusual to hear accounts outlining how insightful people took the reins of floundering organizations and brought them back to life—nearly by their sheer willpower alone. The problem with these stories is that—notwithstanding the inevitable "let me tell you how I saved the day"—none of them reveal a standard, repeatable pattern to their success. Herein lies the myth of "elegant reasoning"—a temptation for leaders to lock themselves in a room, draw on their own intuition and analytics, and dream up a mystical day-saving strategy, which they then bring down from on high like Moses with a new set of tablets. This temptation is fueled by the workforce's tendency to look exclusively to their leaders to define the strategy for everyone to follow.

The key challenge faced by senior executives is establishing a balance between expanding their sphere of influence to include meaningful participation in the strategic formulation and planning process while concurrently building awareness and motivation within the workforce as a whole. The myth of elegant reasoning builds on a misconception that good leaders are able to create compelling, inspiring strategies. But compelling strategies are seldom created; they are, instead, discovered. This discovery can occur as a result of trial and error or a synthesis of ideals and concepts, but in the end really good strategies emerge through both thought leadership and careful consideration in discerning the best path from the various options presented. The value to be found in leading strategy creation is drawing on shared experiences beyond those of senior executives alone, so as to enable selecting the path with the greatest potential to build on the vision and mission of the organization.

To be sure, the idea of expanding strategy formation beyond the most senior executive levels is contrary to several leadership models. For example, within the visionary leadership model only senior leaders participate in the strategic thinking process, while the physical planning rests with line managers. However, in light of the complexities associated with strategy formulation and execution, it would seem clear that benefits and obligations apply to both leaders and followers to be active participants in the entire strategy process. So although the formulation of strategy should begin with executives, it should not stop there. Nor should the execution of the strategy be relegated to followers.

VIEWS ON THINKING, PLANNING, AND LEADING STRATEGICALLY

A number of empirical studies have been conducted to improve understanding of the connection between the formulation and communication of an organization's strategy and the effectiveness of the actions that an organization undertakes to execute its business plan. Specifically, these studies attempt to identify an association between effective awareness efforts on behalf of an organization's strategy and an organization's ability to communicate, inspire, and motivate its workforce to achieve tangible results. Data from these studies suggest a linkage between effective formulation, communication, and measurement of strategies and achieving organizational success. But simply defining a compelling strategy does not dictate success. Consider a 1998 Ernst & Young study that reported, "The ability to execute strategy was more important than the quality of the strategy itself." Additionally, two *Fortune* studies in 1982 and 1999 validated the Ernst & Young findings while further concluding that 70 percent of corporations struggled with strategy planning and execution far more than with formulation (Kaplan and Norton 2001, 1).

To establish a working knowledge for the way effective strategy execution relates to strategy formulation, planning, and leadership, examine two empirical studies: research conducted by Kaplan and Norton, authors of *The Strategy-Focused Organization,* and Malina and Selto's study on the effectiveness of strategy implementations. The following lists summarize the resulting data:

Data from the Balanced Scorecard Collaborative (www.bscol.org 2007)

- 95 percent of a typical workforce do not understand their organization's strategy.

- 90 percent of organizations fail to successfully execute against their strategy.

- 86 percent of leadership teams spend less than one hour per month reviewing progress against strategy.

- 75 percent of senior leadership teams do not have consensus regarding their organization's value proposition—the market segment an organization's strategy targets (product leadership, customer intimacy, operational excellence, and the like), which defines how the organization will differentiate itself relative to its competition. (Kaplan and Norton 2001, 86)

- 60 percent of organizations do not tangibly link activity to strategy.

Data from Malina and Selto (2002)

- A linkage can be drawn between effective management control, strategy alignment, and positive outcomes.

- A linkage can be drawn between effective management control, effective motivation, and positive outcomes.

- Significant distinctions exist among strategy formulation, strategic planning, and leading strategically.

Sanders defines strategic thinking (formulation) as the exploration of external influences such as environment, resources, and competitive landscape that, through a series of intuitive, visual, and creative processes, "result in a synthesis of emerging themes, issues, patterns, connections and opportunities" (1998, 162). Strategic planning can be thought of as the formal decomposition of defined strategies "into distinct steps, each delineated by checklists and supported by techniques" for "implementation through detailed attention to objectives, budgets, programs and operating plans" (Mintzberg, Ahlstrand, and Lampel 1998, 58). Finally, Hughes and Beatty suggest that the "focus of strategic leadership is sustainable competitive advantage, or the enduring success of the organization . . . to drive and move the organization so that it will thrive in the long term" (2005, 9). Recall that sustainability is one of the three essentials for effective leadership. So let's take a closer look at the areas of strategic thinking, strategic planning, and strategic leadership and see if that will further clarify how these factors influence perceptions of effective leadership.

Strategic Thinking Versus Strategic Planning

In many regards strategic thinking conforms to the premise outlined by Mintzberg, Ahlstrand, and Lampel (1998, 58): namely, that strategy emerges from controlled, formal planning with the responsibility for the overall process residing with executive leadership, while execution rests with staff personnel. Within this construct the responsibility for strategic thinking rests with the leadership, while execution, including the detailed planning (budgets, project plans, and so on), rests with the followers. One argument for strategic formation falling on an organization's executive leadership is based on the three-dimensional model of competitive strategy that draws attention to considering an organization's past, present, and future (J. Taylor and Wacker 2000, 98–99):

- A company needs to consider its past so that its people do not forget who they are and what brought them to their present state.

- A company needs to consider its future so that it has a keen eye on trends and leading indicators.

- A company needs to consider the present so that it keeps its eye on the ball.

So the question might be asked, Who other than the most senior executive can adequately consider an organization's past, present, and future? This framework for strategic thinking versus strategic planning may explain why we typically find mid-level leaders associating their strategic planning process with the creation and maintenance of annual expense and capital budgets. For many mid-level managers, their entire annual focus, including new initiatives, business as usual, and competitive efforts, is driven from what was or was not approved in their budgets. A software executive once told me, "We don't make decisions against a strategic plan—we make decisions against an annual budget. If the activity or initiative we want to pursue isn't in the budget, then it waits until the next budget planning cycle." Mintzberg outlines how the capital budget process is often used as an ad hoc control mechanism in the strategic planning process:

> [A new initiative] is conceived by a sponsor at some level down in the hierarchy. There, an assessment is made of its costs and benefits over time. . . . The [initiative] is then proposed to one or more successively higher levels in the hierarchy, where it is supposed to be compared with projects and funded if it ranks sufficiently high to deserve receiving whatever remains in the capital budget. (1994, 87)

Mintzberg continues to distinguish budget planning from strategic planning:

What remains of strategic planning is in fact a set of three independent approaches—a kind of portfolio of planning techniques, if you like. On one side is a numbers game, geared to motivation and control but not to strategy formation. On the other is capital budgeting, a portfolio technique to control capital spending through decision making but not strategy making. And in between is a process that seems to be about strategy making, but more in name than in content. (1994, 89)

Additionally, Shaw, Brown, and Bromiley critique a strategy embodied as a business plan and budget:

Virtually all business plans are written as a list of bullet points. Despite the skill of knowledge of their authors, these plans usually aren't anything more than lists of "good things" to do. . . . Rarely do these lists reflect deep thought or inspire commitment. Worse, they don't specify critical relationships between the points, and they can't demonstrate how the goals will be achieved. (2002, 51)

As you unpack these statements, it should be no surprise that it is always easier to put your hands on an organization's annual budget than on its strategic plan. Likewise, you'd find more measures and processes in place to monitor and track line items in a budget than to monitor and track accomplishments against a strategic plan. Budgets are typically on the tops of desks or pinned to corkboards on the wall. Strategic plans are buried in files and dusted off every few years—most likely just prior to a board planning meeting. The reality is that people in organizations live with budgets every day—they only dream about strategies.

In an attempt to break away from strategies disguised as budgets, some managers gravitate toward a scenario-based planning technique as a way to deal with the uncertainty and fluid nature of business. According to Sanders, "Scenario-based planning results in a number of options or responses to the different scenarios: if this happens, then we go to plan A; but if that happens then plan B or C is the best move; and if it really gets crazy, then we follow plan XYZ" (1998, 142). However, Sanders continues, although scenario-based planning can help an organization consider its future, users of this approach still face some key challenges (142–143):

- Being blindsided by unanticipated developments

- Falling into stasis in the gap between present and future, while the organization waits for something to happen

- Spending endless time analyzing data, planning scenarios, and building consensus

Leading Strategically

It would seem that what we want in our leaders is an ability to create a compelling vision for the future that creates excitement and rallies the troops. The concept of visionary leadership is one where a strategy will inspire the workforce, drawing on emotional and spiritual energy to motivate team members to get on board through an almost mystical, charismatic inspiration. Counter to this notion is that strategic thinking happens through social interaction, based on the shared beliefs and understandings of the members of an organization (Mintzberg, Ahlstrand, and Lampel 1998, 137).

The concept of incorporating societal understanding in creating and fostering strategic thinking has been suggested by CCL—noting that, in the context of an organization's culture, "Complex challenges [such as establishing and executing strategies] require richer and more complex ways of creating direction, alignment, and commitment. The ways people talk, think, and act together—the culture of the organization along with its systems and structures—are what need to become richer and more complex" (Drath 2003).

Finally, it is not uncommon for perceptions regarding the effectiveness of an organization's strategic plan to be influenced primarily by how well it performed against key performance indicators (KPIs) such as sales targets and budget maintenance. However, KPIs have limitations that make them unreliable as the sole measure of an effective strategy. While using KPIs can produce a more balanced view, without a clear strategic map to align performance it may be possible to overlook critical components required for business success, such as measures of customer satisfaction (Kaplan and Norton 2000, 167). Therefore key interest should be applied to resolving any disconnect between the executives' awareness of critical business drivers (value proposition, market focus, and the like) and that of the workforce.

HOW EXECUTIVES STRATEGIZE

The data collected on C-level executives suggest several observations regarding how their personality types, interpersonal relations, and leadership characteristics influence the manner in which they approach strategy definition and execution. First, let's take another look at the MBTI assessment.

Personality Types and Blind Spots

In Chapter 2 I reflected on the leadership characteristics and approach to problem solving and decision making of the predominant personality types (ISTJ, INTJ, INTP, and ENTJ) found among the C-level executives attending the CCL programs in the past several years. Table 3.1 adds further insight to these personality data to help clarify the possible blind spots associated with these personality types (Myers 1998, 14, 18, 23, 25; Hirsh and Kummerow 1998, 10, 11, 22, 25).

I can make a few key observations from this insight. First, senior executives with these personality types need to be careful not to overlook gaining input from others as well as the possible effect on others of their actions. This blind spot isn't all that startling, given that none of the predominant personality types (ISTJ, INTJ, INTP, ENTJ) included a preference for Feeling. However, this is not to suggest that senior executives are insensitive. Remember, everyone can and does use all eight of the preferences to some extent, so everyone who prefers Thinking also has access to Feeling. Also, 18 percent of the population of C-level executives reported a preference for Feeling. People with a preference for Feeling are likely to demonstrate a preference toward empathy and deference to how decisions affect others, and to strive for harmony and positive

LEADERSHIP CHARACTERISTICS	APPROACH TO DECISION MAKING	POSSIBLE BLIND SPOTS
ISTJs (Introversion, Sensing, Thinking, Judging)		
Are clear and steadfast in their opinions because they have arrived at them by carefully and thoroughly applying logical criteria based on their experience and knowledge.	Want to be thoroughly grounded in the facts that are analyzed in a logical framework.	May need to respond to the impact on people and search for more possibilities or more optimal solutions.
INTJs (Introversion, Intuition, Thinking, Judging)		
Are excellent long-range planners and often rise to positions of leadership. They are independent, trusting their own perceptions and judgments over those of others.	Want to use their internal vision for strategies, systems, and structures that they have objectively determined.	May need to include input of others and the details needed to make their visions a reality.
INTPs (Introversion, Intuition, Thinking, Perceiving)		
Quickly see inconsistencies and illogicality and enjoy taking apart and reworking ideas. They naturally build complex theoretical systems to explain the realities they see.	Want to use their internal logic to structure problems and solutions while attending to the facts and specifics.	May need to consider other possibilities and the impact of people.
ENTJs (Extraversion, Intuition, Thinking, Judging)		
Typically are excellent solvers of organizational problems as they are keenly aware of the intricate connections within organizations and are action oriented.	Want to logically analyze and control situations based on an internal understanding of what could be.	May want to include a realistic determination of the facts and to consider the impact on people other than themselves.

Table 3.1 • Senior Executive Leadership Characteristics, Approaches to Decision Making, and Possible Blind Spots

interactions (Myers 1998, 10). But Table 3.1 does present a pattern of senior executives' need to expand their thinking to include these efforts:

- Considering multiple possibilities

- Keeping track of what's needed to make their ideas happen

- Avoiding becoming so enamored of their ideas that they unintentionally skew data or facts to fit their preconceptions

Insights on Strategic Planning

Insights drawn from the *Executive Dimensions* assessment show that while senior executives, their bosses, and their direct reports identified strategic planning as an important leadership characteristic, no one (including the senior executives themselves) identified it as a top competency. Table 3.2 reflects the competency ratings of the *Executive Dimensions* Strategic Planning scale (ratings are 1–5, with 5 being the highest).

Recall that given the high performance typically associated with executives attending CCL programs, scores generally fall within the mid-3s to low 4s. Therefore it is helpful to keep two points in mind when reviewing the data:

- Overall, the scores are in the low end of the typical range (that is, 3.5s).

- To identify possible areas of improvement, it is important to rate scores against all leadership characteristics measured.

So as you consider the data, recall that while strategic planning is one of the most important characteristics for executives, it does not surface as one of the strongest competencies—and thus is perhaps an area where senior executives might consider development opportunities.

Among the questions raised by *Executive Dimensions* to draw out an understanding of an executive's strategic planning performance, the first deals with how the executive works the plan: "Regularly updates plan to reflect changing circumstances." Scores on this question suggest that executives, bosses, and direct reports perceive very good performance

STRATEGIC PLANNING	EXECUTIVES	BOSSES	DIRECT REPORTS
Regularly updates plan to reflect changing circumstances	3.38	3.49	3.28
Translates his or her vision into realistic business strategies	3.74	3.45	3.37
Weighs concerns of relevant business functions when developing plans	3.45	3.46	3.21
Articulates wise, long-term objectives and strategies	3.67	3.46	3.40
Develops plans that balance long-term goals with immediate organizational needs	3.51	3.59	3.38
Develops plans that contain contingencies for future changes	3.25	3.35	3.33
Successfully integrates strategic and tactical planning	3.60	3.51	3.43
Average	3.51	3.47	3.34

Table 3.2 • *Executive Dimensions* Strategic Planning Scale

executing against a strategic plan. The same-level performance is rated by executives, bosses, and direct reports on questions that attempt to measure the ability of the executive to balance tactical day-to-day activities with an eye toward the future: "Weighs concerns of relevant business functions when developing plans"; "Develops plans that balance long-term goals with immediate organizational needs"; "Successfully integrates strategic and tactical planning."

Three questions are designed to illuminate the senior executive's ability to build and move the organization into the future: "Translates his or her vision into realistic business strategies"; "Articulates wise, long-term objectives and strategies"; "Develops plans that contain contingencies for future changes." Scores on these questions reflect less confidence in the senior executives' ability to map and guide the organization strategically. Specifically, executives, bosses, and direct reports provided scores toward the lower end of the range for senior executives' ability to communicate compelling long-range goals for the organization as well as ensure those strategic plans accounted for unforeseen bumps along the way. Data on the *Leadership Index* assessment make it possible to dig a bit deeper into executives' ability to look forward—their farsightedness.

Insights on Being Farsighted

The *Campbell Leadership Index* (CLI) assessment identifies senior executives with strong ratings in farsightedness as having the ability to "assess where the organization is now, identify the resources necessary to attain the organization's goals and provide a road map for using those resources to benefit the company." However, senior executives with a limited ability to look ahead "appear trapped, with little interest in future possibilities. They have difficulty extrapolating beyond present circumstances, and they prefer immediate payoffs to potentially more important long-term benefits" (Nilsen and Campbell 1998, 11). Questions raised in the *Leadership Index* to illuminate an executive's farsightedness are reflected in Figure 3.1.

While the standard scores for both executives and observers (consisting of bosses and direct reports) rated Farsighted as 58 (within the high range). You can gain some interesting insights by looking closer at the detail questions and observer breakout. For example, in Figure 3.1, executives receive relatively high favorable ratings in the questions relating to Forward-looking and Insightful, indicating perceptions of an executive's attentiveness to the future and ability to identify critical trends. However, executives do not receive as high a favorable rating regarding their ability to craft inspiring visions for the future of their organizations (Farsighted). This suggests that while senior executives do in fact demonstrate an ability to look beyond a tactical, results-today mind-set, they struggle when it comes to synthesizing this into a future vision for the organization.

Farsighted Scale

42. Farsighted - Shows great vision in imagining the future.

	Nev	Sel	Occ	Som	Usu	Alw	%Fav
You				2	22	37	13
All Obs	2	25	57	172	320	177	66
Superior			2	21	25	14	63
Peer		6	19	35	65	27	61
Subord	2	15	30	97	197	112	68
Other		4	6	19	33	24	66

47. Forward-looking - Focuses on the future.

	Nev	Sel	Occ	Som	Usu	Alw	%Fav
You				2	6	49	17
All Obs	1	8	31	105	370	238	81
Superior			1	8	37	16	85
Peer		2	8	31	73	38	73
Subord	1	6	19	56	218	153	82
Other			3	10	42	31	85

59. Insightful - Able to detect important points in complex situations.

	Nev	Sel	Occ	Som	Usu	Alw	%Fav
You				1	11	49	13
All Obs	3	8	30	104	411	196	81
Superior		1	2	5	37	17	87
Peer			9	27	91	24	76
Subord	2	5	16	58	239	133	82
Other	1	2	3	14	44	22	77

Figure 3.1 • *Campbell ™ Leadership Index* Farsighted Scale Questions

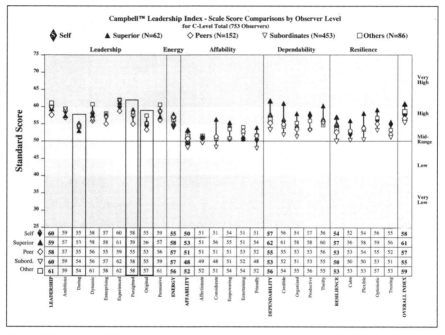

Figure 3.2 • *Campbell™ Leadership Index* Daring, Farsighted, and Original Scales

Another interesting insight from the CLI assessment can be found contrasting scores on the Farsighted scale with Daring and Original, which were among the lower-rated leadership characteristics (see Figure 3.2). While I'll discuss creativity and innovation in more depth in Chapter 5, these data do raise a question about the boldness surrounding executives' future visions. Can executives envision how their industry will operate in the future as they consider new opportunities and challenges?

Insights on Organizational Planning

While the *Campbell Organizational Survey* measures planning at all levels in the organization, scores in the Planning scale generally relate to how senior executives perform on long-range planning, specifically, "how their planning strategies are reflected in the work flow throughout the organization." According to Campbell and Hyne, high COS scores in the Planning scale "are found in organizations where plans are explicitly generated and shared by top leadership and where projects are completed according to plan rather than handled in perpetual crisis mode. Low scores are usually an indication of poor planning at the top, failure to communicate plans, or lack of follow-through" (1995, 16–17). COS scores for Planning centered at the midline, with senior executives' providing a standard rating of 57 and observers 51 (see Figure 3.3).

Review of the COS questions further reveals that three reflect on the manner in which tactical work is engaged with an eye toward project planning (see Figure 3.4). Responses to these questions clearly indicate that executives feel project planning and execution occurs more effectively than observers perceptions would indicate. However, this separation pales in contrast to response to the item "The people in charge here have a clear vision of where we are going." Here we see that executives' favorable perception (80 percent) far surpasses that of observers (59 percent).

From these data, it's useful to ponder a few more questions:

- Does senior executives' drive for results blind them to the inefficiencies that observers perceive in achieving these results?

- Is the perception gap between executives and observers in setting the future direction of the organization real, or is one group unable to picture or recognize clarity of vision?

Summary of Data

From the data reviewed thus far, it's reasonable to surmise that senior executives may get caught in a routine of connecting and drawing insight from only a restricted number of people—their select confidants. Senior

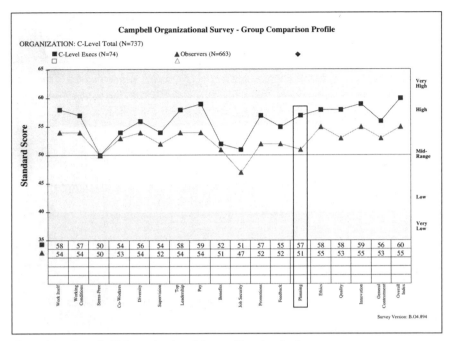

Figure 3.3 • *Campbell™ Organizational Survey* Planning Scale

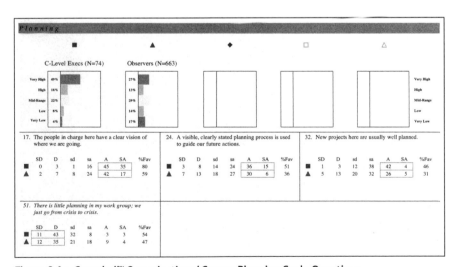

Figure 3.4 • *Campbell™ Organizational Survey* Planning Scale Questions

Note: "Percent Favorable" reflects answers that indicate approval. For positive statements favorable responses would be "Always" or "Usually" and for negative statements favorable responses would be "Never" or "Seldom."

executives may also get caught up in "knowing what they know" and thus unable to discover and address what they don't know. To counter this perception, senior executives may look to stir things up just for the sake of change, perhaps engaging an ill-conceived plan as a fad, making decisions more quickly than the situation requires, or reacting to unforeseen circumstances too abruptly.

OBSERVATIONS ON EXECUTIVE THINKING, PLANNING, AND LEADING

As noted in research by the Balanced Scorecard Collaborative, the typical worker below the middle management level lacks a solid understanding of the organization's strategy. Despite some apparent linkage between effective communication, strategy alignment, motivation, and positive outcomes, we continue to be drawn to the idea of a great leader as someone with a compelling vision who can lead the organization from lackluster performance to excellence. However, the problem with most visionaries is that while they are able to see a desirable future state, they are unable to motivate others to undertake the journey. As Greenleaf points out, "The essential artistry in their leadership, that which makes them more dependable and trustworthy than most, is their intuitive insight, which [unfortunately, often] cannot be fully explained" (2002, 151). The other problem with following visionaries is that while you're inspired to follow, you rarely internalize the reasons for a particular direction—so you can't explain to those following you why you're all going down a certain path.

The Problem with "Follow the Leader"

Case in point: During the cold war Russia lost a nuclear submarine in deep waters and at that time did not have the technology to salvage the ship or recover the crew. Thinking the vessel was safe because of the depth to which it sank, the Soviet Union abandoned the sub. The U.S. government, however, saw an opportunity to get access to valuable Russian technology and secretly approached Howard Hughes to develop and execute a plan to clandestinely retrieve the submarine. As part of his ruse Hughes developed a deep-water oil exploration rig that served to disguise the real intent of the platform—attach to the Soviet sub and raise it from the ocean bottom. Even though Hughes was not actually exploring for oil, several of his competitors believed Hughes had insight into yet undiscovered oil fields beneath the ocean and invested millions of dollars so that they could explore for oil in the same region. They followed Hughes's vision without understanding its rationale and ended up wasting time and money.

At senior executive levels you can see a pattern of one-upmanship or keeping up with the Joneses that damages an organization as executives pursue strategies that they do not fully understand only because their peers with other organizations are engaged in something new or exciting. For example, at a gathering of regional business heads a sidebar conversation arose as to the latest and greatest in business leadership. Before long the topic of Six Sigma came up, with nearly every leader espousing the benefits and virtues of the Six Sigma program. However, one particular executive was somewhat embarrassed that he had little to add to the conversation; his organization had not embraced the new concept (and in fact he didn't really understand what Six Sigma was). But since his peers were all on board with Six Sigma, he felt he'd better get moving as well—so as soon as he returned home, he immediately announced his organization would be implementing Six Sigma and formed a task group to make Six Sigma happen. The problem was (and still is) that this executive had no vision for the benefits embodied in Six Sigma. He only knew it was something other business heads were pursuing and thus something his organization would pursue as well.

However, executives can also create an environment where their organization blindly follows their direction—even when direction was never actually given. Here's an example of what can happen:

The president of a national manufacturing firm was touring a new facility recently built outside Columbus, Ohio. During the tour the plant manager took great care to show off many of the latest advances in production and quality assurance that were engineered into the new facility. Entering the high-tech mold-injection section, the president noticed that the configuration of the equipment and workflow seemed somewhat awkward and casually observed out loud . . . "I would have placed this equipment along that far wall—I bet work would flow much better." Before any conversation could occur regarding the president's observation the tour quickly progressed to the next area of the plant.

Several months later the president returned to the plant for another visit. Upon entering the mold-injection section the president observed that the equipment *had* been moved and noted: "So you moved the equipment. Did it help?" Sheepishly the plant manager told him that the move had not resulted in a more efficient flow since the original layout had already accounted for workflows that were not apparent on a casual review. "Why the hell did you move the equipment, then?" the president barked. "Because you said to," replied the plant manager.

We've all heard countless stories of executives' thinking out loud—with no intention of influencing specific action—only to be startled that their musings actually caused others to take action. Sometimes these actions are just bothersome, like repainting an office the favorite color of the executive. But all too often these actions have more costly implications—disrupted workflows and worse.

Strategic Thinking

To explore how senior executives engage in strategic thinking, consider the following factors:

- The frequency with which strategic thinking occurs as well as the time frame it attempts to address
- Perceptions of the effectiveness of the organization's strategic thinking

Strategic thinking most often occurs at the corporate and executive levels (senior vice presidents, chief operating officers, CEOs, and the like), and the time frames associated with strategic thinking may vary depending on the organization and may be attributed to an organization's perception of its competitive marketplace, the speed it must move to capture markets, and its overall longevity. Perceptions of overall effectiveness of an organization's strategic thinking appear to be connected (albeit anecdotally) to both its success on the ground and to a positive outlook among employees. In some part this perception is tied to how senior executives communicate strategies within their organization as well as to how strongly employees are motivated to embrace and connect with these strategies. In this regard the following considerations may prove helpful:

- Perception of the effectiveness of the organization in communicating an awareness of its strategic thinking

- Perception of the effectiveness of the organization in motivating its workforce to embrace its strategic thinking and align corporate activity and performance accordingly

In many cases strategic communication takes the form of defined and visibly posted mission statements and lists of corporate values. Communication also takes the form of formalized distribution and review of the corporate business strategy inclusive of targeted end states and critical success factors. Motivating a workforce to get behind stated strategic thinking mistakenly takes the form of measuring progress against KPIs that attempt to align activity and track performance against their strategies. The problem with motivating and aligning activity solely on KPIs is the shortsightedness often built into these measures, particularly in light of a company's competitive position. For example, an organization may feel a sense of accomplishment in revenues that reflect a 10 percent growth from last year. However, if the market is realizing 15 percent growth, then the organization has in effect lost 5 percent market share. This would coincide with Kaplan and Norton's assertion that "in the short run, financial results can be affected by temporary factors—weather, interest rates, exchange rate movements, energy prices, and economic cycles. But what determines how the organization does in the long run is how well it is positioned relative to its competitors" (2001, 59). In specific terms effective strategic leadership generates success that can be linked to a well-articulated strategy that is communicated effectively within the organization and impels the workforce to achieve sustainable business results.

CALL TO ACTION

It is a misconception that effective leaders are able to create compelling, inspiring strategies. This misconception has a lot of illusory support, but a misconception it remains.

For nearly every corporate success story or every effective turnaround, credit is often given to that one charismatic leader who through sheer brilliance and elegant reasoning created that one elusive strategy that led the organization to the promised land. This is further embodied in the idea of a "great leader" as someone with a compelling vision who could lead virtually any organization from lackluster performance to excellence (Mintzberg, Ahlstrand, and Lampel 1998, 137).

Nonetheless, as I said at the beginning of this chapter, compelling strategies are almost always discovered, not created (Hughes and Beatty 2005, 35–37). In the end really good strategies emerge through both intuitive thought leadership and careful analytical consideration in discerning the best path among the various options presented. Understanding that strategic thinking is a process of social interaction that embodies the beliefs of the members of an organization raises the question, How can these beliefs be marshaled into an effective strategy? As Lombardo and Eichinger write:

> There are a lot more people who can take a hill than there are people who can accurately predict which hill it would be best to take. There are more people good at producing results in the short term than there are visionary strategists. It is more likely that [an] organization will be out maneuvered strategically than that it will be out produced tactically. Most organizations do pretty well what they do today. It's what they need to do tomorrow that's the missing skill. (2000, 346)

So then the critical challenge senior executives face in leading strategically is that although their brilliance and elegant reasoning enable them to achieve remarkable results for today, they are often unable to develop and motivate toward a vision for tomorrow. However, this challenge reinforces the benefits and obligations for both leaders and followers to be active participants in the entire strategy process—applying both intuitive thought leadership and careful analytical consideration in discerning the best path. This can be problematic because in our culture we expect our leaders to establish direction, set the course, and marshal the resources needed to win the day. However, in the demanding, complex challenges we face, it is unlikely that any one person or small group of leaders will meet this challenge. The value to be found in leading strategy creation is drawing on shared experiences so as to identify the path with the greatest potential to benefit the vision and mission of the organization. This idea of shared participation is brought out by Gadiesh and Gilbert: When CEOs push decision making out to the far reaches of an organization good things happen; fleeting business opportunities are seized quickly and workers are motivated to innovate and take risks (2002, 153).

So while the formulation of strategy might begin at the executive ranks, it should not stop there. Nor should the execution of the strategy be relegated solely to those who follow. Senior executives can increase the effectiveness of their strategic thinking, planning, and leadership by considering the influencers described in the following sections.

Expanding Your Sphere of Influence

Don't give in to the pressure to be *the one* who has the mystic vision for the organization. Bring other voices and insights into your sphere of influence. These voices should be people from various levels of your organization as well as thought leaders from outside your company. As Hughes and Beatty write:

> For anyone working to become a strategic leader, developing and using strategic influence involves forging relationships inside and outside the organization, inviting others into the process, building and sustaining momentum and purposefully utilizing organizational systems and

cultures. It demands that leaders be clear about what drives them; be able to see and understand other perspectives and paradoxically, be open to influence from others. (2005, 124)

Without expanding their sphere of influence, senior executives risk succumbing to blindness of self-sufficiency implied in Plato's *Meno*. Through this dialogue Plato raises the question, "Can anyone ever really learn anything?" If we know enough about an issue to phrase a thoughtful question, he points out, odds are we already have a preconceived idea of what the answer should be (and thus perhaps are predisposed toward a particular answer). However, if we do not know enough about a subject to properly phrase an elegant question, odds are we will not recognize the correct answer, even if it falls into our lap! The counter to *Meno* rests in building a sphere of influence wide enough to include people who challenge your assumptions and stretch your imagination.

Finally, expanding your sphere of influence, particularly moving it beyond those within your organization, will help you counter the imbalance that can be associated with organizational myths. All organizations have myths (stories) about their past accomplishments and defeats. These myths define the character and behavior of the company and in large part reinforce its workforce's perception of the way they are while reflecting perceptions and beliefs of organizational values and culture (Schwartz 1991, 44). In themselves these myths are not consciously fictitious. They may indeed be grounded in fact. However, the further back in time the events are associated with a myth, the more likely the myth departs from truth. Just as there are infinite possible futures, there are "infinite alternative pasts, which compress [in accuracy] as they approach the interval of the present" (Schultz 1995, 30). If these organizational myths cloud your perceptions of the past, they can at times block your ability to consider the future. Drawing insight from others outside your organization can chip away at the organizational myths that may encumber forward movement.

Getting Over Being Perfect

Become comfortable with uncertainty and with results that are less than perfect. As Lombardo and Eichinger suggest, "The essence of dealing comfortably with uncertainty is the tolerance of errors and mistakes, and absorbing the possible heat and critics that follow" (2000, 8). To help with this, make sure your strategy accounts for uncertainties and crises. Even if you're not sure what crisis may arise, make accommodations in your strategies for the unforeseen through strategic foresight.

There is often the misperception that foresight entails predicting or envisioning future events. In truth, "foresight is not the ability to predict the future. It is a human attribute that allows us to weigh up pros and cons, to evaluate different courses of action and to invest possible futures" (Slaughter 1995, 1). So, if you consider strategic foresight a critical leadership competency, how do you develop and refine this skill? One technique for enhancing strategic foresight is to engage in regular scenario planning—outlining two or three potential futures with various possibilities and rehearsing how you might respond to each scenario. Schwartz describes scenario planning as "a matter of training yourself to think through how things might happen that you might otherwise dismiss—to get to know the shape of unfolding reality. To have at hand the answer to the question: 'What if . . . ?'" (1991, 30). To this end scenario planning makes it possible to understand how the future might unfold as a result of your decisions as well as external influencers. Thus the development of a trend, a strategy, or a wild-card event may be described in a scenario of possible futures ("The Art of Foresight" 2004, 4–5), to which the following steps are involved:

- Understanding where you are today and assessing the implications of present actions and decisions (Slaughter 1995, 48)

- Outlining possible future events that would include favorable, unfavorable, and status quo scenarios (Slaughter 1995, 48)

- Establishing markers within your plans to help indicate which scenario might be unfolding (Schwartz 1991, 199)

Risk Management Versus Risk Avoidance

There is a big difference between being risk averse and managing risk. Risk aversion plays out as an executive puts off or neglects to set a course of action for fear that the risk will outweigh the benefits. Risk management looks to identify the possible setbacks and obstacles that might occur in pursuing the benefit and seeks to negate and counter these risks. To help develop a risk management mind-set, get over knowing what you know.

I once had a chance to hear Tom Peters share his thoughts on the type of leaders we need today. Among the key characteristics Peters highlighted was the willingness to speak out with compassion *and* the courage to take chances. Peters maintained that we need the sort of leaders who will boldly do a swan dive from the platform at the risk of a major belly flop, and not the sort who prefer to tip-toe into the shallow end holding their nose. I would add that we need leaders who will take that second, third, and fourth dive from the platform regardless of how many belly flops they have.

Uncertainty avoidance is the natural inclination to plan, predict, and anticipate as many of life's uncertainties as possible so as to avoid undue anxiety and stress. However, uncertainty avoidance should not be confused with risk avoidance. While individuals may want to manage events to prevent unpleasant surprises, these same individuals will willingly pursue thoughtful calculated plans with a less than 100 percent probability of success (Hofstede 2001, 145–149).

To help manage through uncertainty, successful leaders exhibit the following characteristics (Black, Morrison, and Gregersen 1999, 83–86):

- Master environmental complexities by moving forward with confidence and determination, even without clear direction

- Apply the 80/20 rule by leveraging what is known to the situation at hand and allowing the unknown to be discovered and addressed along the journey

- In uncertain times, look to pattern direction based on industry best practices and benchmarking

Today's leaders commit significant energy to the building of compelling strategic visions designed to inspire and guide their organizations into the future. Unfortunately, although strategic vision will help a leader plan for the future, it is strategic foresight that will enable a leader to deal with the inevitable variations that will occur as that future unfolds.

Given the uncertainty of these alternative future images, leaders would do well to add strategic foresight to their toolkit. Marsh and McAllum encapsulate this thought neatly: "When we truly 'stand in the future' we are able to create a view that is unrestricted by the present. We are free to create scenarios of possibility and understanding. We are free to realize that the future is not predetermined, something that we have to react to and cope with—but rather that it offers a range of possibilities, depending on our responses now to those possibilities" (2002, 2).

Bacharach echoes this sentiment: "Uncertainty appears as a fundamental problem for complex organizations, and coping with uncertainty, as the essence of the [leadership] process. Just as complete uncertainty and randomness is the antithesis of purpose and of organization, complete certainty is a figment of the imagination" (quoted in Kramer and Neale 1998, 70).

PERSONAL REFLECTION:
IT'S NOT ALL ABOUT ME!

I've always been drawn to the heroic stories of how a grand visionary skillfully turned a failing organization into an astounding success. Perhaps in my daydreams I saw myself as one of those heroes—saving the day with my brilliance. I've been blessed to have been associated with several major initiatives that were remarkably successful. One project in particular was the launching of the co-branding products at Amex. I was given the luxury of a hand-picked team who knew more about launching new credit products than I would ever know. So while on paper the box with my name was at the top of the page, in reality I worked for the team that was making this happen. But since in theory I was in charge, it was important that I at least gave the impression that I was adding brilliance.

I recall one event in particular that crystallized for me the importance of perspective and that setting vision and direction isn't "all about me." We were meeting in Phoenix to hash out critical details for how the co-branding products would operate. This was an important meeting because several major roadblocks had surfaced as to how the products would function operationally and how the technical systems would accommodate the new features. The meeting included people representing Business Operations and Technology. Here was my chance. The one place I knew I could add value was bridging the divide between businesspeople and programmers. So I put on my superhero cape and sprang into action. I had a grand plan for how we could seamlessly tie in several key operational functions by using some rather sophisticated programming tricks.

Well, it was a disaster. After a few minutes of my rambling it was clear I didn't have a clue what I was talking about. My interjection totally derailed the meeting to the point that we called it a day and decided to pick things back up in the morning. I went back to the hotel on my own and tried to figure out how I could make my grand vision work. The next day when we reconvened the meeting everyone was there ready to start anew. The Business Operations people, the programmers, everyone— that is, everyone except my team.

I stepped out of the meeting room and called my team lead. When she answered her phone I knew there was trouble. She and the team were at the airport waiting to catch their flights back home to Florida. When I asked her why they were bailing in the middle of such an important meeting she responded that it seemed as though I had a handle on what I wanted to do and they would simply go back home and wait for direction. I got the message loud and clear. I was doing more than grandstanding; I was trying to set the direction and vision for the group without any input or insight from them.

I canceled the remainder of the meeting and took the next fight home. There I sat down with the team and apologized for being a fathead and threw my superhero cape in the trash. To my surprise the team had kicked around my ideas from the day before and worked them into a viable approach that helped make the launch a huge success. Most important, we all agreed that should the team ever feel the need to bail on another meeting, they would be sure to include me in the prison break!

The lesson I learned is that just because I might be out in front and leading, I don't have to be the one to come up with the grand plan or vision. In fact, the best planning has always come from working together as a group—with all the members adding their unique insights and perspectives.

PART II

Paradoxes
of Effective Executive Leadership

— PARADOX —

A statement that is seemingly contradictory or opposed to common sense and yet is **perhaps true;** *a self-contradictory statement that at first seems true* **(but may be false);** *an argument that apparently derives self-contradictory conclusions by valid deduction from acceptable premises. (Merriam-Webster 2005, emphasis added)*

— LEADERSHIP PARADOX —

Competing demands for leaders to accept leadership practices that conventional wisdom maintains will yield favorable results, but that in fact fall short of promised outcomes; opposing pressures for leaders to avoid seemingly failing practices that will in reality have a compelling impact.

4

Values, Ethics, and the Performance Paradox

Studies have found that nearly 93 percent of corporations have written codes of conduct. Yet despite documented codes of conduct and formal (often mandatory) ethics training, the result has been a barely perceptible impact on behavior in public, private, or government sectors (J. Conley and Wagner-Marsh 1998, 252–253). As we continue to experience high-profile instances of poor ethical behavior like that displayed by leaders at Enron, WorldCom, and many government offices, there appears to be a performance paradox confronting corporate leaders as they weigh two distinct ROI calculations: *return on investment* and *risk of incarceration.*

In the endless pursuit of bottom-line results, the first ROI, senior executives can find themselves operating closer and closer to the edge of right and wrong, as in the second ROI. The result is that their judgment can become impaired as they risk career, reputation, and organizational well-being for what on the surface may seem a worthwhile opportunity—but in retrospect could never have justified the sacrifices that follow from poor ethical actions and decisions.

Without question we live in a world that is at the same time both constant and constantly renewing. We see this push and pull as we encounter new challenges, ideologies, and wider global influences that compel us to rethink traditional values and beliefs (Stackhouse et al. 1995, 32). For many, ethics is a matter of social tolerance and relative moral upbringing—what is ethical behavior for one group of people, another group could consider unacceptable (Wren 1994, 408). This flux becomes problematic in the heat of day as we constantly face challenges living a life that is successful and ethical. In a real sense morality in society constantly confronts actions that are equally "right, good, and fitting" and that "more often that not pull in contrary directions" (Stackhouse et al. 1995, 31).

What then is needed to align the performance paradox of doing whatever it takes and resolving the conflicts that can occur with our values and ethics? The answer begins with understanding the spheres of influence that shape perceptions of right and wrong. An examination of respected research on values and ethics will begin the quest.

VIEWS ON VALUES AND ETHICS

In *Leadership in Organizations,* Yukl provides an explanation for the shifting base of ethical behavior, both individual and corporate:

> Despite the growing interest in ethical leadership there is considerable disagreement about the appropriate way to define and assess it. . . . One difficulty in evaluating the morality of individual leaders is the subjectivity inherent in determining which criteria to use and their relative importance. The final evaluation can be influenced as much by the qualities of the judge and by the qualities of the leader. Judgments about the ethics of a particular decision or action usually take into account the purpose (ends), the extent to which behavior is consistent with moral standards (means), and the consequences for self and others (outcomes). (2002, 402)

Unpacking Yukl's comments reveals the problem of defining an ethical standard from which to guide behavior as twofold: the lack of a consistent standard by which to judge actions, and the sense that the means will somehow justify the ends. To help bring this issue into focus, here's some background on the origin of values, along with some contemporary examples of ethics in action.

The Universal Constant of Gravity Versus Values and Ethics

According to legend, Newton, while sitting under an apple tree, was struck on the head by a falling fruit. Imagination stirred, he considered the existence of heavenly forces that govern the motion of plants and planets. From this experience Newton would eventually articulate these heavenly forces mathematically through the "universal constant of gravity." Newton's laws of motion have served as the unchanging principles that guide the study of astrophysics. However, unlike the laws of physics, the laws of man (the definitions of values that govern the actions of humankind) have changed dramatically since Newton's day, becoming more relative with changing political, economic, and social influences (Joas 2000, 2). While many of these changes in values have been beneficial, in some regards this moral relativism has shaped today's values toward a dangerously self-serving mind-set.

A case in point is Judith Brandt's book *The 50-Mile Rule: Your Guide to Infidelity and Extramarital Etiquette* (2002), which serves as a primer for anyone wanting to have an extramarital affair. In advertising her book, Brandt offers readers nonjudgmental information on adultery that shows not only how to go about being unfaithful but how to lessen the chances of being caught. As an enticement Brandt offers the age-old carnival call—"Come on, everybody's doing it"—by highlighting some statistics:

- Only 5 percent of affairs result in marriage between the affair partners.

- An estimated 10 percent of all children born to married women are raised by husbands who aren't the biological father—but don't know it.

- At least 5 percent of all married men and women cheat in any given year.

Points of view such as Brandt's raise a burning question: Is there such a thing as a moral and ethical absolute? Is it possible to define a universal law of ethics that is timeless, unwavering in the shifting ebbs and flows of human influences? If so, what then is our response to the assertion that "values" are simply standards of behavior that are culturally based and therefore a matter of individual choice? ("Moral Relativism—Neutral Thinking?" 2003).

The Origin of Values

Generally our values are learned, and we employ them to "guide the positions we take on various social, ideological, political and religious issues" (Rokeach 1979, 43). Examples of values are "wisdom, courage, reverence, love, compassion, kindness, gratitude [which] are seen as being inherent in human nature" and that can be categorized as follows (Behrman 1988, 7):

- "Absolute" values of perceived "good or evil" that affect the innate character and will of a person—and "are not affected by culture or situation; they are what informs our conscience and makes us feel guilty, even when we are violating no law or social ethics." Honesty and truthfulness are examples.

- "Societal" values that impact how a group behaves. An example might be the might-makes-right mantra of the USSR—that is, "the government has the power, and therefore whatever it says is good is good."

- "Pragmatic" values that reflect the technique for how things are done. Examples may be understood and acceptable doctor-patient or lawyer-client relationships.

Joas suggests that "values arise in experiences of self-formation and self-transcendence" (2000, 1) and have as their genesis that "point where faith is lost in the historizing variants of a way of thinking that asserts the identity of the true and the good" (21). Thus Joas chronicles the evolution of values as distilled by several noted philosophers:

- Nietzsche, who subscribed to the concept that good was no more beneficial to man than evil and that morality was a hindrance to man's fullest evolution (23)

- Scheler, who refined an "ethics of imperatives" to reconcile acts of good committed out of pure love verses acts of compliance exercised out of obligation (86–88)

- Dewey, who saw the genesis of values as "the creative work of [one's] imagination," suggesting the human "will" responded to controlling desires and choices based on the moral demands self-imposed (115)

- Habermas, who proposed that morality was a safety net used in emergency to avoid corporal repercussions and temporal ramifications (185)

Ethics in Action

While it's easy to find examples of poor ethics in the corporate and political world, unfortunately the issue of poor ethical behavior isn't limited to corporations or government. The Josephson Institute's *Report Card on the Ethics of American Youth* (2006) highlights some disturbing trends in high school students' attitudes on ethics. For example, 60 percent of high school students admitted to cheating on exams, and 23 percent said they had stolen money from a parent or relative. Perhaps the most startling comparison of American youth and corporate leaders is seen in how young Americans believe that a person needs to cheat and lie to get ahead (65 percent of males; 54 percent of females). If these data points aren't enough of a wake-up call, consider that nearly 92 percent of students polled rated their own ethical standards as high—while at the same time acknowledging cheating, lying, and stealing to get ahead.

The apparent lapse in the moral compass of youth is not limited to academic endeavors. A 2005 study titled "The Sport Behavior of Youth, Parents, and Coaches: The Good, the Bad, and the Ugly," conducted by researchers at the University of Minnesota in Minneapolis and the

University of Notre Dame, identified similarly alarming trends among young athletes (Shields et al. 2005, 47–48; Brown 2005, 1):

- Almost 10 percent acknowledged cheating.

- More than 10 percent admitted to having tried to hurt an opponent.

- More than 30 percent indicated they had argued with a sport official.

- More than 10 percent reported they had made fun of a less-skilled teammate.

- More than 25 percent reported they had acted like "bad sports."

As with the Josephson Institute research, young athletes indicated a belief that "cheating is an acceptable behavior, and 32 percent consider arguing with officials to be part of the game" (Brown 2005, 1). Perhaps most concerning in the young athlete study is the poor ethical behavior exhibited by parents and coaches. For example:

- 13 percent of parents acknowledged angrily criticizing their child's performance.

- 8 percent of coaches encouraged their athletes to hurt an opponent.

- 7 percent of coaches condoned cheating.

- 33 percent of coaches admitted to yelling at players for making mistakes.

- 20 percent of coaches had made fun of a team member with limited skills.

- 4 percent of coaches reported they had hit, kicked, or slapped a poorly performing young athlete.

While the frequency with which students and young athletes are cheating, stealing, or lying is disturbing, what should really grab our attention is the perception from our youth that this type of behavior is not only acceptable but required in order to succeed. The sense of right and wrong, the ethics of individual and corporate behavior, has taken a sharp decline toward self-serving misbehavior not only in our youth, but also in modern society as a whole. The question often asked today isn't, Is it wrong to steal? but, Under what circumstances is stealing justified?

From a theological perspective, the Book of Proverbs raises this same question: "Men do not despise a thief, if he steals to satisfy his soul when he is hungry" (Proverbs 6:30, *The Ryrie Study Bible* 1976). While the act of stealing is clearly defined as immoral, the conditions that incited the act are not without consideration. Biblical commentator Mathew Henry draws this distinction in reference to the same passage (1996, 676):

> As for the sin of stealing, if a man were brought to it by extreme neces-
> sity, if he stole meat for the *satisfying of his soul when he was hungry,*
> though that will not excuse him from guilt, yet it is such an extenuation
> of his crime that *men do not despise* him, do not expose him to
> ignominy, but pity him. Hunger will break through stone-walls, and
> blame will be laid upon those that brought him to poverty, or that did
> not relieve him. [Although] he have not that to say in his excuse, *if he be*
> *found* stealing, and the evidence be ever so plain upon him, yet he shall
> only make restitution *seven-fold.* (emphasis added)

Note, however, that Henry does not use the excuse for stealing (extreme necessity) as a means to *justify* the act. Price helps us draw a distinction between excuse and justification by using the example of two individuals who arrive late to a meeting (2006, 24–25). A subordinate arrives late because he was inadvertently locked out of his room by housekeeping. "Although he did what he should not have done, he is not to blame for his inappropriate behavior." Contrast this example with senior executives who likewise arrive late to a meeting because they had "more important matters to which they needed to attend." Thus senior executives do not offer an excuse for being late (I was doing something more important) but stand justified in their action because of the demands and responsibilities of the position. Herein lies a treacherous slope—the inclination for senior executives to believe they are exempt from generally accepted norms of behavior because of the privilege associated with their position of power.

But the inclination to justify or excuse inappropriate behavior is not confined to those in positions of power. Historian Herbert Schlossberg suggests that one possible explanation for the decline in ethical behavior is that we are living in an "age of envy [where] fewer people than ever are ashamed of being envious, apparently believing that the fact of their envy is proof that social injustice has been done. The cultural message is strong: 'Why shouldn't I have what others have?'" (quoted in Swenson 1992, 193).

When Values and Ethics Collide

Shifting ethical standards and changing opinions regarding morality constantly redefine what is accepted as right and wrong behavior. This is perhaps nowhere more evident than in the workplace, where employers and employees alike are regularly challenged to align their actions with codes of conduct. Yet even with formal codes of conduct in place, the elasticity of behavior fluctuates so regularly that the phrase "situational ethics" has entered into the business vocabulary.

Still there exists a basic sense of right and wrong, illustrated by McSwain's assertion that "the ethical ambiguity of the workplace [is] not so much knowing the right as knowing how to be influential in encouraging right behavior" (1995, 719). But are there occasions in which our values (what we believe to be true and right) conflict with acceptable "ethical" behavior? If so, can we establish a standard of ethical behavior based on values unaffected by changes in societal attitudes?

A Case Study for Values Versus Ethics

Contemporary life offers any number of examples in the struggle to align values and ethics: what we believe with how we act. For example, the suspicion has been raised that Colin Powell's departure from the Bush cabinet was due in large part to a conflict between his beliefs and presidential policy. For example, Hitchens offers this comparison: "From William Jennings Bryan to Cyrus Vance, history [has suggested] a remedy for secretaries of state who become demoralized or disillusioned with the policies pursued by their presidents: *resignation*" (2004).

However, from this side of history such assertions regarding contemporary events are calculated conjectures as best. So let's consider a more distant historical event to help us build a framework for understanding how our values are established and how acceptable ethical behavior at times challenges us to reevaluate either what we believe or how we behave. An example that has passed some measure of critique with time is the biblical account of Na'aman as told in the Book of Kings.

Na'aman was a powerful, highly successful commander of the Syrian army and had great favor with the king of Syria. However, Na'aman had a problem. He was a leper. Word had come to Na'aman that there was a man of God in Israel who was reported to have divine powers to heal. With the king's blessing Na'aman set out to find this man of God, known as Elisha. Upon finding Elisha, and reluctantly following his instructions, Na'aman was miraculously healed.

The mighty warrior humbled himself and acknowledged the God of Elisha by attesting he would never again "offer burnt offering or sacrifice to any god but Elisha's God" (Kings 5:17, *The Ryrie Study Bible* 1976). In the moment of his healing Na'aman's beliefs (his values) were changed and, in some regards, his behavior as well. However, Na'aman knew that when he returned home to Syria his new beliefs would be pitted against acceptable Syrian behavior (local values). Thus Na'aman confessed to Elisha: "In this matter may the Lord pardon your servant: when my master [the Syrian king] goes into the house of Rimmon to worship there, leaning on my arm, and I bow myself in the house of Rimmon, when I bow myself in the house of Rimmon, the Lord pardon your servant in this matter" (Kings 5:18).

The story of Na'aman helps visualize the difference between ethics and values. Recall that values are beliefs "we take on various social, ideological, political and religious issues" (Rokeach 1979, 43), while ethics are actions we engage in based on informal or formal standards and procedures that relate to matters of conduct and culture (CLC 2003, 1). In Na'aman's case his values were significantly changed by his experience with Elisha. This experience had a positive impact on Na'aman's behavior (driven by ethics) in his practice of sacrifice. However, not all of his behaviors would be influenced; namely his obligation to comply with values and traditions of Syria.

Na'aman's issue is clearly one many executives face today. How do they respond when faced with the issue of compromising their values (beliefs) with acceptable or required behavior? Even corporations understand the need to link values to actions. The Corporate Leadership

Council (CLC) suggests that to be effective, corporate codes of conduct must "link ethics with employee behaviors by including ethics in statements of corporate values, drafting competency sets based on these values, and subsequently, by creating a value-based culture" (CLC 2003, 6). From this we see corporations' linking corporate values to ethics (codes of conduct) in such areas as integrity, respect, teamwork, quality, and citizenship.

HOW SENIOR EXECUTIVES APPROACH VALUES AND ETHICS

From the review of senior executives' personality data in Chapter 1, it is clear that C-level executives have a strong proclivity for achieving results. But how are these results achieved—at what cost and at what sacrifice? Digging deeper into the assessment data on C-level executives yields useful insights to these questions. Specifically, two assessments—the *Campbell Leadership Index* (CLI) and *Executive Dimensions*—both seek to measure leadership style pertaining to credibility, while the *Campbell Organizational Survey* (COS) measures how employees perceive their manager's and top leader's ethical behavior.

Credibility

The *Campbell Leadership Index* identifies being credible as "able to allocate organizational resources and manage details." Thus, leaders

> with high Observer scores on the Credible Scale appear trustworthy and believable, and they live within the accepted standards of right and wrong. They appear candid and honest, and their actions and opinions are based on visible and openly stated beliefs. They inspire trust in others. [Leaders] with low Observer scores on the Credible Scale are not necessarily seen as untrustworthy or unreliable, but may appear to make decisions that affect others without explaining the reasons. They appear to work from hidden agendas and therefore are unpredictable. Because of this perceived secretive tendency, they may have little credibility in important areas. (Nilsen and Campbell 1998, 20)

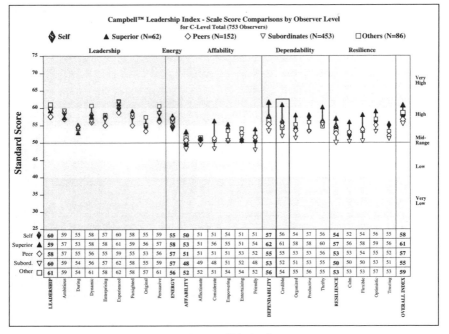

Figure 4.1 • *Campbell™ Leadership Index* **Credible Scale**
Note: These instruments chart scores along a standard format of a bell curve—where the mean is 50 and a standard deviation is 10.

The standard scores on the CLI Credible scale reflect a wide dispersion, ranging from a high of 61 for superiors to a low of 52 for subordinates (see Figure 4.1). To understand this spread better it is helpful to review the item-level detail questions associated with the Credible scale (see Figure 4.2). In the question "Ethical—Lives within society's standards of right and wrong," both superiors and subordinates provide highly favorable ratings. However, a significant difference in superior and subordinate ratings emerges on the questions of "Candid" and "Scheming." This may reflect that subordinates typically do not have as great an access to senior executives' thought processes and decision making as do superiors and as a consequence, subordinates may provide lower ratings in these areas.

Likewise, recall from the review of *Executive Dimensions* that senior executives and observers identified credibility as a leadership

Credible Scale

9. Candid - Open and honest when dealing with others.

	Nev	Sel	Occ	Som	Usu	Alw	%Fav
You		1	6	42	25		
All Obs	1	26	48	120	361	196	74
Superior		2	6	26	28		(87)
Peer	6	7	25	77	37		75
Subord	1	18	34	77	216	107	(71)
Other	2	5	12	42	24		78

20. Credible - Worthy of trust, believable.

	Nev	Sel	Occ	Som	Usu	Alw	%Fav
You				1	43	30	
All Obs	6	14	29	73	284	344	84
Superior			3	2	17	39	92
Peer	1	3	3	16	69	60	85
Subord	5	8	18	49	172	199	82
Other		3	5	6	26	46	84

23. Deceptive - Conceals the truth for selfish reasons.

	Nev	Sel	Occ	Som	Usu	Alw	%Fav
You	34	36	2	1	1		
All Obs	352	240	49	77	30	1	79
Superior	46	11	3	2			92
Peer	68	57	8	13	4	1	83
Subord	196	147	31	56	20		76
Other	42	25	7	6	6		78

38. Ethical - Lives within society's standards of right and wrong.

	Nev	Sel	Occ	Som	Usu	Alw	%Fav
You				4	34	36	
All Obs	1	4	17	51	258	419	90
Superior				1	16	45	(98)
Peer		2	1	8	55	85	93
Subord	1	2	11	38	163	236	(88)
Other			4	5	24	53	90

83. Scheming - Develops sly and devious plans.

	Nev	Sel	Occ	Som	Usu	Alw	%Fav
You	33	33	1	6	1		
All Obs	357	225	52	79	28	6	78
Superior	42	16	1	2	1		(94)
Peer	79	56	4	9	3		89
Subord	191	133	42	58	21	4	(72)
Other	45	20	5	10	3	2	76

96. Trustworthy - Inspires trust and confidence.

	Nev	Sel	Occ	Som	Usu	Alw	%Fav
You				6	47	21	
All Obs	3	21	36	103	348	237	78
Superior			2	6	32	22	87
Peer	1	3	7	23	77	40	77
Subord	1	16	26	63	206	139	76
Other		1	3	11	33	36	82

Figure 4.2 • *Campbell™ Leadership Index* Credible Scale Questions

Note: The scores reflect the raw favorable percent from each observer group: answers that indicate approval. For positive statements such as "Open and honest when dealing with others," favorable responses would be "Always" or "Usually." For negative statements such as "Develops sly and devious plans," favorable responses would be "Never" or "Seldom."

competency that was both important and a strength for executives. Table 4.1 reflects the ratings that were provided for the Credibility scale in the *Executive Dimensions* assessment, which rates responses on a five-point scale, with 5 being the highest rating. The results suggest that senior executives demonstrate the behaviors described in following sections.

Ethics

While significant distinctions appear between self and observer Credible ratings in the CLI, there is little separation in the Ethics ratings in the COS (see Figure 4.3, p. 124)—where the self-ratings reflect 58 against an observer score of 55. While both ratings fall within the high section for the standard scores, recall that the COS measures the perceived ethical behavior of an organization's leadership as well as the organizational environment. Campbell and Hyne help make sense of the *Organizational Survey* scores of the Ethics scale by providing the following interpretation:

> High scores are usually found in organizations with strong expectations for ethical behavior that are then reinforced by the actions of management. Low scores are often found in organizations where there has been a recent controversial issue such as a termination or other situation that

CREDIBILITY	EXECUTIVES	BOSSES	DIRECT REPORTS
Uses ethical considerations to guide decisions	4.05	4.10	3.73
Through words and deeds encourages honesty throughout the organization	4.10	4.12	3.74
Speaks candidly about tough issues facing the company	3.93	4.00	3.88
Tells the truth, not just what important constituents want to hear	4.08	4.14	3.78
Can be trusted to maintain confidentiality	4.12	4.37	3.94
Places ethical behavior above personal gain	4.25	4.50	3.94
Follows through on promises	3.92	4.01	3.70
Acts in accordance with stated values	4.11	4.18	3.86
Average	4.07	4.17	3.82

Table 4.1 • *Executive Dimensions* Ratings on the Credibility Scale

is perceived as unfair to some individual or group. Unexplained but apparently selfish or self-serving decisions by members of top leadership can also lead to low scores. (1995, 17)

As with the Credible scale in the CLI assessment, the Ethics scale of the COS assessment provides more depth regarding individual ratings of both senior executives and observers. Figure 4.4 provides such a view, revealing that both senior executives and observers do not feel pressure to engage in unethical or dishonest conduct. However, senior executive and observer ratings diverge widely on the question that relates to honesty as a way of organizational life—only 64 percent of observers rate this favorably, compared to 79 percent for senior executives. This pattern appears even more strongly in the question on how the organization handles issues of right and wrong; with a 48 percent favorable rating

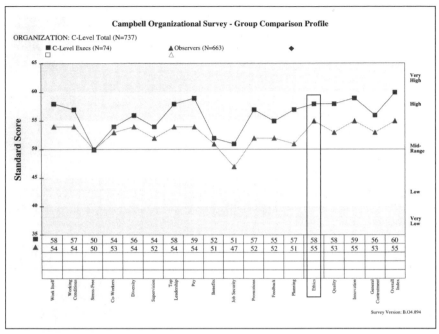

Figure 4.3 • *Campbell™ Organizational Survey* Ethics Scale

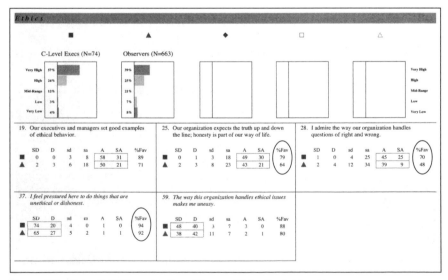

Figure 4.4 • *Campbell™ Organizational Survey* Ethics Scale Questions

Note: "Percent Favorable" reflects answers that indicate approval. For positive statements favorable responses would be "Always" or "Usually" and for negative statements favorable responses would be "Never" or "Seldom."

from observers and a 70 percent favorable rating from senior executives. Clearly, these two questions evoked startling differences in perceptions between senior executives and subordinates.

Summary of Data

So what can be gleaned from the data collected around ethics and credibility? First, Campbell and Hyne point out that there is a very strong intercorrelation between COS scores on Ethics and scores on Quality, Innovation, Planning, Feedback, Top Leadership, and Supervision (1995, 55). From this you might anticipate that high ethical conduct will influence favorable perceptions regarding work performance and decision making. Also, while the characteristic of Sound Judgment might speak to the perception that senior executives will do things correctly and Results Orientation addresses the perception that things will get done, the leadership characteristic of Credible relates to how others trust and believe the senior executive will do the right thing—the right way.

EXECUTIVE BALANCE IN VALUES AND ETHICS

Here I cover situational ethics, accountability, integrity, and keeping confidences as they relate to the paradox of balancing values and ethics in executive performance.

Values-Based Ethics and Accountability

One suggestion that has surfaced in attempting to balance the performance paradox is that ethics should be situational, complying with the acceptable norms of the moment. However, as Chewning points out, there are inherent dangers with this concept when so-called situational ethics create an environment where bad ethics can become good and good ethics can become bad simply by varying the situation and allowing "the human participant" to serve as ultimate judge of right and wrong (2000, 67). It would seem then that without a clear benchmark

from which to establish ethical standards, there would be a natural inclination to look inward for a self-directed moral compass.

While the notion of turning inward to set standards of ethical behavior should trigger alarms on nearly every moral compass, many noteworthy leadership theorists propose just such a self-aggrandizing ideal.
For example, consider a comment made by Greenleaf, architect of the
servant-leadership discipline. During a lecture to aspiring college students, Greenleaf encouraged his audience to look to themselves in
redefining moral values, stating: "The level of consensus necessary for
traditional morals to be accepted as law no longer holds. Therefore your
generation may well be the first to face the condition of producing your
own. For better or worse you will have to achieve it on your own, with
your own resources" (1998, 100).

Over time many philosophers have attempted to connect the human
struggle with good and evil to an evolutionary drive to divorce the definition of morality from a higher (divine) set of standards. The influence
of this thinking has contributed to a hedonistic approach to defining
codes of conduct. In this conundrum we find ourselves with such questions as, Is stealing always wrong? and, Is it acceptable to cheat to get
ahead?

Is it unreasonable to believe that a constant, timeless baseline for
ethical behavior could serve to guide human actions regardless of societal influences? Stackhouse and his colleagues provide insight to this
question: "Ethics to be sure is an important discipline, but it finally cannot stand alone. Ethics needs theological help, in part because it needs an
ultimate center of integration. The ultimate issues about what is right,
what is good and what is fitting demand a foundation in a living reality
that transcends ordinary human capabilities" (1995, 32). However, simply knowing right from wrong rarely translates into high ethical behavior. To this point Stackhouse and his colleagues continue, "ethics is not a
recipe by which one can add one part rightness, one part goodness, and
one part fittingness" (32). What is needed is a mechanism for building
accountability—accountability to one another as well as accountability
to a higher calling, an absolute standard of right and wrong.

Integrity Issues in "Follow the Leader"

By definition a leader is out in front, visible for all to see. Over time those being led may begin to emulate the leader's behaviors and patterns. In the animated movie *Robots,* about a world run by machines, a major character is Big Weld, the founder and president of a company that makes parts for robots. All executives reporting to Big Weld dress and look like small copies of him, even copying some of his mannerisms— much as real-life followers copy the behaviors and actions of executives.

I became painfully aware of this phenomenon when I transferred from Amex's Florida Operations Center to the one in North Carolina. My family and I came to the Carolinas in the fall of 1996. As winter approached I recall asking around about how much snow we might see that year. I should have braced myself for the inevitable when everyone assured me the Carolinas rarely see much snow. That year we were hammered. The first snowstorm caught Amex off guard, and we barely had enough staff available to handle the work. So when the next threat of major snow occurred, Amex decided to have employees sleep over at the operations center the day before so that we'd have enough staff on hand to accommodate the work. We did the sleepover right, bringing in cots, movies, and lots of food. While the group I oversaw did not directly support customer interactions, I felt that because I was part of the senior leadership team I should chip in and stay the night, so I volunteered to run the movie projector. The sleepover worked really well. We did get hit with a ton of snow, but enough staff had stayed the night before so that we could handle the work.

A few weeks passed before another threat of major snow was in the forecast. So another sleepover was planned. However, this time most of my staff volunteered to stay over, even though they did not have direct contact with customers and could easily do their work from home if they were snowed in. After the snow event came and went I asked my team why they had opted to stay. I expected to hear something noble like, "We wanted to be here to serve the customer if we were needed." But what I heard was, "We stayed because you stayed"! Because it was important to me to be at the operations center, it became important to my team.

This is a similar pattern in the area of ethics and integrity. If the person in front exhibits and demonstrates high ethical character, group members will, in turn, emulate this behavior. Likewise if poor ethical behavior is the norm, others will follow suit, perhaps even finding willing partners for engaging in poor ethical practices.

Keeping a Confidence

As the saying goes, "It can take a lifetime to earn trust and a moment to lose it." Executives' ability to maintain the confidence of those they lead is tied directly to their credibility and the organization's perception of ethical behavior. This is reflected in the following story.

> The senior leadership team at a large bank was known for their ability to work together as a team and get things done. The bank had recently experienced significant growth that was attributed to the senior leadership team's decisive action and bold moves. However, it had one major problem—the team couldn't keep a secret. Some of the key decisions the bank was engaged in involved possible acquisitions and new lines of business. The very nature of the work dictated maintaining a tight lid on negotiations and ideations. Yet details of these sensitive initiatives always seemed to leak out. Likewise, word of delicate personnel decisions around hiring, promotions, and terminations that were reviewed and discussed within the senior leadership team regularly made its way into the bank's grapevine.

> For the bank president it became a crisis of confidence in her senior leadership team—so she decided to flush out the leak. She privately shared with each senior executive specific details about a very sensitive initiative, knowing that only that executive would be privy to that particular detail. Then she patiently waited to see which detail appeared in the bank's rumor mill. Once the specific detail surfaced she knew who was unable to keep a confidence—and who would no longer be on her team.

CALL TO ACTION

Lombardo and Eichinger summarize the themes of this chapter nicely: "Values and ethics are shorthand statements of the core or underlying principles that guide what [we] say and do . . . [and] provide guidance on how we act and how we make choices" (2000, 134). So, to begin aligning the ever-constant performance paradox of doing whatever it takes with ever-shifting standards for values and ethics, we need to begin with understanding the influencers that shape our perceptions of right and wrong. From this understanding senior executives can align their actions with a solid ethical standard from which to guide behavior by considering three key influencers: accountability, openness and transparency, and integrity for keeping commitments and maintaining confidences.

Accountability

In addressing the topic of ethics in the COS assessment, Campbell and Hyne suggest that for individual leaders accountability for adhering to an agreed-upon, known standard of behavior should begin with the leaders' first examining their own values and ethics, and then making this known to those around them (1995, 238). Lombardo and Eichinger offer a similar suggestion when they write, "define your standards of behavior [ethics and values] and make them known to those around you" (2000, 134). The obvious power in making known how you feel about specific values and ethics can be lost without reflection. Once you take a stand that a certain type of behavior is acceptable (or unacceptable), then those around you will look for you to pattern that behavior. This approach is the same as the one recommended for breaking a bad habit, when sharing your decision with those around you can be a valuable source of strength and accountability in helping you keep to your commitment. So if an executive makes the assertion that a certain code of conduct, say, "complete disclosure of all financials—good and bad" for example, those around the executive will first look for that behavior on the part of the executive, and then that behavior will be patterned by those who follow. Here again Lombardo and Eichinger offer valuable insight:

> We all have a set of values and ethics but many times we haven't thought out our values and ethical stance well; we are on autopilot from childhood and our accumulated experiences. All organizations have a set of reasonably consistent values and ethics they prefer to operate under.

Organizations require reasonable conformity with those collective standards. [Leaders] who are models of ethics and values have thought their values through, are clear about them, can deal with close calls by applying them, understand other value stances, speak up on these matters, and are reasonably consistent and in tune with those around them."
(2000, 137)

Additionally, as highlighted earlier, one observation CCL has noted is that as executives move up the corporate ladder their interaction with others in their organizations becomes more and more constrained. In other words, the higher up you go, the less likely a subordinate or direct report will tell you when you're behaving like a jerk—or worse, like a crook. It is very difficult for subordinates or direct reports to tell senior executives that they are being inconsistent in their actions—changing their behavior based on their mood, their last meeting, or what insightful tidbit of information just came across their desk. It is critical for senior executives to find someone on an equal footing, perhaps a peer in another organization, who can help keep them accountable to the values they want to live out. Most important, it should be someone who cares enough to tell them when their behavior begins drifting away from the values they want to live by.

Also, it is important to be willing to reflect on your ethics to regularly compare your ethics with acceptable norms. Times do change, and there is something to be said for keeping up with the times. The story is told at CCL of discussions in the 1970s about the appropriate length of the then-popular miniskirts. The challenge was to suggest a length that was long enough to be modest but short enough to be interesting. A conversation on this topic today might take a different tone. So while it is helpful to be able to change with the times, it is equally important to stand your ground. Some values and ethics should perhaps remain timeless—and it's important to understand what those values are and stand by them.

Openness and Transparency

The perception of an executive's credibility is tied directly to how open and transparent the executive is in decision making and actions. As noted earlier, the perception of organizational politics can erode the effectiveness of a leader. It is critical then that senior executives manage perceptions so that organizational politics are not seen as attempts to buy favors or influence. It is equally important for senior executives to be mindful of how their actions are perceived. For example, do their motives appear to be (or perhaps are) selfish and self-serving? This is especially important remembering that C-level executives have a disposition toward achieving results, and it is important for them to guard against the "performance at all costs" mind-set.

In being open and transparent, be sure to give clear, well-reasoned explanations for your decisions and what you're looking to achieve. One idea that can help in this is to let people see what you do by bringing observers into your sphere of influence to watch your decision-making process. While this will not always be practical, as often as you can, invite someone outside your regular leadership team to sit in on a staff meeting or a meeting on a particular initiative. Not only might you realize some valuable insight from the observer, the observer will be able to better see the details involved in your actions and communicate to the organization on your behalf. But one caution is needed—above all else be genuine. Don't invite an observer into your sphere of influence only so you can put on a show. People have a way of seeing through insincerity, and the end result is likely to heighten people's mistrust of your integrity.

Finally, be quick to acknowledge mistakes and take responsibility for your own missteps. Don't pass the buck or look for someone or something to take the blame. Openly accept mistakes as learning opportunities and encourage others in the organization to do the same. Not only will this reflect on your own openness and transparency, in the end it could save you from being surprised by bad news—you'll get timely reports of other people's errors that might otherwise have been swept under the organizational carpet.

Integrity

Here again Campbell and Hyne offer two insights that are helpful for groups and organizations as they consider managing perceptions around integrity (1995, 238): "As a group, identify areas of concern. Document issues and implications. Decide on steps to take to alter practices. . . . Review code of ethics and consequences of unethical actions. Take action on concerns and complaints. Be candid."

Within the framework of integrity it is possible to distill two critical components to which executives must pay attention—keeping commitments and maintaining confidences.

Keep Commitments. Another saying worth remembering is "Undercommit and overproduce." In senior executives' pursuit of results it is reasonable to expect that occasionally expectations will not be met. While this is understandable and perhaps even a good indication that you're aggressively moving forward, be careful that overcommitment doesn't become habitual. You'll be much better off when you keep your word—especially for commitments that are personal in nature (say, "We'll review your mid-year performance on Friday" or, "Let's talk about that next assignment this week"). No matter how good your reasons why a particular commitment could not be met seem to you, to the person who was counting on you the reason may not carry any weight at all. What is remembered is that you didn't hold up your end of the deal.

Keep Confidences. Maintaining a person's confidence is perhaps one of the most trusted forms of integrity in personal and professional settings. While few people would intentionally betray a confidence, misunderstandings or legitimate concerns can sometimes let the word out. To protect against this, be sure that if someone asks you to keep something confidential, you establish an understood, spoken-out-loud agreement that you cannot keep something in confidence if it appears illegal or unethical, or would endanger someone's health or safety. Once this caveat is on the table, then be sure to keep information you accept as confidential in confidence.

PERSONAL REFLECTION:
A TRUE UNIVERSAL CONSTANT

Clearly society has countless systems and conventions in play, replete with checks and balances designed to keep leaders on the straight and narrow—Sarbanes-Oxley quickly comes to mind. Still we continue to see senior executives fall from grace—making poor ethical decisions on a regular basis. To make matters worse, leaders often try to close the barn door after the horse has been stolen. Consider President Bush's mandate that all White House officials attend "ethics briefings" following the mishandling of classified CIA materials (VandeHei 2005) or the House's requirement that members of Congress attend "ethics training courses" in the aftermath of several high-profile corruption scandals (Seabrook 2005). It would seem that if we learned anything from the era of Prohibition (when the manufacture, distribution, and consumption of alcohol were outlawed), it was that we cannot legislate a society's moral behavior.

What then is our response to endlessly shifting values and sliding ethics? Should we be concerned with the values embraced by a younger generation that suggest cheating is okay to get ahead? Or is the younger generation simply applying situational ethics as the code of conduct they've observed in their parents?

It would seem that what is needed is a universal constant, a higher purpose if you will, that would serve as a grounding point of our values and ethics. This universal constant would not only influence our behavior but would give heart to our conscience. It's not enough to simply say "stealing is wrong" unless we understand why stealing is wrong. Without our values and ethics (motives) centered on a universal constant, our actions will be subject to the times in which we live. And history would suggest that if this is the case, then in the end our actions will inevitably be influenced by our own selfish desires.

5

Creativity, Innovation, and the Operational Excellence Paradox

Creativity and innovation may sound synonymous, but there is a subtle though noteworthy distinction between them. Creativity centers on ideation—that is, the process and dynamics associated with generating ideas. Innovation, on the other hand, is the practical application of creative outcomes to productive results (Shalley and Gilson 2004, 3; Krause 2004, 1). An example that highlights the distinction between creativity and innovation can be found in the way the U.S. Navy greatly improved its performance by borrowing a creative idea from the British.

At the beginning of the nineteenth century, naval gunnery accuracy rates were abysmal, averaging less than 2 percent (meaning that of 9,500 shots fired, less than 190 hit their intended targets). However a creative British admiral, Percy Scott, had developed an ingenious method of elevated gears and telescopic sightings that allowed gunners to continually adjust fire to account for the rolling of the ship. The result was a remarkable increase in gunfire accuracy. However, as Tushman and O'Reilly point out, Admiral Scott was more interested in creative endeavors than in product development and was content with simply outfitting his own ship rather than the entire British Navy. Admiral Scott was, however, inclined to share his ideas with others, including a young U.S. Naval lieutenant named William Sims. What Lieutenant Sims lacked in creativity, he more than made up for in innovative thinking and tenacity. Over the course of many months and many bureaucratic roadblocks, Lieutenant Sims eventually convinced President Theodore Roosevelt to take up the idea of continuous-aim gunfire and thereby increased the accuracy of U.S. warships by 3,000 percent (Tushman and O'Reilly 1997, 4–7).

This distinction between creativity and innovation raises an interesting issue. To build sustainable success (one of the three essential elements of effective executive leadership), organizations need to run two concurrent strategies (Basadur 2004, 104):

- Build and maintain operational efficiencies that will allow margins for investment, but . . .

- Sustain continuous innovation through productive implementation of creative energies

These competing demands—being operationally efficient and at the same time fostering creativity and innovation—bring about a perplexing paradox. For an innovative organization to thrive competitively it must build infrastructure and processes to facilitate delivery of goods and services at a compelling value. Nonetheless, an organization that is able to provide goods and services at a compelling value will stagnate and die unless it is able to harvest and exploit its creative and innovative energies.

Meanwhile, for innovative organizations that build standard, repeatable processes to deliver goods and services at a compelling value, these operational processes often constrain the very creative energies that led to the organization's success. The converse is true for organizations that have efficiently streamlined their operations to provide remarkable price points but in the end are overtaken by competitors with a new and innovative offering.

The paradox for leaders is to balance the competing promises and demands inherent in creative and innovative ideas to capture new markets and operational excellence to ensure delivery of compelling value. Thus the point can be made that while creativity of leaders is helpful, for innovation to occur in an organization, leaders need to focus their own creativity and that of their teams toward practical and beneficial results. In this delicate balancing act, leaders need to be diligent to develop and carry out operational processes that ensure "value entitlement"—where customers are entitled to receive quality goods and services at compelling prices and producers are entitled to realize reasonable margins and sustainable growth.

To explore this leadership challenge, the first stop is what thought leaders have had to say about executive creativity and innovation.

VIEWS ON CREATIVITY AND INNOVATION

Attempts to characterize *creativity* often isolate personal traits associated with someone of noted giftedness. For example, Gelb outlines some of the characteristics of Leonardo da Vinci: curiosity, a disposition toward experiential learning, the ability to embrace ambiguity, and an appreciation for connecting the dots (1998, 9). Likewise, Renzulli's research out of the National Center of the Gifted and Talented has suggested that giftedness is a combination of above-average talent, creativity, and commitment to results—and that remarkable accomplishments are demonstrated when a gifted person fully exercises at least two of these traits (Shavinina 2003, 79–89). Consider the remarkable athlete who despite a poor work ethic is able to take advantage of inborn ability and creativity to achieve results, or the average student who through strong study habits and creativity is able to consistently perform at the top of the class.

However, characterizations of *innovation* generally focus on implementations of remarkable outcome. For example, Henry Ford's application of mass production concepts in assembly line production was hardly creative. Many of the concepts Ford employed had already been in play in various forms. But particularly compelling was Ford's innovative approach in applying these creative concepts to yield results (Sternberg, Kaufman, and Pertz 2004, 464). Ford himself highlighted this point, saying, "I invented nothing new. I simply assembled into a car the discoveries of other men behind whom were centuries of work" (quoted in Hargadon 2005, 33). However Ford's giftedness came more from his tenacity and refusal to give up—even though Ford's first two attempts to build cars, the 1899 Detroit Automobile Company and the 1901 Henry Ford Motor Company were "market and financial failures" (Silzer 2002, 5).

So, if creativity and innovation are critical resources for organizational success, the natural question emerges: How do we make creativity and innovation happen? For organizational innovation to become a reality, leaders and teams must direct their creativity toward results. To this end Shalley and Gilson suggest that the "role of leaders is to ensure that the structure of the work environment, the climate and culture and the human resource practices . . . are such that creative outcomes can and do occur" (2004, 35). What type of creativity emerges in an organization is contingent not on the leadership but on an organization's environment (Sternberg 1999, 471). In particular, environments that exhibit "expert knowledge and information, and the granting of degrees of freedom and autonomy" foster greater creativity (Krause 2004, 100). If creativity is about generating ideas and innovation is about producing results, organizations need equal focus on both processes.

Before crafting an action plan for harnessing an organization's creative and innovation energy, it is helpful to understand two key factors:

- How certain obstacles will at times inhibit these processes

- How an organization's culture will influence creativity and innovation

The body of knowledge dedicated to understanding creativity and innovation is astounding. For the purposes of this review, I'll focus on a finite section of research that looks at several key areas: reward and recognition, trust, organizational self-awareness, and customer intimacy.

Reward and Recognition

Much research has been focused on studying the impact of extrinsic rewards on creativity. For example, research has shown that the "effects of monetary incentives and recognition on creativity are not uniform across different jobs and employees" (Baer, Oldham, and Cummings 2003, 581). It is clear that the way jobs are structured influences creativity. For example, the more complex and demanding the job, the greater the creativity exhibited (Shalley and Gilson 2004, 37). Specifically, individuals in complex jobs by definition require greater cognitive skills and therefore typically don't see gains in creativity or innovation from extrinsic rewards and recognition. However, individuals in less complex jobs, requiring less cognitive skills, do see positive results in creativity and innovation from reward and recognition programs (Sternberg 1999, 307). It is also clear that people are drawn toward environments where creativity (and perhaps their individual contributions) are recognized, supported, and valued (Breen 2004, 77).

A number of theories attempt to explain why this difference exists, but when it comes to reward and recognition, there definitely is no such thing as "one size fits all." Collins helps summarize the complexity and breadth of research on the influence of rewards on creativity by suggesting, "the more tedious the task, the more influential motivators are to the creative process. . . . Different motives will act distinctly on different components of the creative process" (2005, 305). This can be particularly challenging in organizations that have a strong egalitarian culture. However, to a measurable extent, some level of motivation (reward) will connect people with a particular topic and thereby increase their interest and thus creativity.

Trust

According to Kahtamaki, Kekale, and Viitala, trust evolves systematically as an organization moves through the various stages of its life cycle (2004, 75–86). For example, early in an organization's life, trust is embedded with the founder, whose vision and passion inspire and drive people forward. As an organization matures, trust in the founder is replaced with trust in individuals because of their roles, responsibility, and even procedures. Eventually, as an organization grows, its entrepreneurial spirit gives way to the need to standardize operations. In this stage, trust becomes institutionalized as trust in the organization replaces confidence in a particular individual.

So when people trust in their leaders, who in turn affirm confidence in their workforce's competency, innovation takes form in new solutions and breakthrough products. However, when trust is institutionalized, innovation is often replaced with simple problem solving.

Self-Awareness

Sternberg, Kaufman, and Pertz have outlined an interesting model for creative leadership that connects how an organization embraces creativity with how the organization perceives the strength or vulnerability of its market position. Within this model of creative leadership, two positions are suggested for how an organization will propel itself forward: "Stay the Course" (2004, 457–463) and "Change or Die" (463–468).

"Stay the Course." These organizations believe they are in the right place at the right time with the right product. Their culture is strong, steady, and very resistant to change. Acceptance of new ideas and concepts is heavily influenced by past successes (Tushman and O'Reilly 1997, 8) and more so by past failures. Within the "Stay the Course" position are several strategies for how organizations engage creativity and innovation.

The "pedal in place" strategy focuses on not losing any ground or status. This strategy might be found in an organization with quantifiable consumer demand, solid success, and limited competition. You could almost hear the board's admonition to a newly appointed president: "You're taking the reins of a company that's running very well as is. Whatever you do—don't foul it up!" Clearly in this configuration very little creativity will occur.

The "right place—wrong offering" strategy suggests that the organization has done well to earn its current position in the marketplace but needs to consider multiple vantage points so as to redefine its value proposition. An example can be seen in how aspirin, once used primarily for pain relief, is now used more as a measure for preventing heart failure.

The "advancement" strategy suggests that all the right components that have influenced the organization's success are still in play. Thus, increased success is achievable by simply adding more fuel to the engine. Often this is seen in variations to successful products through calculated improvements timed to extend value as well as consumer demand. An example might be a series of sequels to a hit movie or a spin-off from a popular TV series.

"Change or Die." These organizations face significant challenges that threaten their prosperity, or even their continued existence. In these conditions, leaders are drawn toward transformational creativity and innovation to reaffirm the organization's value proposition and establish market dominance. Here organizations have several strategies for engaging creativity and innovation.

"Redirection" strategies suggest that the organization needs to divert its efforts from its current momentum. This does not necessarily suggest altering the organization's value proposition itself, but rather the constructs for which the value is positioned. For example, when Mattel changed its advertising from targeting parents to targeting children, the new approach saved the company from bankruptcy.

"Glory days" strategies attempt to replicate a value position at a time when the organization was successful and then attempt to move forward. This model is typically seen in political circles, where sentiment and historical revision rule the day.

"Visionary" strategies look to move an organization to a point on the horizon that is invisible to most observers. These are generally groundbreaking innovations.

Customer-Inspired Innovation

Customers can be a great source of creativity and innovation, especially those customers who are defining new market trends. For example, Juniper Networks seeks out customers who can direct Juniper's efforts toward new frontiers, rather than simply enhancing legacy systems. According to Christine Heckart, Juniper's vice president of marketing,

"We pick customers higher up the mountain—companies that are facing the problems first." By aligning with these leading-edge customers, Juniper is able to gain insight into future trends and customer demands (L. Conley 2004, 66).

Without question, customers are a critical stakeholder group for the organization, and overall customer satisfaction is a bellwether for the organization's performance and effectiveness (Daft 2004, 22). Savage and his colleagues echo this point on stakeholder management:

> Without an appropriate framework, managers are likely to respond in the traditional ad hoc manner to stakeholders—greasing the squeaky wheel. Instead, executives need to go beyond traditional strategic management issues, such as likely competitor's actions or market attractiveness. They should also evaluate the environment for those external, internal, and interface stakeholders that are likely to influence the organization's decisions. (1991, 63)

So while it is extremely insightful for an organization to seek out trend-setting customers, it is equally critical to stay close to the long-time, loyal customers it already has. However, drawing insight from existing customers can pose a distinct set of challenges. Sometimes it would seem that organizations believe that they become closer to their customers by simply conducting regular satisfaction surveys or focus groups. I once asked a senior executive how well she understood her organization's customer base. She then shared with me a lot of interesting data and facts about customer demographics, the frequency and volume of customer purchases, and the latest data from a customer satisfaction survey. But when I asked how she came to "know what they know," her response was the usual round of marketing and sales analysis, surveys, and executive summaries from focus groups. Few organizations and fewer senior executives ever walk the proverbial mile in their customers' shoes; they rely on developing an understanding of their customers by calculated data analysis and sophisticated surveys. But there is a world of difference between asking customers how they engage with your organization and actually observing customers in action.

To truly understand how customers use your products and services, you need to adopt an anthropologist's approach for getting close to customers—observing customers in action rather than simply asking questions. In their *HBR* article "Empathic Design," Dorothy Leonard and Jeffery Rayport suggest that when we limit our understanding of customers to responses to survey questions and focus groups we short-circuit the creative and innovation potential because in general customers are "so accustomed to current conditions that they don't think to ask for a new solution" (1997, 104). To help draw out an understanding for how customers engage your organization and use your products and services, Leonard and Rayport outline several components of "empathic design" that can help an organization gain creative and innovation insights from observing customers in action (105–107):

> **Triggers of use.** "What circumstances prompt people to use your product or service? Do your customers turn to your offering when, and in the way, you expected?" Example: Cheerios being used as a snack for toddlers rather than a breakfast food.
>
> **Interactions with the environment.** "How does your product or service fit into your users' own idiosyncratic systems—whether they be a household routine, an office operation, or a manufacturing process?" Example: At CCL we gained valuable insight for how our Internet-based assessment system interacts with organizational firewalls and e-mail systems.
>
> **Customization.** "Do users reinvent or redesign your product to serve their own purposes?" Example: Auto manufacturing taking note on how consumers customize their cars for looks or performance and then introducing these features in new models.
>
> **Intangible attributes of the product.** "What kinds of peripheral or intangible attributes does your product or service have?" Example: Moen's use of a cultural anthropologist to observe how consumers use their water faucets revealed novel insights for intangible uses of Moen products (Johnston and Bate 2003, 63–64).

Leonard and Rayport summarize the potential insights that can be gained from observing customers in action instead of simply asking customers questions by the comparison shown in Table 5.1 (111).

INQUIRY	OBSERVATION
People can't ask for what they don't know is technically possible.	Well-chosen observers have deep knowledge of corporate capabilities, including the extent of the company's technical expertise.
People are generally highly unreliable reporters of their own behavior.	Observers rely on real actions rather than reported behavior.
People tend to give answers they think are expected or desired.	Observers determine reactions based on nonverbal cues of their feelings and responses through body language, in addition to spontaneous, unsolicited comments.
People are unlikely to recall their feelings about intangible characteristics of products and services when they aren't in the process of using them.	Using the actual product or a prototype, or engaging in the actual activity for which an innovation is being designed, stimulates comments about such intangibles as smells or emotions associated with the product's use.
People's imaginations—and hence their desires—are bound by their experience; they accept inadequacies and deficiencies in their environment as normal.	Trained, technically sophisticated observers can see solutions to unarticulated needs.
Questions are often biased and reflect inquirers' unrecognized assumptions.	Observation is open-ended and varied; trained observers tend to cancel out one another's observational biases.
Questioning interrupts the flow of people's natural activity.	Observation, while almost never totally unobtrusive, interrupts normal activities less than questioning does.
Questioning stifles opportunities for users to suggest innovations.	Observers in the field often identify user innovations that can be duplicated and improved for the rest of the market.

Table 5.1 • Asking Customers Questions Compared to Observing Customers in Action

Influencing Creativity and Innovation

Table 5.2 (based on Krause 2004, 84–86) summarizes several research findings regarding how senior executives might positively influence the effectiveness of their organization's creativity and innovation.

INFLUENCE ON CREATIVITY AND INNOVATION	DESCRIPTION	POSSIBLE ACTION PLAN
Connection with the work and the leader	Employees connect positively with leader's passion for work and its impact. This causes employees to internalize a leader's norms and values.	Ensure everyone on the staff can connect with customers—vicariously if need be, through testimonials and impact studies (Tushman and O'Reilly 1997, 51).
Information sharing	Enable greater frequency and clarity of information sharing relevant to innovation and creativity.	Provide regular communication from senior executives regarding strategies and initiatives.
Degrees of freedom and level of autonomy	Afford employees input, space, and discretionary authority needed for innovation.	Provide staff at all levels (faculty, staff, and operations) with the freedom to investigate, form hypotheses, and experiment with various innovations.
Support for innovation	"By definition, processes of generating and testing ideas contain errors" (Sternberg 1999, 85). Support for innovation acknowledges that a level of failure is anticipated and used as a learning opportunity.	Stay commited to nurturing new ideas through the growing stage.
Openness in decision making	"Innovation by its very nature calls into question the existing balance of power within an organization" (Krause 2004, 86).	Demonstrate commitment to intellectual capital (people) and not departments by redeploying people whenever innovation reengineers physical structures.

Table 5.2 • Executive Influence on Creativity and Innovation

HOW SENIOR EXECUTIVES APPROACH CREATIVITY AND INNOVATION

Recall from Chapter 1 that four personality types were predominantly reflected in the study population of C-level executives: ISTJ, INTJ, INTP, and ENTJ. In this section, I draw on the work of Lynne Levesque to show how senior executives' personality type relates to their creative and innovative energies. As a preamble, however, it's useful to step back for a moment and lay some groundwork for how your personality type might influence your creative energy.

Personality and Creativity

The *Myers-Briggs Type Indicator* (MBTI) personality assessment is built on the work of noted Swiss psychologist Carl Jung, who believed that all of us have certain creative instincts and we are able to enhance our creativity by fully understanding our personality preferences (Levesque 2001, 9). Jung also believed that people develop two distinct talent-sets: an external talent-set (more dominant) that influences how we gather, assimilate, and act on information, and an internal talent-set (auxiliary) that shapes how we perceive the world around us and drives our self-discovery. According to Levesque, leaders need to be able to balance their understanding of what's going on in the world around them while at the same time being able to pause to reflect on what's *really* happening. In her words, "Being effectively creative and productive [innovative] requires an interaction between collecting information and making decisions about it, as well as acting and reflecting" (2001, 26). Her work with personality and creativity suggests that leaders of different personality types assume specific dominant creative roles.

INTJs: Visionaries

Leaders with a personality type of Introversion, Intuition, Thinking, Judging (INTJ) will assume a dominant creative role of "visionary" (Levesque 2001, 95–101). This plays out when senior executives consistently challenge the status quo and look for provocative and profound ideas. Visionaries likewise are able to make connections to data, trends, and facts that many don't see—and use this insight to propose novel approaches. Visionaries are good at:

- Asking provocative questions that push others to see the world differently; striving to find profound solutions to complex problems

- Future thinking and scenario planning

- Offering multi-disciplined perspectives

Visionaries may inadvertently inhibit the creative process because they:

- Tend to ignore people's feelings

- May chase after new ideas just for the sake of change, and thus may latch onto fads

- Can become perfectionist and hesitate to share ideas and information openly

- May become too attached to a particular idea or course of action and be unable to assess its merits or probable effectiveness

ISTJs: Navigators

Leaders with a personality type of Introversion, Sensing, Thinking, Judging (ISTJ) will assume a dominant creative role of "navigator" (Levesque 2001, 55–63). In general navigators "have trouble getting their hands around creativity," seeing their role as being the person who "makes things work right." Navigators are more inclined toward innovative energies (applied creativity), and they are good at:

- Adapting and fine-tuning others' ideas and concepts

- Making things work

- Operationalizing systems and processes

- Drawing on their detailed imagination and nonlinear insight

Navigators may inadvertently inhibit the creative process because they:

- Tend toward perfectionism

- May have problems expressing ideas and concepts

- Will avoid conflict and become overly cautious

- May be uncomfortable with uncertainty and loss of control

INTPs: Inventors

Leaders with a personality type of Introversion, Intuition, Thinking, Perceiving (INTP) will assume a dominant creative role of "inventor" (Levesque 2001, 133–139). Inventors have "keen, questioning, penetrating minds" that enable them to think logically and objectively when solving problems. Inventors have a great deal in common with pilots except that their thought process is much more internal, being more introspective in their reasoning. Inventors are good at:

- Analyzing data, facts, and ideas with original approaches

- Maneuvering innovatively around constraints

- Learning very fast as a result of intellectual curiosity

- Thinking about things as systems

Inventors may inadvertently inhibit the creative process because they:

- Tend to overlook emotional needs and values

- May see problems as either black or white

- Will avoid making decisions

- May be seen as absent-minded, lacking focus

ENTJs: Pilots

Leaders with a personality type of Extraversion, Intuition, Thinking, Judging (ENTJ) will assume a dominant creative role of "pilot." The external (most visible) pilot talent-set reflects a personality type that is focused on completing a task and getting things done—a trait that's been clear throughout this review of C-level executives. Pilots excel at building energy and focus within a team and are especially gifted at inspirational communication. Pilots are also good at:

- "Synthesizing information and proposing new combinations and new ways at looking at the situation" (115)

- Accepting change—they like to shake things up and are constantly looking for ways to improve performance

- Making things happen through their strong will

  Pilots may inadvertently inhibit the creative process because they:

- Are so driven to produce, their requests may stifle the creative energies of others

- Can become overly dependent on a specific set or sources of data

- May step in too quickly to "save the day" and short-circuit the team's energy

- Often appear too abrasive or confrontational

- May see everything as a problem that needs to be solved

Leading Change

This background on executives' creativity talent-set provides insight into how senior executives lead innovation within their organizations. But how do senior executives lead change? The Leading Change scale in the *Executive Dimensions* assessment provides a glimpse of the way senior executives lead the creative and innovative energies in themselves, their direct reports, and their organizations. Table 5.3 breaks out the specific questions raised and the responses provided.

Recall that responses falling in the mid-3s are a very good score and are typical of senior executives who attend CCL programs. The interesting data here are the relatively higher scores for the questions "Supports activities that position the business for the future" and "Pushes the

LEADING CHANGE	EXECUTIVES	BOSSES	DIRECT REPORTS
Correctly judges which creative ideas will pay off	3.41	3.29	3.26
Supports activities that position the business for the future	3.90	3.96	3.85
Pushes the organization to adopt new initiatives	3.89	3.74	3.73
Offers novel ideas and perspectives	3.44	3.53	3.64
Fosters a climate of experimentation	3.12	3.26	3.22
Average	3.55	3.56	3.54

Table 5.3 • *Executive Dimensions* Leading Change Scale

organization to adopt new initiatives." These higher scores suggest that executives, their bosses, and direct reports perceive senior executives as effective in moving the organization to engage new approaches as well as toward a future vision. However, scores from executives, bosses, and direct reports in the area of "Fosters a climate of experimentation" are lower—perhaps suggesting that senior executives often take a calculated, guarded approach to implementing new ideas.

Leading Creativity

Three characteristics in the *Campbell Leadership Index* (CLI) focus on how senior executives lead creatively—Daring, Enterprising, and Original. Figure 5.1 shows the *Leadership Index* scores of these characteristics in relation to the assessment as a whole. As you can see in the graph, Daring and Original are among the lowest-ranked characteristics in the Leadership orientation grouping.

To understand these scores better, it's useful to look more closely at the item-level questions that the CLI poses for each characteristic. The questions in Figure 5.2 (p. 152) are those asked to draw out perceptions regarding a senior executive's competency in Daring and Originality. In

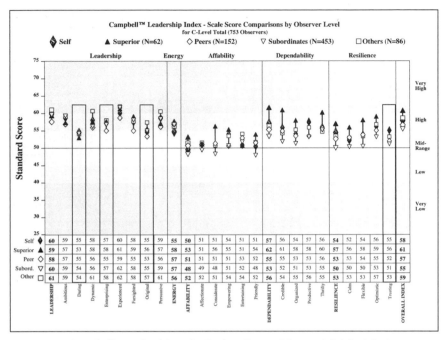

Figure 5.1 • *Campbell™ Leadership Index* Daring, Enterprising, and Original Scales

the item-level questions for the Daring characteristic, senior executives received solid favorable ratings in the questions on trying new and novel activities and trying new experiences. However, it is interesting to contrast these scores with those around risk taking and being conservative, where senior executives received much lower scores. It seems that while senior executives are willing to try new things, their willingness is calculated against pragmatic risk/reward trade-offs. This pragmatic approach may be precisely the leadership dimension needed at more senior levels, given the potential scope of the damage that could result from a failed adventure. However, two thoughts come to mind. First, going back to decision making—do the scores on risk taking and being conservative reflect senior executives' proclivity toward risk management or risk avoidance? Second, it would be interesting to consider senior executives' scoring on their Daring scale earlier in their careers and lives. Thinking back on my own history, I engaged in many more activities and took more risks when I was younger than I would now. In part I would like to believe this is because I'm wiser now. But in truth, I can't do many of the

Daring Scale

3. Adventuresome - Likes to try new and novel activities.

	Nev	Sel	Occ	Som	Usu	Alw	%Fav
You	1	4	20	36	13		
All Obs	18	63	183	326	160		65
Superior	2	3	18	25	14		63
Peer	1	14	35	70	32		67
Subord	13	41	107	194	95		64
Other	2	5	23	37	19		65

22. Daring - Willing to try new experiences.

	Nev	Sel	Occ	Som	Usu	Alw	%Fav
You		4	2	26	33	9	
All Obs	2	34	60	217	323	115	58
Superior		2	4	21	23	12	56
Peer		8	14	40	66	23	59
Subord		22	34	131	199	66	59
Other	2	2	8	25	35	14	57

80. Risk-taking - Takes on new untested or hazardous activities.

	Nev	Sel	Occ	Som	Usu	Alw	%Fav
You	2	4	4	23	37	4	
All Obs	15	79	89	244	224	97	43
Superior		4	11	20	18	9	44
Peer	2	10	21	55	41	21	41
Subord	10	55	49	147	132	57	42
Other	3	10	8	22	33	10	50

15. *Conservative - Cautious about changing the status quo.*

	Nev	Sel	Occ	Som	Usu	Alw	%Fav
You	5	34	14	15	6		
All Obs	37	226	142	219	107	20	35
Superior		12	11	25	12	2	19
Peer	4	43	37	43	22	2	31
Subord	29	146	77	129	56	15	39
Other	4	25	17	22	17	1	34

Original Scale

19. Creative - Produces many novel ideas, products, or methods.

	Nev	Sel	Occ	Som	Usu	Alw	%Fav
You		8	22	36	8		
All Obs	2	25	55	212	322	134	61
Superior		5	19	26	12		61
Peer	6	15	45	59	27		57
Subord	2	17	27	128	201	75	61
Other	2	8	20	36	20		65

55. Imaginative - Has a flair for seeing the world differently.

	Nev	Sel	Occ	Som	Usu	Alw	%Fav
You		2	9	23	37	3	
All Obs	5	40	110	245	244	109	47
Superior		4	13	18	22	5	44
Peer		11	22	53	41	25	43
Subord	5	24	60	150	150	64	47
Other		1	15	24	31	15	53

61. Inventive - Comes up with clever new products or ideas.

	Nev	Sel	Occ	Som	Usu	Alw	%Fav
You		2	11	26	28	7	
All Obs	3	33	70	245	301	101	53
Superior		1	5	23	27	6	53
Peer		11	14	51	51	25	50
Subord	3	17	45	149	182	57	53
Other		4	6	22	41	13	63

71. Original - Thinks and acts in fresh, unusual ways.

	Nev	Sel	Occ	Som	Usu	Alw	%Fav
You		2	3	28	33	8	
All Obs	2	31	72	237	301	109	55
Superior			4	23	26	9	56
Peer		11	20	47	56	18	49
Subord	2	19	39	146	178	68	54
Other		1	9	21	41	14	64

Figure 5.2 • *Campbell™ Leadership Index* Daring and Original Scales Questions

Note: "Percent Favorable" reflects answers that indicate approval. For positive statements favorable responses would be "Always" or "Usually" and for negative statements favorable responses would be "Never" or "Seldom."

activities I used to—and the time I take to recover from a misstep is much greater now than it was when I was younger.

In reviewing details on the Original scale in Figure 5.2, it is helpful to start by considering the questions themselves—as they focus on both creative (ideation) and innovative (producing products and methods) energies. The lower-rated question within the Original characteristic reflects perceptions of the imaginative manner in which the senior executives approach problems and opportunities.

If you align insights from the Original and Daring scales with the understanding that senior executives are highly focused on achieving results, you might speculate that observer responses may be reflecting on the C-level executives' ability to generate novel results such as products and methods. Looking deeper into the CLI characteristic of Enterprising in Figure 5.3 provides support for this speculation, with highly favorable ratings for action- and results-oriented outcomes.

A review of these questions indicates that these characteristics may be more aligned with innovative and get-the-job-done traits such as resourceful, notable achievements, confidence, and so on. This becomes clearer when we review the significance in high and lower scores for the characteristics of Daring, Original, and Enterprising outlined in Table 5.4.

Enterprising Scale

	14. Confident - Believes that future challenges can be met successfully.							35. Enterprising - Clever in developing and carrying out new plans.							56. Impressive - One whose achievements stand out.							79. Resourceful - Deals skillfully with unexpected challenges.						
	Nev	Sel	Occ	Som	Usu	Alw	%Fav	Nev	Sel	Occ	Som	Usu	Alw	%Fav	Nev	Sel	Occ	Som	Usu	Alw	%Fav	Nev	Sel	Occ	Som	Usu	Alw	%Fav
You				3	38	33				2	19	44	9				10	24	36	4				10	53	11		
All Obs	4	11	42	339	357		92	17	47	165	359	164		70	6	14	48	183	312	188	67	2	1	26	117	449	157	81
Superior	1	4	28	29			92	3	13	34	12			74	1	4	16	29	12		66	1	8	38	15			85
Peer	2	9	78	63			93	3	14	36	67	31		65	1	5	13	38	65	28	62	8	28	89	26			76
Subord	4	6	25	197	221		92	12	30	100	205	106		69	4	7	27	108	184	123	68	1	1	15	68	272	96	81
Other	2	4	36	44			93	2		16	53	15		79	1	1	4	21	34	25	69	1	2	13	50	20		81

Figure 5.3 • *Campbell™ Leadership Index* Enterprising Scale Questions

LEADERSHIP CHARACTERISTIC	STANDARD RATING			
	Sr. Executives	Superiors	Peers	Subordinates
Daring *High Scores:* Try new and novel activities; willingly seek new experiences; like change and spontaneity. *Low Scores:* Appear cautious, resist change, are steady and predictable.	55	53	55	54
Original *High Scores:* Imaginative, source of new ideas. *Low Scores:* Critical of new ideas— will not rock the boat.	55	56	53	55
Enterprising *High Scores:* Derive order from chaos; develop new paths from unexpected challenges. *Low Scores:* Difficulty seeing new opportunities; uncomfortable with change.	57	58	55	57

Table 5.4 • *Campbell™ Leadership Index* Characteristics Relating to Creativity and Innovation

Note: Campbell Leadership Index results are reported in a standard score format, that is, with a bell-shaped distribution where the mean is 50 and a standard deviation is 10. Thus a score of 50 is considered typical or normal, a score of 40 is considered very low, and a score of 60 is considered very high. Sixty-eight percent of the individuals in the database score between 40 and 60, and nearly all scores fall between 25 and 75.

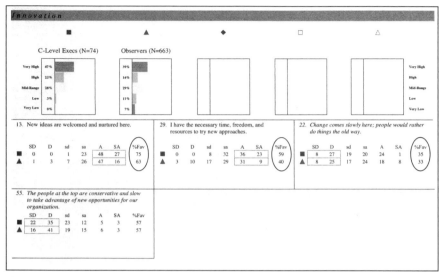

Figure 5.4 • *Campbell™ Organizational Survey* Innovation Scale Questions

The *Campbell Leadership Index* results show that senior executives seem to demonstrate a proclivity toward innovation—tangible products from creative outcomes. Now let's review how senior executives lead innovation within their organizations.

Insights on Innovation and Organizational Effectiveness

The *Campbell Organizational Survey* (COS) seeks to draw out perceptions for how the organization encourages and nurtures innovation. Figure 5.4 reflects the item-level questions for Innovation. Organizations scoring in the high range of the Innovation scale "usually indicate that individuals feel they have the freedom to try new approaches and, if successful, that the organization will adopt these improvements [while] low scores usually indicate a conservative environment where change is discouraged and innovators feel stifled" (Campbell and Hyne 1995, 17).

Standard scores for Innovation fell within the high range for senior executives (59) and the mid-range for observers (55). Looking at the item questions for Innovation, a noticeable perception gap shows up between senior executives and observers on two key points: welcoming and nurturing new ideas, and the flexibility and freedom to tackle new approaches. While the favorable ratings for nurturing new ideas were high for both senior executives (75 percent) and observers (63 percent), the perception gap between these scores suggests that senior executives see this factor in a more positive light. This is also true for the question on flexibility to tackle new approaches, and the perception gap is more problematic as the senior executives' rating is in a higher range (59 percent) than that of observers' (40 percent). From these scores it is possible to speculate that senior executives' more positive favorable ratings may come from the fact that their positions grant them greater autonomy, access, and decision-making authority to identify and pursue innovation activities. Likewise, the nature of senior executives' position suggests an expectation that they will guide their organizations toward innovative initiatives.

Another interesting observation emerges from a review of perceptions for how the organization approaches new opportunities. Senior executives and observers share similar perceptions (57 percent favorable) regarding the organization's agility, flexibility, and timeliness in pursuing new ventures. However, it appears that the manner in which these new ventures are approached may see little to no change, in view of the lower favorable ratings associated with the questions of how readily the organization embraces change to its internal processes and procedures.

Summary of Data

From the review of assessment data, it appears that some senior executives are more inclined toward creative endeavors, while others lean more toward innovative initiatives. And obstacles may arise if senior executives overplay either creative or innovative energies as they look to shake things up just for the sake of change—perhaps chasing after the next fad or being so driven to produce results that they may cut off the creative energies of others or may step in too quickly to save the day and short-circuit their team's energy. Also, some senior executives' no-nonsense, structured approach may come across as too abrasive or confrontational, and some may see everything as a problem that needs to be solved.

Finally, it is helpful to draw a distinction between how a senior executive approaches creative and innovative endeavors and the manner in which the organization encourages and nurtures these characteristics. Thus in some regards, a senior executive's position may by its very nature enable (or even dictate) a level of innovative prerogative, but organizational inertia may resist change regardless of its sponsor's position or level.

OBSERVATIONS ON EXECUTIVE CREATIVITY AND INNOVATION

Creativity and innovation are topics that easily evoke personal experiences or observations. Let me share a couple of mine . . .

No Points for Original Thought

In the early 1990s I had the privilege of working with a team of extremely bright and dedicated people at American Express in the development of a new credit card—Optima True Grace. Over the course of nearly a year the Amex design team worked out various value positions, marketing plans, business operations, and deployment strategies for the new card. By all accounts, the launch of the True Grace card in the winter of 1994 was very successful, resulting in a healthy increase in new account bookings for American Express. However, within a few short months, a major competitor replicated many of the salient features of the new Amex card. The net effect was an immediate decline in new account bookings of the True Grace card—and its eventual withdrawal from the marketplace a few years later.

As the Amex design team reviewed the market influences that had such a dramatic impact on the initial success and eventual decline in the Optima True Grace card, a sobering assessment surfaced: "There are no points for original thought!" While the creative concept for the new product was compelling, we were not able to innovatively establish a sustainable competitive advantage. (This was before we realized we now live in a world of temporary competitive advantages—as described by Jay Galbraith [2002].) Thus we encountered a real-life case study on the distinction between creativity and innovation. If the challenge of continuously creating new and more innovative customer-value propositions isn't daunting enough, today's leaders need to be equally adept at recognizing and sidestepping organizational barriers to creativity and innovation, especially from skilled "entremanures."

Entremanures

Perhaps this sounds familiar:

> You're attending a meeting where several senior managers are brainstorming ideas for how a critical business challenge might be addressed. As ideas are brought up, one of the newer managers offers a novel approach that she's seen work at another organization. As the idea gets airtime among the senior managers, the energy for the novel approach comes to an abrupt end when one of the old-timers observes:

> "Yes, that's an interesting idea, but I doubt it will fly here because . . . we tried that before . . . we're different . . . it's too risky . . . yadda yadda. . . ."

Brainstorming sessions often wind up with a myriad of "yes-buts"—that is, comments to the effect that "*Yes*, that's an interesting idea, *but* it will not work because . . . " (Michalko 2001, 24). This may be due to a strong culture that influences new ideas based on past successes and past failures. Regardless of the reason, the entrepreneurial nature of brainstorming and ideation has slowly been replaced with the voice of an *entremanure*, that is, "a person who believes you can kill any idea if you pile on enough dung" (Hammett 2005a, 16).

Some of the best entremanures are able to squash an idea with a smile and a pat on the back. Before you realize what happened, the creative idea that woke you up at 4 A.M. is now a pile of rubble on the floor. Still, some subtle signs can clue you in that an entremanure is hard at work.

Entremanures have an uncanny gift for appearing to be actively heading forward, while in fact they're simply running in place. You might find run-in-place entremanures in well-established organizations that have a solid track record of success and perceived market dominance. To a certain degree, they are trapped by the organization's own inertia—a success-fueled momentum that keeps their focus on continuing with tried-and-true activity.

Entremanures in this environment often mistake small incremental changes for innovative advances. You could almost hear them chastise anyone wanting to shake things up with the admonition: "Things are working pretty well as is. Don't foul it up with any crazy ideas!"

Entremanures often have better hindsight than foresight. This regularly plays out in reminiscing back to times when the organization (or they themselves) experienced great success. However, they often have a misguided view of the past, selectively distorting prior events and actual outcomes. They may display this by taking undue credit for the work of others and overstating results while omitting shortfalls, and they're especially active in highly charged political circles.

One key advantage entremanures do bring to the table is their keen focus on resolving problems as quickly as possible. They do this by isolating problems into core components so as to simplify resolution. While this tends to facilitate quick results, it does not always yield the best solutions because those who take this approach fail to look past the easy answers to fully understand causes and possible options. This shortsightedness is also a detriment when positive results occur serendipitously— as an entremanure is delighted with the results (and subsequent credit) but tends to ignore the cause or sustainability.

CALL TO ACTION

Senior executives need to balance the paradox of creativity, innovation, and operational excellence. Most of them appear to be more geared toward innovation (applied creativity) than toward abstract thought. Still it is possible for an organization to delicately balance its creative and innovative energies—as highlighted by Beinhocker in his comments regarding a cultural icon (1997, 36):

[Walt Disney's] theme parks and other businesses are run in a deeply conservative fashion. A strong culture supports Disney's mission of providing family entertainment. In operations, no detail is too small, right down to the personal grooming of the parking-lot attendants. This culture is ingrained in the organization and constantly reinforced through management processes.

At many organizations, such a conservative culture and such tightly controlled operations would snuff out creativity. Yet Disney manages to be one of the most innovative companies in the world. It pioneered animated films and destination theme parks, built EPCOT, linked media and retail with its Disney Stores, and took an early lead in cable television. Disney manages the tension between conservatism and innovation by maintaining an almost cult-like attention to detail and discipline, but at the same time forgiving honest mistakes made in the pursuit of innovation.

To make creativity sustainable, senior executives must emphasize that creativity is important (Shalley and Gilson 2004, 37). However, the type of creativity that emerges in an organization is contingent not only on the leadership but also on the environment (Sternberg 1999, 471)— and environments that exhibit "expert knowledge and information, and the granting of degrees of freedom and autonomy" foster greater creativity (Krause 2004, 100). To this end it is useful to consider the axioms in the discussion that follows.

Creativity Versus Innovation

The point to make is that while creative people are important to have around, for innovation to occur within an organization leaders need to be able to harness their own creativity and that of their teams to practical, beneficial results. To this end, Shalley and Gilson suggest that the "role of leaders is to ensure that the structure of the work environment, the climate and culture and the human resource practices [for example, reward and recognition] are such that creative outcomes can and do occur" (2004, 35). This gives rise to the first axiom of creativity versus innovation:

Axiom #1: *Creativity is influenced by environment.*
Innovation is influenced by leadership.

The Tyranny of Success

In some regards an organization's success can become its own worst enemy. As Tushman and O'Reilly (1997) point out, successful organizations often become entranced by their own press. An indicator of this is the way successful organizations often fail to acknowledge the beautiful preponderance of skills, personal styles, and culture that are so appealing to onlookers. In the end an organization can become ensnared in the inertia that occurs when small companies grow and expand (Sternberg, Kaufman, and Pertz 2004). Tushman and O'Reilly make the same point: "As long as there is no gap between expectations and performance, a successful system will actively attempt to remain stable." Thus an organization at rest (that is, stagnant) will stay at rest until acted upon by the force of creativity, and once set in motion the directional focus of the organization will be influenced by innovative energies. That is, assuming that organizational inertia conforms to physical laws of motion, an organization at rest will stay at rest until acted upon by an equal or greater force—and an organization in motion will likewise stay in motion until acted upon by an equal or greater force. Likewise, an organization in motion (that is, engaged in focused direction) will stay in motion until redirected by creative energies. This analogy yields the second axiom of creativity versus innovation:

> **Axiom #2:** *Creativity sets an organization in motion.*
> *Innovation gives that motion focused direction.*

Trust in Leaders Versus Trust in Organizations

As noted earlier, Kahtamaki and his colleagues (2004) trace the evolution of trust in an organization across its life cycle, from the person of the founder, through individual roles, to the organization itself. The result is that the organization in the last, institutional phase of its life experiences fewer creative solutions and less of the innovative breakthroughs that once came from an environment where people trusted their leaders and affirmed individual confidence in their competency. The strong institutional processes and procedures characterized by clever problem solving lead to the third axiom of creativity versus innovation:

Axiom #3: *Trust embodied in a leader influences innovative breakthroughs. Trust embodied in the organization will at best foster clever problem solving.*

Reward and Recognition

If creativity and innovation are critical resources for organizational success, the natural question emerges: How do we make creativity and innovation happen? Research addressing this question (summarized earlier in the chapter) has found no simple answer, as job structure has a strong influence on creativity.

This might help explain why reward structures that attempt to influence creativity are hit-or-miss at best. Perhaps this is because creativity is closely tied to passion—an individual's heart and spirit. This may also explain why the most compelling creative outcomes are inspired. It would be interesting to critique creative outcomes done as works for hire as opposed to outcomes generated from inspiration.

In contrast, innovative thinking may be more influenced by extrinsic motivators. Anecdotal evidence of this is plentiful: when organizations provide incentives for quality improvement ideas, they get lots of ideas. From considering the distinction between generating creativity and generating innovation, the fourth axiom emerges:

Axiom #4: *The best creative outcomes are those that are inspired. The best innovative thinking can be facilitated with compelling incentives.*

If creativity is about generating ideas and innovation is about producing results, organizations need equal focus on both processes. To this end organizations and senior executives may find the following suggestions helpful in positively influencing and fostering creativity and innovation:

- Identify and address distractions that inhibit creativity and innovation. This includes providing a safe environment for people to speak up and air frustrations. This also places a premium on regular, clear, and concise communications regarding critical business decisions and their impact.

- Build compelling HR systems and processes for recognizing and rewarding creativity and innovation. Understandably, not every creative idea can be implemented. However, visibly acknowledging creative efforts will in turn foster more of them.

- Use the deep relationships and touch points with key clients and customers as a source of inspiration and insight as to current and future market demands.

- Executives should consider:

  - Spending time reflecting and processing information internally to avoid simply accepting the opinions of respected experts

  - Being guarded as to how to word questions to avoid giving the impression of being critical or nonsupportive

  - Making thoughts visible and verbal; physically drawing out ideas and speaking them out loud (Levesque 2001, 123–127)

As demonstrated in this chapter, executives appear to be more hard-wired toward innovative energies—fostering the creative thinking within their employees and using these outcomes to set new paths for their organizations. The four key axioms discussed in this section appear in Table 5.5 as a review to help senior executives in their innovative endeavors. The axioms highlight how at times creativity and innovation combine as a force multiplier to enable sustainable success (Hammett 2005c).

AXIOM	CALL TO ACTION
Axiom #1 Creativity is influenced by environment. Innovation is influenced by leadership.	Do whatever you can to foster an environment that produces as much creative energy as possible. Harness the organization's creative energies through effective leadership of innovative applications of those creative energies.
Axiom #2 Creativity sets an organization in motion. Innovation gives that motion focused direction.	Organizations need to balance standardization and customization: • Standardize to capture cost savings • Innovate to capture market share
Axiom #3 Trust embodied in a leader influences innovative breakthroughs. Trust embodied in the organization will at best foster clever problem solving.	Be careful not to mistake problem solving for breakthroughs—realistically assessing the outcomes of your creative and innovative energies may help determine if employees are in it for the organization or its leaders!
Axiom #4 The best creative outcomes are those that are inspired. The best innovative thinking can be facilitated with compelling incentives.	Inspire ideas—reward results!

Table 5.5 • Axioms for Creativity and Innovation

PERSONAL REFLECTION: SEE THE CUSTOMER, BE THE CUSTOMER

Although I've already recommended drawing on customers for creative and innovative inspiration, it's worth emphasizing. From my vantage point there can be no better source than customers for creativity and innovation, and the most effective methods to integrate customer input into your creative processes center around analyzing how your customers engage your organization and observing customers as they use your products and services.

See the Customer . . .

The first place to gain insight about your customers is in your service quality metrics. How your customers choose to engage your organization can serve as a great source of inspiration for new value propositions. If your service quality metrics highlight usage patterns for specific times or events, analyzing these patterns might generate new concepts. For example, a restaurant analyzing take-out and dine-in orders might uncover a potential home delivery concept.

Be the Customer . . .

Another source of inspiration may come from observing customers in action, and also from actually becoming a customer yourself. Observing how customers use products can uncover a multitude of alternative uses and concepts: aspirin as a preventative for heart failure; Ensure as a dietary supplement regardless of age; Cheerios as a snack for toddlers. Additionally, becoming a customer can open remarkable insights like those discovered when Amex provided cards to its employees. Not only did Amex's account base increase dramatically, it instantly gained invaluable consumer insight.

6

Gifted Leadership's Paradox of Developing Future Leaders

Here's a trivia question: Can you name a superstar Hall of Fame athlete that went on to be the head coach of a winning team? Give up? So do I. I'll confess that I'm not a sports historian and I may not have all the facts, but the point I want to make is this: We remember the great athletes for their accomplishments on the field of play and we remember the great coaches for the championships they won—but we rarely place both in the same category. We can name any number of outstanding players who retired from competing and took a job coaching. Likewise, many Hall of Fame coaches at one time played the game. But few really outstanding athletes went on to become really outstanding coaches.

Now I'm certain this point of view will get the most critique and feedback of anything in this book. In fact, among my peers and coworkers this question has raised significant debate. Considering the Hall of Fame coaches who once played the game, the question is, Would they have gotten to the Hall of Fame on their athletics alone?

So do great athletes make great coaches? The short answer is no, according to *Boston Globe* sports columnist Bob Ryan. In an August 2005 NPR interview on how well Wayne Gretzky might do in taking over as head coach of the Phoenix Coyotes, Ryan elaborates: "If you were a betting man, you would bet against him [Gretzky] being a success. The evidence is overwhelming to suggest that, as a general rule superstars, no matter what the sport, do not make good coaches" (quoted in Norris 2005).

But how does this play out in business? Do great senior executives make great coaches? Recall the three components that define effective executive leadership:

- Achieving desired results

- Ensuring long-term sustainability

- Enhancing the well-being of the workforce

From the data and research reviewed thus far, it's clear that "achieving results" is a strong competency of senior executives. Likewise, effective leadership is about allowing, encouraging, and supporting the well-being of the workforce. Those leaders who are attentive to their followers' needs for emotional and spiritual expression release their teams to incorporate all of themselves in their work, producing a synergy that fulfills the individuals and benefits the organization.

Still there is a missing component: the long-term sustainability of the organization. Truly great coaches are measured not by a particular game they won or by a single successful season but by the longevity of their success over multiple winning seasons. While the success formula of a winning coach has many facets, one is the way coaches are always focused on team building. They build teams in the traditional sense of getting the most from the players they currently have—but they focus equally on identifying, selecting, and developing up-and-coming players.

So does a *great* senior executive make a *great* coach? Let me phrase this question another way: How successful are great senior executives in identifying and developing future leaders? This question becomes particularly relevant as we consider the impact that baby boomer retirement and the creation of new jobs will have on the workforce in the next decade. Virtually all industrialized nations are experiencing shrinkage in working-age populations. Where will future leaders come from in a reduced workforce?

VIEWS ON DEVELOPING LEADERS

A number of associations and think tanks have conducted in-depth studies that provide insight into the way current leaders are meeting the challenge of developing the next generation of leaders. A select review of this research follows.

The Handwriting on the Wall

Presenting on the state of leadership development at the 2005 American Society for Training and Development conference, Sylvester Taylor, director of assessment development at CCL, observed that the corporate world is experiencing a "leadership gap"—leadership ranks are stretched too thin, intense recruiting wars for talent are under way, and too little thought is given to formal development systems (S. Taylor 2005, 2). Some organizations have recognized the need to develop a pipeline of capable leaders with the skills, experience, and competencies necessary to step up and lead the organization into the future, but far too many companies have not seen the handwriting on the wall. Consider the following comments (Tucker, Kao, and Verma 2005, 1):

- A recent Conference Board survey reported that senior executives gave *talent identification and growth, engaging employees in the company's vision, values, and goals,* and *leveraging diversity* surprisingly low rankings—sixth, eighth, and seventeenth, respectively—in their lists of top management concerns for the year 2008.

- A Society for Human Resource Management survey revealed that less than one-third of employers are adjusting their talent management policies and practices to the aging of their workforces, and 60 percent of organizations don't account for workforce aging in their long-term business plans.

- Recent surveys also indicate that most HR leaders are spending less than 25 percent of their time preparing for the workforce of the future, and that few organizations believe that HR has the skills required to manage a diverse and global workforce.

These findings are truly remarkable in light of warnings and admonitions regarding the impending talent gap. According to Peter Engstrom, vice president of corporate knowledge with SAIC, in 2006 baby boomers will begin to retire at a rate of one every seven seconds (2005). He adds that this retirement rate will continue for the next fifteen years! Meanwhile, IBM's 2005 Global Human Capital Study suggests that within the next five years 19 percent of the American executive and managerial workforce will retire (Rogers 2005, 3). And Weiss and Molinaro write, "Executive leaders are beginning to recognize the leadership gap problem and as a result are worried about motivating leaders and engaging them to participate actively in making changes" (2005, 11–12).

We are fast approaching (and in some cases are already in) "an era in which demand for leadership greatly exceeds the supply." Successful organizations will be those who develop "an approach that will allow [them] to keep their own leadership pipeline full and flowing" (Charan, Drotter, and Noel 2001, 1).

At CCL we are seeing evidence that the impending talent gap is sparking a renewed interest in succession planning and talent management, but we also see a common misperception as to exactly what people mean when they say "succession planning" and where organizations should start in building a compelling talent management process. Specifically, the goal of succession planning is not only to align an organization's available talent to meet the current needs of the organization but to ensure effective development of talent for the organization's future needs by "having the right people in the right places at the right times to do the right things" (Rothwell 2001, 6–7).

Some organizations confuse their existing talent management planning with formal succession planning—when in fact what they have is little more than an elegant replacement strategy. The distinction is that a replacement strategy focuses on finding talent to replace existing leadership positions, whereas real succession planning involves ensuring that the pipeline of leaders has the capacity to tackle tomorrow's issues. Rothwell compares replacement planning to risk management (continuity planning to ensure some level of leadership will be in place), while succession planning involves proactively developing leader capabilities from within the organization (2001, 7). In other words replacement planning is ensuring an organization maintains the same level and caliber of leaders currently in place without considering that the leadership skills needed for the future may be different. Succession planning on the other hand focuses on the long-term sustainability of the organization by "perpetuating the enterprise by filling the pipeline with high-performance people to assure that every leadership level has an abundance of these performers to draw from, both now and in the future" (Charan, Drotter, and Noel 2001, 167).

So how weak is the bench strength of talent, and how do senior executives go about beefing up their leadership pipelines? Several studies coming out of CCL help shed light on these questions.

The Present State of Leadership Development: A Changing World

A keynote of CCL's "State of Leadership Development" study was identifying what leadership skills and perspectives are critical for success and how strong the organizational bench is in these critical skills and perspectives. Figure 6.1 provides an overview of the study's findings, reflecting that those skills identified as critical for the success of an organization (resourcefulness, results, decisiveness, building relationships, and so on) are in short supply (weak bench strength).

Figure 6.1 clearly shows that while organizations have a solid bench of leaders with competencies such as respecting differences and being quick learners, these particular competencies, while helpful, were not identified as critical for the long-term success of the organization. Competencies such as building relationships, leading employees, and decisiveness were identified as critical to the long-term success of the organization but also noted as having a weak presence on the leadership bench.

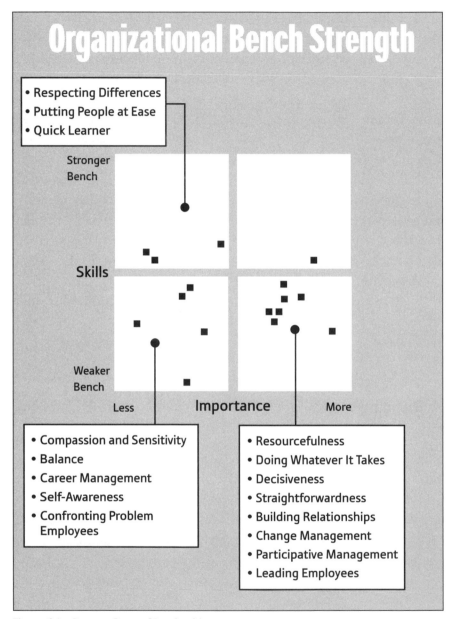

Figure 6.1 • Present State of Leadership

Additionally, in the summer of 2005 CCL produced results from a study conducted to understand future trends in leadership. Key findings from this study help bring to light the changing world that the next generation of leaders will face. Specifically, CCL's report highlights that leadership challenges are becoming more complex in "requiring new processes and perspectives found outside current knowledge and resources . . . [and] resulting from an unexpected event requiring an immediate and often drastic organizational response" (Martin 2005, 6). Likewise, these challenges are becoming more drawn out, requiring many months or even years to fully resolve. Addressing these challenges will require more collaboration and interdependence, as Figure 6.2 shows, than we have traditionally seen in many organizations. They include working across functions, increasing speed of response, making more effective decisions, and enhancing coworker relationships (Martin 2005, 9).

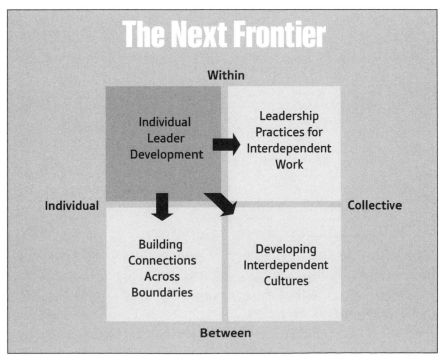

Figure 6.2 • Building Organizational Capacity for Leadership in the Face of Complex Challenge

These CCL studies point to two critical observations: leadership competencies needed to drive the organization into the future are in short supply, and the next generation of leaders will need to master a new set of competencies to be successful in an ever more complex world.

Aligning Leadership Development with Business Strategy

As I mentioned earlier, while some organizations understand the importance of developing a pipeline of capable future leaders, many are lagging in this respect. It's clear that succession planning is important, but what is less clear is where to start in building a compelling succession planning process. A critical outcome of the succession planning process is an articulation of key business challenges (current and future) and the leadership competencies needed to address these challenges. Using research from Martineau and Hannum (2004), defining a leadership development framework for succession planning begins by focusing on the following objectives:

- Clarifying organizational goals and objectives for succession planning

- Identifying the target audience for development

- Determining desired impact (what outcomes are sought) and time frames

- Understanding success criteria (how the organization will know its efforts are working)

Clearly a critical first step in developing a succession planning process is to identify the key business challenges the organization presently faces as well as those challenges it may face in the future (Charan, Drotter, and Noel 2001, 172; Weiss and Molinaro 2005, 100; Rothwell 2001, 53). CCL's research and practice on developing strategic leaders help us visualize how the understanding of business needs influences a leadership strategy. Hughes and Beatty bring this alignment into focus by defining *business strategy* as "the pattern of choices an organization makes to achieve sustainable competitive advantage" and *leadership strategy* as "the organizational and human capabilities needed to enact the business strategy effectively" (2005, 28).

As a starting point in developing a succession planning and talent management strategy, identify the three or four critical business needs your organization is currently facing. Then determine whether these are the issues you're most likely to face in the future by taking the following steps:

1. Understand where you are today and assess the implications of present actions and decisions.

2. Outline possible future events, including favorable, unfavorable, and status quo scenarios.

3. Establish markers within your plans to help indicate which scenario (favorable, unfavorable, or status quo) might be unfolding.

Central to the succession planning process is bridging the gap between current and future business challenges and needed leadership competencies. To assist in identifying these leadership needs, CCL has developed its Model of Leader Competencies, shown in Figure 6.3, which draws on more than thirty years of research and experience in the practice of leadership development (McCauley 2006, 13). The Model of Leader Competencies reflects characteristics associated with the job and with the person (knowledge, skill, self-concept, attitudes, values, and motivation), and explains the core competencies that an organization or individual would assess and develop by focusing on three dimensions: leading the organization, leading oneself, and leading others.

The following questions help frame which leadership competencies are critical in light of an organization's strategic vision and foresight:

- What leadership competencies are needed to enable your key business drivers?

- What shifts need to occur to facilitate meeting today's and tomorrow's business challenges?

- What do we need more of or less of?

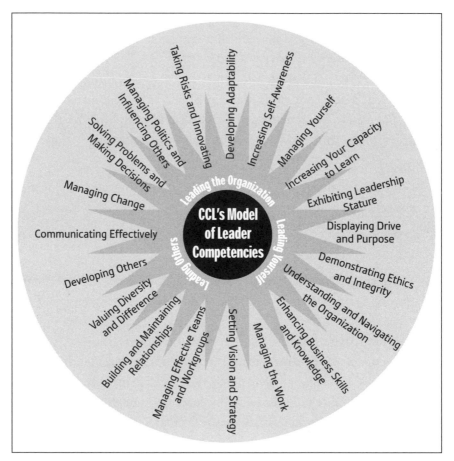

Figure 6.3 • CCL® Model of Leader Competencies

With an understanding of the organization's current and future business challenges and a framework of needed leadership competencies to address these challenges, the organization is better prepared to craft a compelling succession planning and talent management program. So succession planning focuses on deliberately selecting, acquiring, and developing leader capabilities that will enable the organization to achieve its mission both now and in the future.

HOW SENIOR EXECUTIVES DEVELOP LEADERS

One of the key challenges HR and OD professionals face is getting buy-in from senior executives for a talent management and succession planning initiative. Even when presented with the most recent trend reports for shortages in labor, some executives are not motivated to action. Developing awareness for how senior executives think about and approach developing talent is critical, and is often overlooked or misunderstood by HR and OD professionals. This understanding will prove insightful for HR and OD professionals who are seeking to establish sustainable talent management initiatives throughout their organization.

Selective Need to Relate Interpersonally

As reported in Chapter 1, senior executives have a low need for interpersonal contact, which plays out in being choosy about how, when, and where they associate with others. Senior executives are also very cautious about how they use or share authority and in the end will avoid becoming too close with others in their workplace. Senior executives may likewise believe that the manner in which they want others to treat them is how they should treat others (Waterman and Rogers 2004, 1). The end result is that close personal relationships (particularly within the work context) can become frustrating and senior executives perceive these relationships as potentially interfering with their jobs. Thus senior executives work better in small groups with regular contacts, or perhaps even alone, and despite the extent to which their work performance depends on input from others, they do not overly rely on others.

This arm's-length approach to interpersonal relationships in the workplace presents a twofold challenge for senior executives who desire to build their organization's bench strength. First, both the isolation of their position and their personal predisposition prevent senior executives from identifying up-and-coming leaders by firsthand observation. The result may be that senior executives rely on input from a narrow sphere of influence as to who the organization's high-potential employees—its "hipos"—are. Second, because their perspective on the world is both successful and narrow, senior executives may be drawn to finding and grooming hipos who are mirror images of themselves.

Developing, Empowering, and Leveraging Differences

The *Executive Dimensions* assessment includes a scale called Developing and Empowering that can shed light on the way senior executives deal with managing their organization's leadership pipeline. Table 6.1 highlights the questions asked in *Executive Dimensions* for this scale. For the most part senior executives received quite good scores—averaging in the 3.5s on the five-point scale.

However, in two areas direct reports indicate a lower perception of competency for executives: "Acts as a mentor, helping others to develop and advance in their careers" and "Develops staff through constructive feedback and encouragement." Lower scores on these questions may suggest that direct reports do not feel as though senior executives are focused on helping others advance their careers or that providing feedback and encouragement is a particular strength for senior executives.

In the review of values and ethics, I made the point that it is critical for senior executives to manage the perception of organizational politics so that their efforts are not seen as attempts to buy favors or influence. It is equally important for senior executives to be mindful of how their actions are perceived—that their motives neither are nor appear to be selfish and self-serving. This is especially important in view of the strong predisposition toward achieving results that C-level executives have. This may be perceived by subordinates as an attempt to advance an executive's own career at the expense of others. Similarly, the review of creativity and innovation raised the related point that an executive's focus on results may come across as too pragmatic and insensitive, which may show up as an inability (or unwillingness) to provide helpful, encouraging feedback.

DEVELOPING AND EMPOWERING	EXECUTIVES	BOSSES	DIRECT REPORTS
Delegates work that provides substantial responsibility and visibility	3.49	3.54	3.54
Acts as a mentor, helping others to develop and advance in their careers	3.51	3.62	3.27
Supports the decisions and actions of subordinates	3.66	3.69	3.55
Utilizes others' capabilities appropriately	3.48	3.43	3.35
Develops staff through constructive feedback and encouragement	3.33	3.39	3.10
Encourages individual initiative in determining how to achieve broad goals	3.56	3.56	3.56
Average	3.51	3.54	3.40

Table 6.1 • *Executive Dimensions* Developing and Empowering Scale

Leadership Characteristic of Empowering

The *Campbell Leadership Index* (CLI) poses three questions to draw out an understanding of a leader's competence in building staff:

- **Empowering.** Enables others to achieve more than they thought possible.

- **Encouraging.** Motivates through encouragement and emotional support.

- **Supportive.** Helps others be successful and confident.

As Figure 6.4 shows, the standard score of the Empowering scale is within the mid-range of the CLI, and while not a specific developmental issue, compared to scores on other leadership characteristics no one would suggest that Empowerment is a particular strength of these exec-

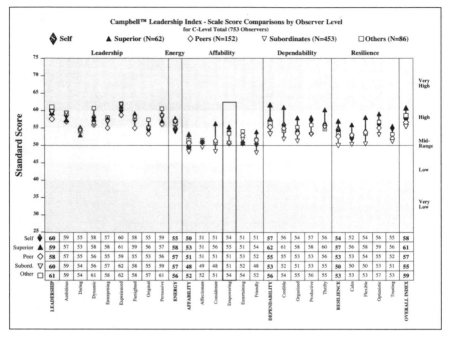

	LEADERSHIP	Ambitious	Daring	Dynamic	Enterprising	Experienced	Farsighted	Original	Persuasive	ENERGY	AFFABILITY	Affectionate	Considerate	Empowering	Entertaining	Friendly	DEPENDABILITY	Credible	Organized	Productive	Thrifty	RESILIENCE	Calm	Flexible	Optimistic	Trusting	OVERALL INDEX
Self ◆	60	59	55	58	57	60	58	55	59	55	50	51	51	54	51	51	57	56	54	57	56	54	52	54	56	55	58
Superior ▲	59	57	53	58	58	61	59	56	57	58	53	51	56	55	51	54	62	61	58	58	60	57	56	58	59	56	61
Peer ◇	58	57	55	56	55	59	55	53	56	57	51	51	51	51	53	52	55	55	53	53	56	53	53	54	55	52	57
Subord. ▽	60	59	54	56	57	62	58	55	59	57	48	49	48	51	52	48	53	52	51	53	55	50	50	50	53	51	55
Other □	61	59	54	61	58	62	58	57	61	56	52	52	51	54	54	52	56	54	55	56	55	53	53	53	57	53	59

Figure 6.4 • *Campbell™ Leadership Index* Empowering Scale

utives. Higher scores in Empowering would suggest that senior executives are seen as helping others "achieve higher levels of performance than they thought possible . . . [allowing] subordinates and colleagues to take risks and [supporting] them in new endeavors." Most notable, higher scores in Empowering reflect a perception that senior executives are very open to sharing both power and accountability with their peers and direct reports. Lower scores, on the other hand, suggest a perception that senior executives are "concerned with their own advancement [and] may be too narrowly focused on the tasks at hand to consider how to motivate and involve others" (Nilsen and Campbell 1998, 17).

The item-level questions within the Empowering scale, shown in Figure 6.5, indicate a perception gap among the observers for each question. Most notable is the difference in ratings between superiors and peers on the questions on enabling others to achieve and helping others be successful. It seems possible that since subordinate ratings on these questions are in line with the ratings for all observers, peers either don't

Empowering Scale

33. Empowering - Enables others to achieve more than they thought possible.							34. Encouraging - Motivates others through encouragement and emotional support.							91. Supportive - Helps others be successful and confident.							
	Nev	Sel	Occ	Som	Usu	Alw	%Fav	Nev	Sel	Occ	Som	Usu	Alw	%Fav	Nev	Sel	Occ	Som	Usu	Alw	%Fav
You		1	2	16	44	11				1	16	44	13					10	52	12	
All Obs	8	30	63	213	322	116	58	3	46	72	187	314	131	59	23	53	150	380	144	70
Superior		1	2	20	33	6	63		1	3	12	37	9	74		1	12	33	16	79
Peer	1	6	13	55	59	17	50		8	16	36	75	17	61	3	10	40	73	25	65
Subord	7	19	43	120	189	75	58	3	33	46	123	168	80	55	17	32	86	233	83	70
Other		4	5	18	41	18	69		4	7	16	34	25	69	3	10	12	41	20	71

Figure 6.5 • *Campbell™ Leadership Index* Empowering Scale Questions

Note: "Percent Favorable" reflects answers that indicate approval. For positive statements favorable responses would be "Always" or "Usually" and for negative statements favorable responses would be "Never" or "Seldom."

witness senior executives' enabling and helping others or peers do not experience the senior executives as particularly helpful or enabling for themselves (the peers). This isn't too difficult to imagine in view of the competitive or self-sufficient environment typical in senior ranks.

Promotions and Organizational Effectiveness

The *Campbell Organizational Survey* (COS) also measures perceptions of an organization's effectiveness in advancement opportunities (promotions are seen as fair—based on results rather than favoritism or politics). As shown in Figure 6.6, standard scores on the COS for promotions were in the high range (57) for senior executives and the mid-range (52) for observers. High scores in the Promotions scale are "found among individuals who feel that their current job and their current supervisors are helping them develop personally so they will have more options in the future." Low scores "can indicate that workers feel trapped in their current situation by organizational politics, by a lack of support from their supervisor or by external forces such as tradition or rapidly changing technology" (Campbell and Hyne 1995, 16).

Reviewing the item-level questions on the Promotions scale, presented in Figure 6.7, shows significant perception gaps between senior executives and observers on every question. I see two interesting observations to draw from this insight. First, it is obvious that senior executives have a much higher appreciation of how the organization develops, nurtures, and grows its talent pool. This perspective may stem from the

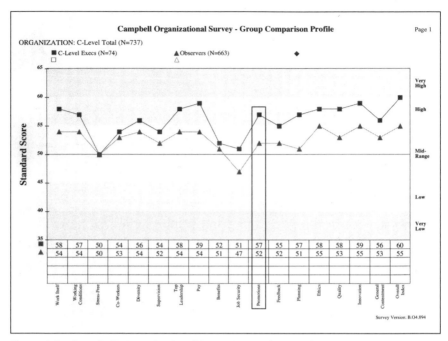

Figure 6.6 • *Campbell™ Organizational Survey* Promotions Scale

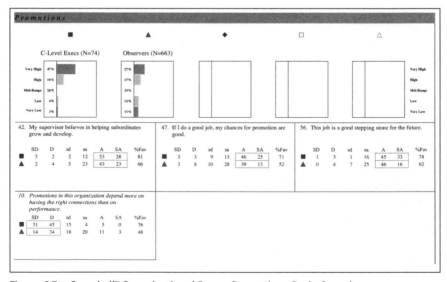

Figure 6.7 • *Campbell™ Organizational Survey* Promotions Scale Questions

senior executives' own personal success in climbing the organizational ladder—or from an overassessment of the organization's receptiveness to existing talent management systems. However, the second observation evoked by this data is more revealing. Keeping in mind that the scores on the COS are standardized against the larger population as a whole, two facts are glaring: observer scores of 52 are within the mid-range for all observers, and the observers perceive the organization as significantly less effective in developing talent than the senior executives do.

Summary of Data

Senior executives have a tendency to manage relationships at work with an arm's-length approach; that is, they do not get too close or too personal with their coworkers. This can at times constrict senior executives' sphere of influence and limit the quality of insight they receive. This isolation can also inhibit senior executives' ability to identify individuals who might be in the up-and-coming next generation of leaders. Likewise, senior executives' predisposition to get the job done may come across as too pragmatic and insensitive to the needs and aspirations of others. This may lead to a perception that senior executives are more concerned with advancing their own careers than with helping others move up the ladder. Also, the end result may be that senior executives are drawn toward finding and grooming mirror images of themselves—or, what's worse, may succumb to organizational politics and favoritism when it comes to promotions and advancements.

The assessment data on empowering and promoting reveal significant perception gaps between senior executives and their superiors, peers, and subordinates. Within the peer group, one possible cause for this gap may be that peers rarely see senior executives helping advance others' careers. Peers might also see the senior executives as a competitive threat for limited higher-level positions. That view would be unlikely to lead to a great deal of helpfulness in career advancement between senior executives and their peers. Finally, from an organizational perspective, observers have a significantly less favorable perception than that of senior executives with regard to developing and nurturing talent.

OBSERVATIONS ON EXECUTIVE DEVELOPMENT OF LEADERS

A recent wave of books, articles, and publications has addressed the topic of succession planning and talent management. I've been caught up in this wave myself, chairing the 2005 International Quality and Productivity Center conference, which was titled "Talent Management and Succession Planning." From this wealth of material, three observations come to mind that may be helpful to senior executives as they consider how to develop the next generation of leaders: consider becoming a player/coach, engage fourth-generation leadership development, and guard against "Mini-Me-ism."

What About Player/Coaches?

Do great athletes make great coaches? Returning to the question, sports columnist Bob Ryan points up an interesting phenomenon: the *player/coach*. For example, consider Rogers Hornsby, who won the 1926 World Series as a Cardinals player/manager, and Mickey Cochran, who won the World Series in 1935 as a Tigers player/manager. Perhaps most notable was Bill Russell, who played with and coached the Celtics to two championships.

Senior executives have the unique opportunity to be in the game and at the same time actively seek out and develop the next generation of leaders. In essence, senior executives are player/coaches. As senior executives look to build an organization that has a long-term sustainable business model, they also need to look to build the talent pool of leaders who have the skills to continue running the organization.

It is interesting how many senior executives have little or no direct involvement in identifying, developing, and nurturing their organization's next generation of leaders. In trying to understand why senior executives were so far removed from the succession planning process, one senior HR executive explained it to me this way: "For our senior executives, succession planning is worse than planning your own funeral.

You're also planning who's going to take your place in the family photo when you're gone."

If you're a leader relatively low in the ranks of an organization, succession planning can be a great tool for your own forward progress. Knowing that you have viable candidates who can step into your current shoes frees you to pursue higher-level positions. But after a while the headroom grows limited, and it's not so comforting to look back at a stable of energetic, capable leaders waiting in line for your job. Adopting a player/coach model may help senior executives maintain their player status while at the same time actively developing the talent pool of leaders who will be able to take the organization into the future.

Fourth-Generation Leader Development

I had the privilege of attending a session at the Mercedes training facility in New Jersey as CCL Senior Faculty Roger Conway shared his thoughts on talent management and succession planning. I was drawn to a phrase Dr. Conway used—"fourth-generation selection for development." According to him, in first-generation development, we typically saw someone in Purchasing advising leaders on what type of leadership development they were entitled to based on their level. So senior leaders were entitled to more elaborate development than those lower in the ranks, all of which was marshaled by a purchasing agent. In second-generation development we saw HR becoming more involved, bringing structure to the same selection process with pretty much the same results—senior leaders received more development than those in lower ranks.

In third-generation development (what we have today) we often see a qualitative (or worse, arbitrary) selection process that centers on identifying and developing hipos. But how do you define high potential? Rothwell defines hipos as "individuals who are capable of advancing two or more levels beyond their present placement, individuals who are slated for key positions or those who have not reached a career plateau" (2001, 203). This definition permits a distinction between an individual who is a high performer and one who is a high potential. While every hipo should be a high performer, the converse is not necessarily the case: not every high performer will be a hipo. CCL, on the other hand, considers hipos to be individuals who are able to learn from experience, and this learning can occur in various ways. Regardless of which definition you choose, organizations tend to take a common approach concerning hipos—"don't ask, don't tell." In many organizations the identification and selection of a high-potential candidate pool is a closely guarded secret. Few people outside HR and certain senior executives are privy to who has been identified as a hipo. Oftentimes, the hipos themselves are not fully aware that they are on the "A" list. The most common explanation given for the secrecy is that no one wants to have to explain to people why they aren't on the "A" list.

This is one of the issues that drew my attention to the idea of fourth-generation development. In fourth-generation development, employees are encouraged to engage in a level of self-directed leadership development; in essence, taking the responsibility of managing their own development and career planning. Then, based on this individual activity, the organization's HR and senior executives are able to identify those up-and-coming leaders who have the initiative, drive, and commitment desired and provide them with ongoing leadership development opportunities.

Informal Succession Plans and the Pitfalls of Mini-Me-ism

In *Effective Succession Planning*, Rothwell suggests that without a formal succession plan in place two key factors will play out in the hiring and promotion processes: favoritism and politics. "Instead of promoting employees with the most potential or best track record, top managers— or, indeed any level of management employee—may use the corporate ladder to promote friends and allies while punishing enemies, regardless of talent or qualifications" (2001, 69).

A possible checkpoint for determining how seriously your organization's succession planning is influenced by favoritism and politics may be to critique how closely newly appointed employees mirror the character of their hiring manager. Here again, Rothwell warns, "When SP&M [succession planning and management] is left informal and thus unplanned, job incumbents tend to identify and groom successors who are remarkably like themselves in appearance, background and values" (2001, 69). CCL's work on diversity and particularly the 1995 Glass Ceiling survey echoes this point, suggesting one of the most critical barriers to creating a diverse workforce is that traditional managers typically feel more comfortable with their own kind.

Let me share a lighthearted case study to illustrate this point: the succession planning of Dr. Evil, Austin Powers's movie nemesis. Dr. Evil's succession plan was elegant yet simple—find someone similar to himself in behavior and character—Mini-Me. Mini-Me looked, dressed, and even had mannerisms like Dr. Evil, down to the same pinky-to-the-corner-of-the-mouth gesture. Clearly Dr. Evil was fond of Mini-Me, and why not? Mini-Me was Dr. Evil's exact copy (except a bit smaller).

So how many Mini-Mes has your organization recently hired or promoted? Take a critical look at your organization's most recent additions. Do they have the same background and education? Are they from the same industry, market, or even geography? If so, this might be an indication that your informal succession plans are giving way to mirror copies of incumbent leaders.

Two dangers are inherent in informal succession planning. First, it's possible that the informal process, while outwardly producing talent that reflects that of incumbent leaders, is in fact masking a critical inability of new leaders to step up and assume leadership. Second, an informal succession plan may be little more than an elegant replacement strategy; building capacity for today's challenges but deficient to tackle tomorrow's issues.

For example, while Mini-Me was a reflection of Dr. Evil, in many ways he didn't quite measure up (no pun intended). In this way Dr. Evil had a copy of himself without having to worry that the copy would someday aspire to take Dr. Evil's job before he was ready to move on. It's not uncommon in situations where incumbent leaders lack self-assurance that the selection of a successor often reflects people who are similar—but no immediate threat. Conger and Nadler highlight this point when they summarize work done by de Vries, Miller, and Maccoby suggesting that leaders who have strong egos and are inextricably linked to their work "seldom mentor others and prefer protégés of lesser capabilities who may not have the skill required to lead the company" (2004, 52). So while Mini-Mes look like their bosses, it is highly possible that they lack the skills and competencies to step up and lead.

Likewise, informal succession plans may focus on simply finding talent to refill existing leadership positions. Confusing replacement planning with succession planning may endanger an organization's ability to seed its next generation of leaders. Returning to Rothwell's characterization of replacement planning as akin to risk management—I would extend Rothwell's assertion by suggesting that replacement planning ensures that an organization maintains the same level and caliber of leaders currently in place, while succession planning ensures development and nurturing of leadership skills needed for the future. Charan, Drotter, and Noel emphasize this point in *The Leadership Pipeline* (2001, 167), defining the goal of succession planning as "perpetuating the enterprise by filling the pipeline with high-performance people to assure that every leadership level has an abundance of these performers to draw from, both now and in the future."

CALL TO ACTION

Despite not having effective talent management and succession plans in place, nearly 90 percent of executives surveyed from around the world rated leadership as the most important factor in global growth. The result is that even some of the "best employers are struggling to build their leadership pipeline, with 50 percent of companies reporting a significant shortage of available leaders" (Gandossy and Kao 2004, 12). It may be that the comments offered in *Chief Learning Officer* are already playing out: "The lack of an up-to-date view of employee skills means that when the baby boom generation retires, many companies will find out when it is too late that a career's worth of experience and talent has walked out the door, leaving insufficient talent available to fill the void" (CLO Media 2005).

The call to action for senior executives is not simply to do an honest assessment of their organization's succession planning and management processes but to take personal ownership for the effectiveness of the team-building initiatives. To reflect openly and honestly on how talent is recruited and promoted helps determine if the leadership pipeline will not just win the day but win the future as well. Most important, senior executives need to reflect on how their succession plans influence their employees. As Weiss and Molinaro comment, the diversity of an organization's workforce will and should evolve—as new talent is developed to meet the ever-changing demands of the marketplace and reflect the ever-changing demographics of customers. While this change can be difficult, the richness of culture and values from this diversity will infuse and propel the organization forward—ensuring leadership capacity for today and tomorrow.

CCL has developed the *Leadership Development Impact Assessment,* which provides a disciplined approach for ensuring organizational investments in leadership development address critical business needs. Drawing from the CCL framework, Table 6.2 provides succinct steps for an organization to develop its succession planning and talent management processes.

PERSONAL REFLECTION: THE HIDDEN CHALLENGE OF MOTIVATION

A story often misattributed to Mark Twain tells of a young man who left home convinced that his father knew nothing, only to return a few years later amazed at what the old man had learned in such a short time. I think of this young man regularly these days as I try to help my children prepare and embrace their first jobs while at the same time I continue to learn from my own father. It seems that whenever I offer advice to my kids I can't help hearing my dad's voice coming out of my mouth while

PROCESS STEP	DESCRIPTION
1. Identify business challenges.	Define those leadership competencies needed to meet current and future business challenges. Questions that may draw out this understanding: • What is your organization's vision of success? • What are its performance targets? • What must you do to achieve this vision of success?
2. Identify and prioritize leadership needs.	Outline what leadership resources are needed to meet mission challenges. Consider leadership needs requiring development of personal attributes of leaders by addressing the following questions: • How are your leaders' behaviors preventing the organization from meeting this business need? • How will leadership development help the organization address critical business objectives? • What internal systems changes may be needed to support this leadership initiative?
3. Align leadership competencies with business objectives.	Align leadership needs with the competencies effective leaders demonstrate when meeting those needs. A helpful tool is CCL's research-based database of leader and leadership competencies. (These competencies provide outcomes or targets for all subsequent leadership development.)
4. Determine target audience and level of mastery per leader competency.	Determine the level of mastery per leader competency that will be obtained through the leadership development initiatives. Will leaders master basic knowledge of leadership concepts and a critical awareness of their leader strengths and needs? Or will development be extended to provide opportunities to demonstrate mastery in the workplace, enabling leaders to truly retool their leadership style for new and different workplace challenges?

Table 6.2 • Leadership Development Road Map

PROCESS STEP	DESCRIPTION
5. Conceptualize the delivery framework.	Outline the framework needed to meet the target outcomes. What learning events are needed to assist participants in gaining mastery of the target leadership competencies at the specified level of mastery? How should they be sequenced and delivered?
6. Prepare evaluation metrics.	Put together a broad conceptualization of what it would take for stakeholders to declare the leadership development initiatives a success. Questions to consider: • What types of evidence will major stakeholders accept as proof of impact? • What type of evaluation will major stakeholders find powerful?

at the same time hearing my own distant words coming back to me from my kids. In a surreal sense I have the advantage as well as the challenge of experiencing three generations—with me right in the middle. These are the same challenges today's executives face as they lead and motivate the next generation of leaders.

But we have a hidden challenge to face in addressing the pending leadership gap. In addition to the numbers gap—that is, not enough workers to fill open positions—we will also face a challenge in motivating the next generation to take up the mantle of leadership. I have been amazed at the stories I hear throughout the United States and abroad of a younger workforce that is less and less interested in moving into leadership positions. We might not be surprised at this reluctance. The younger generation has watched their parents work more and more hours, spend less and less time at home, and in many cases see their efforts rewarded with layoffs, downsizing, and health and marital problems. So why would anyone expect younger workers to willingly jump into leadership positions?

In fact, in some industries the younger workforce is interested only in earning enough to support their immediate interests. The owner of a real estate agency in the Northwest told me that he has a number of agents who work only as long as necessary to earn enough commissions to support them through the skiing season and then they're off to the mountains. They return to work only when their money runs out or the snow melts. When I asked the owner why he didn't just hire other agents who would be more committed to the job, he replied that he couldn't find them. He's seeing the same phenomenon I've been talking about—the lack of people to fill the job.

The challenge of managing a diverse intergenerational workforce is nothing new. In 1991 Howe and Strauss outlined a new U.S. generation gap resulting from the baby boomer population (those born from 1943 to 1960) whose views were dramatically different from those of previous generations (1991, 67). For example, there was a time when that generation trusted no one over thirty; however, in 1991 this trend reversed to not trusting anyone under thirty (Howe and Strauss 1991, 25).

So while it's easy to outline what managers are looking for in new employees, the bigger question is, What does a younger workforce want from its employers? Several sources offer suggestions for how employers are to work with Gen Y-ers. For example, Luporter outlines several key factors Gen Y-ers are looking for in their first job: an engaging work environment, growth opportunities, challenging job assignments, and flexible work hours (2000b, 1). Critical to leading Gen Y-ers is to understand that their motivations center on "What's in it for me?"—plus a need to know why an assignment is given, clear communication, and "compelling engagement of technology" (Luporter 2000a, 1).

Still, today's younger employees have their own unique dispositions. Barna and Hatch help us understand how this new generational workforce, labeled Mosaics (born after 1984), can be characterized by the following dispositions (2001, 65–70):

- Less emotionally sensitive

- More self-confident

- Less pessimistic about the future

- Emphasize tribal bonds—working as a team or unit

- Have higher demand for leveraging technology to its fullest

- Are adopting a mixture of cultures to suit their predispositions (as in "Absolute truth is a foreign concept")

How do supervisors lead and motivate Mosaics? While Mosaics may be less pessimistic about the future than Gen Y, they may not always have foresight in planning their actions. Helping younger workers better connect present-day decisions and actions with future outcomes will greatly aid building a sense of mission. Additionally, CCL suggests that younger workers will take on greater confidence as they take on positions of greater responsibility. This is highlighted by Drucker in his observation of the Salvation Army as an organization that is effective at placing young leaders in positions of authority and responsibility (GuideStar 2007).

It would seem that if we are to inspire the next generation of leaders, we need to be able to help younger workers connect their present actions with future consequences. We also need to be aware of and sensitive to the younger workforce's affinity toward tribal and group bonds and perhaps take advantage of this understanding when assigning greater responsibility and accountability that helps instill connection to the organization's mission and vision. Wayne George, executive director of Youth for Christ, a faith-based organization that works with middle and senior high schools, outlined what he sees as the three critical needs kids are looking for today:

- Kids want to be known by name—they want those in authority to know who they are and call them by name.

- They want their efforts to be acknowledged and appreciated.

- They want to make a difference—they want to be a part of something that's important.

Fascinating—it would seem that what middle and high school kids are seeking is exactly what we are all looking for.

7

The Paradox of Balance in Work and Life

The great lie promoted in the late 1990s, as companies sought higher margins by trimming their workforces, was designed to lessen the sting for displaced employees by telling them, "Who you are is not what you do." Somehow it seemed that by espousing this quip, companies believed, an employee who had dedicated long years to advancing the organization's mission would be able to find equal fulfillment in some other endeavor—hopefully before the severance package ran out. In truth, who you are is exactly what you do—and this couldn't be truer for anyone than it is for senior executives.

Senior executives find a great deal of satisfaction in the work they perform. Their contributions and achievements are not only a source of pride but a large part of who they are. However, executives' spheres of influence become imbalanced when they limit their energies solely to the workplace. These imbalances play out in poor health and eroded family relations, and ultimately in declining work performance. Ironically, as these imbalances begin to appear, senior executives may attempt to bring more energy to the area where they feel they have the best chance of seeing quick results—namely, their work. Over time the stress that arises feeds on itself until something breaks loose.

According to CCL, "The increasingly competitive nature of global business, the pressures to succeed quickly and the fear of failing, the physical demands of late nights and constant traveling, and the increasing difficulty of balancing work with personal and family needs are just some of the things that fill executives' lives with stress" (McDowell-Larsen 2002, 18). Our ability to identify and manage these stresses will not only affect organizational success but the very fabric of society—the family. In the effort to balance family and work demands it is important to understand that just as the sources of stress come from both individual and organizational influences, the solutions to managing these stressors are likewise an individual and organizational matter. This chapter takes a further look at possible solutions, after examining some of the research on the topic.

VIEWS ON BALANCE FOR ALIGNING WORK AND LIFE

A decade ago Maslach and Leiter asserted that burnout in corporate America had reached "epidemic" levels, not only threatening the health of the workforce but placing the underpinnings of U.S. organizations in peril as well (1997, 1). Today the pace of work is more hectic than ever, with increasing demands for performance and global competition, so that workplace stress and burnout may very well have reached pandemic levels. As organizations and employees seek ways to reduce stress, the topic of workplace burnout is finding prominence in popular journals and research agendas.

With the increased workloads, loss of control over schedules, and breakdown in community connections, it's no wonder that more executives are burning out (Maslach and Leiter 1997, 14–18). That is, "over time, the stresses that executives must inevitably endure can exact a considerable toll on their psychological and physiological health. It's common to hear recently promoted senior executives say that since their advancement they have stopped exercising regularly, have gained weight, and have seen their cholesterol and blood pressure levels rise" (McDowell-Larsen 2002, 18). But the impact of stress isn't relegated to executives—families are likewise feeling the effects.

In *The Fifth Discipline* (1990), Peter Senge recounts a 1990 *Fortune* article that highlighted the difference between families of highly successful executives and families of non-executives. The *Fortune* article reported on an Ann Arbor study that "found that 36 percent of children of executives undergo treatment for psychiatric or drug abuse each year, vs. 15 percent of children of non-executives in the same companies" (1990, 306). It is critical then that we understand individual and organizational sources of stress and the possible solutions to managing and negating these stressors if we are to enjoy healthy families and sustainable organizations.

Individual Causes of Stress

Perhaps one of the greatest individual causes of stress is what Senge labels the self-feeding archetype of "success to the successful"—an imbalance of the desires and pulls associated with work demands and the desires and pulls of family obligations. In systems thinking it is the challenge of "demand management"—unlimited demands set against limited resources. For the executive this demand management is a catch-22—the very actions and character traits that enable success on the job (perseverance, commitment, drive) can actually work counter to contributions to family success. The "success to the successful" archetype also plays out as executives are drawn toward the areas where they experience the greatest influence and have the most visible and immediate rewards—which are typically found in the workplace. Thus the converse can be true as executives shy away from areas where they feel they will be less successful and the rewards may be longer in materializing (their family). How executives identify and respond to this stress is critical to their families and their organizations.

The first step in dealing with stress and balancing work and family is to decide what's important for you and make a commitment that your energies will focus on these priorities. CCL emphasizes this point, highlighting that "people often define work-life balance as having sufficient time for all they want to experience: career, family, friends, community, and leisure pursuits" (Gurvis and Patterson 2005, 3). In setting these priorities, Senge suggests two points to consider. First, once you've made your decision regarding your priorities, don't be shy about letting others know what's important to you. Stand your ground confidently. It is also important to understand that there may be periods in your life when your priorities may shift—albeit for a time. For example, while family may be your top priority, there may be a time when a particular effort at work will consume more time than normal. However, this possibility raises Senge's second point to consider—that family priorities will almost always be threatened or even overwhelmed by the persistent demands of work (1990, 307–309).

Organizational Causes of Stress

Returning to the Ann Arbor study on successful executives and family health, possible causes for the higher rates of problems in executives' families were the personal characteristics of successful executives (commitment to work, perfectionism, and efficiency). But organizations themselves potentially contribute to the problem by directly or indirectly encouraging work habits that entice employees to sacrifice time with their families (Senge 1990, 306). These pressures arise primarily from the narrow focus on organizational goals and objectives to the exclusion of personal goals and objectives. In other words, "if all that matters is the organization's goals, there is simply no space for weighing the cost of those goals for an individual or the individual's family" (307).

Organizations must undo divisive pressures and demands that make balancing work and family so burdensome (Senge 1990, 311). O'Neil suggests organizations need to consider decentralizing power, implementing more adaptable styles of leadership and more flexible structures that are "family friendly" (1994, 254). Thus when we consider how to manage and relieve workplace stresses, "contrary to popular opinion [it] is not the individual but the organization that needs to change (Maslach and Leiter 1997, 21). The first place to start in this effort is to "make it acceptable for people to acknowledge family issues as well as business issues and to interject these into pertinent discussion, especially discussions involving time commitments" (Senge 1990, 312).

Leaders likewise need to acknowledge the pressures our 24/7 world places on employees and help people unplug. Candice Carpenter, former CEO of iVillage, worried about refreshing her people before they burned out: "I've stood at the elevator with people going on vacation and actually taken the laptop and cell phone out of their hands and said, 'Great, now you can have a vacation'" (Palus and Horth 2002, 65). Finally, CCL offers a few practical steps that organizations can take to help keep stress-related issues at bay (McDowell-Larsen 2002, 20):

- Establish a work environment that is supportive of the need for employees to have times of rest and reflection as well as to balance work and family priorities

- Give people at all levels of the organization more personal control and opportunities to use the full range and depth of their abilities

- Provide opportunities for development (learning)

- Make it easier for employees to engage in regular exercise

Disconnecting from the 24/7 World

One of the most important actions we can take in managing stress is to aggressively pursue times of rest and renewal (O'Neil 1994, 165). To this end O'Neil highlights three steps as a guide for effective rest and renewal: step back and gain perspective, take time away from sources of stress and tension, and develop methods for keeping renewal ongoing.

Stepping Back to Gain Perspective. Downtime is essential for rest and renewal in that it allows us to step back like a martial artist or dancer to gain energy and perspective for the next move or action. As O'Neil points out, "For highly driven people, one of the hardest things about stepping back is feeling comfortable with unstructured time." This is because we see time as a precious commodity that must be used effectively. Few us of know how to "waste time productively"—which becomes problematic because unstructured time is critical to effective rest (O'Neil 1994, 172). Thus when we actually take time for rest and renewal we do not always gain the impact we had hoped.

Unplugging Effectively. Unplugging from the 24/7 world has become as much a stress-inducing effort as the work demands we face from day to day. For some executives, time away from work simply masks an inability to unplug and rest. The *New York Times* categorized four patterns of vacation cheaters (O'Neil 1994, 170–172):

- "Power players" don't even try to leave the office—they take everything from the office with them on vacation, and they stay plugged in to their work and use vacation time to either catch up or get a jump on work demands.

- "Stress fighters" spend their whole vacation in hectic activity such as dieting or heavy exercise. They are on a mission, not a vacation.

- "Schedulers" have every moment of their vacation planned with tours, sightseeing, and time-filling activities.

- "Fugitives" desperately seek to escape work with parties and time-consuming activities designed to avoid thinking about work.

The heart of rest and renewal is the time in which deep learning and reflection occur (O'Neil 1994, 165). Restful times away from work can be seen as "any amount of time you spend away from your usual productive round of activities, as long as that time is spent in pursuit of deep learning. One factor that many executives may overlook is taking time to be alone. Storr notes that although psychology points to the importance of interpersonal relationships, "some development of the capacity to be alone is necessary if the brain is to function at its best, and if the individual is to fulfill his or her highest potential. . . . Learning, thinking, innovation and maintaining contact with one's own inner world are all facilitated by solitude" (quoted in O'Neil 1994, 178).

Keeping Renewal Ongoing. When we return to work after times of rest it will be difficult to maintain the renewal. Although we ourselves took time from work, work didn't take time from us—and our e-mail and paper in-boxes will undoubtedly be overflowing. To keep renewal ongoing O'Neil suggests a few simple actions (1994, 185–215):

- Stroll without somewhere to go
- Pause to count your breaths
- Take every step purposefully
- Make daily time to reflect and meditate
- Take time for mini retreats (twenty minutes or so) as well as restful (learning and reflective) weekends

HOW SENIOR EXECUTIVES ACHIEVE BALANCE

Once again, reviewing the data collected on C-level executives will demonstrate how they approach balancing work and life demands. Of particular interest, the *Campbell Leadership Index* (CLI) devotes an entire section to assessing energy and resilience. However, let's begin with reviewing how personality type influences executives' approach to achieving balance in their lives.

Personality Type and Balance

Judith Provost's work on the way different personality types approach achieving balance provides a useful insight into senior executive life. For example, in contemplating leisure it's helpful to consider two points of view. There are those who find what they do so enjoyable that their work habits actually spill over into their off time. An example might be a librarian who enjoys reading for pleasure. However, for many of us leisure time is an opportunity to fill a void that we do not find at work. This compensatory approach might play out as engaging in strenuous physical activity after hours for an executive who spends a great deal of time sitting in meetings (Provost 1990, 25–26). Yet some psychologists believe that for some people there is a fine line between work and play. These individuals are able to find both intrinsic and extrinsic rewards from their jobs and in a real way are able to play at work (26).

Referring to the four predominant personality types found among the population of C-level executives reviewed here, Provost outlines several observations for how people with the personality types of ISTJ, INTJ, INTP, and ENTJ approach their leisure time (1990, 47–52):

ISTJs (Introversion, Sensing, Thinking, Judging)

Serious and often solitary in their leisure, ISTJs apply their concentration and thoroughness to leisure activities. They prefer activities with purpose and concrete outcomes or measurably increased skill. They're deliberate in their approach to play and tend to be little given to spontaneity. Examples of play activities for ISTJs include chess, Trivial Pursuit, computer games, aerobics, or golf.

INTJs (Introversion, Intuition, Thinking, Judging)

INTJs often enjoy games of strategy. They like to challenge their intuition through attending films and cultural events or reading. Their independent nature may lead them to individualistic sports such as swimming and backpacking. They tend to be critical of their own performance in leisure activities since mastery is important to them. Often serious and purposeful in their leisure choices, they might find satisfaction in visiting museums, running marathons, or studying a new subject.

INTPs (Introversion, Intuition, Thinking, Perceiving)

INTPs' tendency to be quiet and reserved is expressed in their preference for solitary leisure choices; they may not enjoy parties or conventional kinds of socializing and sports. They often enjoy activities with an intellectual focus—reading, cultural events, or chess. Although solitary leisure is essential to them because of their reflective nature, it may often be neglected, because their intuition draws them into many work activities—which they then feel must be completed competently. Other options for them include backpacking, hiking, or meditation.

ENTJs (Extraversion, Intuition, Thinking, Judging)

ENTJs may be hearty, outgoing leaders in many activities, organizing a group of friends or their community. Play is usually possible for them only after they feel that their work is finished. They usually enjoy parties and competitive sports. Other options: attending sporting events, racing sailboats, or planning social events in which they can mix business with pleasure, such as golf with clients or associates.

Keep in mind that all sixteen personality types were represented in the sample of C-level executives. Therefore, it may prove helpful to consider, with the aid of Table 7.1, how senior executives approach specific leisure needs according to personality type (Provost 1990, 44).

LEISURE NEED	TYPE	TYPICAL ACTIVITY
Psychological: intellectual challenges, freedom, self-confidence	All types	Activities that foster pursuit of individualistic ideas
Educational: information, self-knowledge, discovery	Intuition	Perpetual learner of something new—perhaps through reading, independent study, school
	Sensing	Learning about the world through travel, interest groups
	Feeling	Participating in self-discovery or growth workshops
	Thinking	Acquiring technical knowledge such as computer skills
Social: relationships with others	Feeling	Affiliation, personal interactions
	Extraversion	High level of activity with others
Relaxation: stress release	All types	Compensation and balance for all types; activity varies with type and lifestyle
Physical activity and health	Sensing	More naturally attuned to body
	Intuition	Maybe less aware of their physical well-being and health
Aesthetic: pleasure in design	Feeling	Harmony in nature, design, and the arts (especially INFP, ISFP)
		Sense of beauty found in order (especially ISTJ, ISFJ)
	Intuition	Ingenious pattern of ideas, films, arts, books
	Thinking	Finding interest in elegant logic and activities such as chess

Table 7.1 • Relationship of Personality Type to Leisure Needs and Activities

Energy and Resilience

The CLI provides several views to assess how senior executives approach balancing work and life demands. Particularly useful are the scales of Ambitious and Dynamic within the Leadership orientation, the Energy orientation, and the scales of Calmness, Flexibility, Optimism, and Trust within the Resilience orientation. Figure 7.1 provides an overview of how these scales compare to the CLI overall.

As Figure 7.1 shows, scores on the Ambitious and Dynamic scales are approaching the "very high" range. Looking closer at the item-level questions for the Ambitious and Dynamic scales in Figure 7.2, two data points demand attention. First, on the Ambitious question of "Forceful—Appears strong and assertive in front of others," an interesting perception gap opens up between subordinates, who provided a 74 percent favorable score, and the 56 percent favorable score that the superiors provided. While definitive conclusions cannot be drawn from the data, this perception gap may be related to a greater power distance between a senior executive and a subordinate than, say, the same executive and an immediate superior. This power distance may likewise explain the perception gap of ten percentage points between senior executives and their peers on the Dynamic question of "Enthusiastic—Has an eager, spontaneous approach." However, in this case the perception gap may be due to the shortened power distance between senior executives and their peers, with peers seeing themselves on a par (or perhaps a bit higher) in the area of Enthusiasm.

The data in the item-level detail on the Energy orientation in Figure 7.3 help draw out perceptions regarding the senior executives' physical activity and health. Overall, scores on the Energy item-level questions are within the high range of the CLI. Only in the question of "Athletic—Engages in vigorous activities" did senior executives see lower favorable scores. However, in light of the higher favorable scores in questions of Active, Hardy, and Healthy, it is clear observers perceive senior executives as maintaining high energy levels.

The CLI Resilience orientation provides insight into the executives' mental durability, emotional balance, and ability to handle ambiguity by

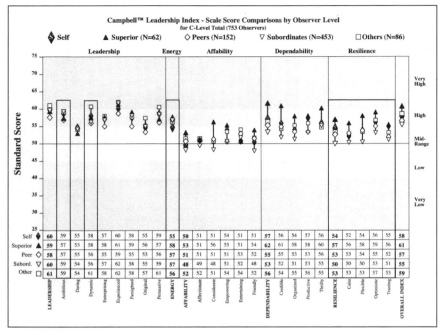

Figure 7.1 • *Campbell™ Leadership Index* Scales Reflecting Approach to Balance

Figure 7.2 • *Campbell™ Leadership Index* Ambitious and Dynamic Scales Questions

Note: "Percent Favorable" reflects answers that indicate approval. For positive statements favorable responses would be "Always" or "Usually" and for negative statements favorable responses would be "Never" or "Seldom."

Energy Scale

1. Active - Is energetic and lively.

	Nev	Sel	Occ	Som	Usu	Alw	%Fav
You			6	32	36		
All Obs	5	14	74	315	344		88
Superior			10	29	23		84
Peer	1	5	14	74	58		87
Subord	4	5	42	182	219		89
Other		4	8	30	44		86

7. Athletic - Engages in vigorous activities.

	Nev	Sel	Occ	Som	Usu	Alw	%Fav
You	3	7	12	14	25	13	
All Obs	16	102	93	173	242	107	48
Superior	1	8	8	14	19	9	47
Peer	2	20	22	31	55	19	50
Subord	13	65	46	108	147	65	48
Other		9	17	20	21	14	43

50. Hardy – Has lots of endurance, is robust and resilient.

	Nev	Sel	Occ	Som	Usu	Alw	%Fav
You	1	1	12	48	12		
All Obs	7	24	69	402	250		87
Superior	1	1	5	26	29		89
Peer	1	2	12	92	45		90
Subord	4	17	42	241	148		86
Other	1	4	10	43	28		83

52. Healthy – Physically fit, promotes well-being.

	Nev	Sel	Occ	Som	Usu	Alw	%Fav
You			1	4	51	18	
All Obs	2	15	17	50	406	259	89
Superior		1		1	37	23	97
Peer	2	3	12	84	49		89
Subord	2	10	13	26	250	150	89
Other	2	1	11	35	37		84

57. Inactive - Physically quiet, shows little energy.

	Nev	Sel	Occ	Som	Usu	Alw	%Fav
You	32	34	3	2	3		
All Obs	341	289	54	8	1		84
Superior	33	16	7	5			80
Peer	63	64	8	16	1		84
Subord	207	176	31	33	5	1	85
Other	38	33	8	5	2		83

84. Sedentary - Lives an inactive life with no exercise.

	Nev	Sel	Occ	Som	Usu	Alw	%Fav
You	34	26	6	5	2	1	
All Obs	404	214	59	54	11	1	83
Superior	35	15	8	2		1	82
Peer	86	42	10	10	1		86
Subord	239	132	35	33	8		83
Other	44	25	6	9	2		80

Figure 7.3 • *Campbell™ Leadership Index* **Energy Scale Questions**

way of several questions in the Calm, Flexible, Optimistic, and Trusting scales. Examine Figure 7.4. In the Calm scale, you can see a significant perception gap in the question on "Easy-going," where superiors reflect a 66 percent favorable rating versus subordinates' 47 percent favorable. Similarly, significant perception gaps show up in the Flexible scale on the questions of "Adaptable," where senior executives' self-ratings were far above observer ratings; as well as on "Headstrong" (superiors' 52 percent favorable versus subordinates' 35 percent) and "Stubborn" (superiors' 61 percent versus subordinates' 38 percent).

Some general observations: In each perception gap, superiors express a higher favorable rating than other observers, which is especially significant with subordinates. This suggests that there may be an issue of self-awareness on the part of executives as to the image they portray (hurried) and their openness to input (unyielding, entrenched). This is an interesting dichotomy when also reflected on the scales of Optimism and Trust. Here again several questions reveal the existence of a significant perception gap: namely on the questions of "Moody" and "Temperamental" in the Optimism scale and "Suspicious" and "Trusting" on the Trust scale. As noted earlier, superiors' ratings were always higher than those of observers—emphasizing a possible issue with the senior executives' self-awareness as to how they are interacting with their superiors, peers, and subordinates.

Calm Scale

8. Calm - Unhurried, unruffled.

	Nev	Sel	Occ	Som	Usu	Alw	%Fav
You		7	9	10	44	4	
All Obs	6	74	84	157	344	87	57
Superior		4	4	15	28	11	63
Peer		9	20	36	66	20	57
Subord	6	52	53	91	204	47	55
Other		9	7	15	46	9	64

29. Easy-going - Has a calm and unhurried manner.

	Nev	Sel	Occ	Som	Usu	Alw	%Fav
You	2	10	11	23	28		
All Obs	25	88	108	153	294	84	50
Superior	1	5	3	12	31	9	66
Peer	1	15	20	35	58	23	53
Subord	20	56	77	87	170	43	47
Other	3	12	8	19	35	9	51

87. Serene - Calm and unruffled.

	Nev	Sel	Occ	Som	Usu	Alw	%Fav
You	1	5	8	21	38	1	
All Obs	16	60	93	176	341	63	54
Superior		2	5	14	34	7	66
Peer	1	13	17	40	43	18	53
Subord	15	38	64	102	203	28	51
Other		7	7	20	41	10	60

Flexible Scale

2. Adaptable - Easily adjusts to changing conditions.

	Nev	Sel	Occ	Som	Usu	Alw	%Fav
You		1	6	50	17		
All Obs	7	29	152	418	143		76
Superior			5	46	11		92
Peer		4	39	76	31		71
Subord	7	22	88	248	86		74
Other		3	20	48	15		73

44. Flexible - Handles change and ambiguity well.

	Nev	Sel	Occ	Som	Usu	Alw	%Fav
You		1	8	52	13		
All Obs	21	60	173	382	116		66
Superior		4	13	34	11		73
Subord	19	37	98	230	68		66
Other	1	7	22	42	14		65

51. Headstrong - Difficult to reason with, opinionated.

	Nev	Sel	Occ	Som	Usu	Alw	%Fav
You	6	22	16	26	4		
All Obs	84	216	96	221	101	32	40
Superior	16	16	9	17	4		52
Peer	23	43	26	43	10	6	44
Subord	39	121	57	134	79	23	35
Other	6	36	4	27	8	3	50

90. Stubborn - Fixed in purpose or opinion; is difficult to change.

	Nev	Sel	Occ	Som	Usu	Alw	%Fav
You	9	22	17	22	4		
All Obs	99	218	125	190	101	18	42
Superior	23	15	7	12	5		61
Peer	22	45	31	38	15	1	44
Subord	41	129	78	118	72	14	38
Other	13	29	9	22	9	3	49

Optimistic Scale

25. Discouraged – Feels gloomy and unhappy.

	Nev	Sel	Occ	Som	Usu	Alw	%Fav
You	29	35	3	7			
All Obs	391	289	32	37	2	1	90
Superior	30	26	3	3			90
Peer	77	59	7	7	1	1	89
Subord	239	171	18	24			91
Other	45	33	4	3	1		91

66. Moody - Shows sudden changes of emotion.

	Nev	Sel	Occ	Som	Usu	Alw	%Fav
You	5	45	14	9	1		
All Obs	164	345	71	123	40	10	68
Superior	25	23	6	8			77
Peer	33	75	15	21	6	2	71
Subord	83	208	43	81	30	8	64
Other	23	39	7	13	4		72

68. Optimistic - Sees the best in people and situations.

	Nev	Sel	Occ	Som	Usu	Alw	%Fav
You			10	52	12		
All Obs	26	50	177	394	103		66
Superior		3	12	40	7		76
Peer	5	7	38	79	22		67
Subord	19	39	109	224	60		63
Other	2	1	18	51	14		76

78. Resilient - Recovers quickly from failures or adversity.

	Nev	Sel	Occ	Som	Usu	Alw	%Fav
You		1	4	55	14		
All Obs	3	20	89	490	147		85
Superior	1	5	39	17			90
Peer	2	28	94	26			80
Subord	2	13	53	298	85		85
Other	1	4	3	59	19		91

93. Temperamental - Moody, irritable, and overly sensitive.

	Nev	Sel	Occ	Som	Usu	Alw	%Fav
You	12	48	11	2	1		
All Obs	246	323	65	83	30	3	76
Superior	37	14	8	3			82
Peer	48	75	10	14	5		81
Subord	130	193	44	56	25	3	72
Other	31	41	3	10			85

98. Well-adjusted - Handles personal and emotional problems well.

	Nev	Sel	Occ	Som	Usu	Alw	%Fav
You		1	5	57	11		
All Obs	1	13	36	90	403	203	81
Superior		2	5	32	23		89
Peer		2	5	23	81	41	80
Subord	1	8	26	54	242	116	80
Other		1	5	8	48	23	84

Trusting Scale

21. Cynical - Doubts the goodness of others.

	Nev	Sel	Occ	Som	Usu	Alw	%Fav
You	12	35	16	11			
All Obs	108	347	119	138	37	4	60
Superior	11	32	8	9	2		69
Peer	22	69	25	28	5	3	60
Subord	53	212	78	83	26	1	58
Other	22	34	8	18	4		65

77. Resentful - Feels injured, insulted, or exploited.

	Nev	Sel	Occ	Som	Usu	Alw	%Fav
You	23	38	9	3	1		
All Obs	281	323	64	63	15	3	81
Superior	26	24	5	4	2		82
Peer	54	68	13	14	2	1	80
Subord	165	202	40	33	8	2	82
Other	36	29	6	12	3		76

92. Suspicious - Inclined to distrust others.

	Nev	Sel	Occ	Som	Usu	Alw	%Fav
You	14	36	15	7	2		
All Obs	147	370	88	105	33	5	69
Superior	24	26	2	8	2		81
Peer	28	81	15	21	5		73
Subord	70	228	60	66	22	5	66
Other	25	35	11	10	4		71

95. Trusting - Believes in the goodness of others.

	Nev	Sel	Occ	Som	Usu	Alw	%Fav
You		3	9	50	12		
All Obs	28	59	150	418	92		68
Superior	1	2	10	40	9		79
Peer	6	11	33	88	13		67
Subord	19	43	91	242	54		66
Other	2	3	16	48	16		75

Figure 7.4 • *Campbell™ Leadership Index* Calm, Flexible, Optimistic, and Trusting Scales Questions

Organizational Perception of Stress

The last set of data to review here is the organizational perception of stress assessed in the *Campbell Organizational Survey* (COS). The COS Stress-Free scale attempts to understand "perceived levels of job stress and its impact, such as physical ailments or poor performance, and whether healthy escape values are available" (Campbell and Hyne 1995, 10). To draw out this understanding, the COS raises the questions shown in Figure 7.5.

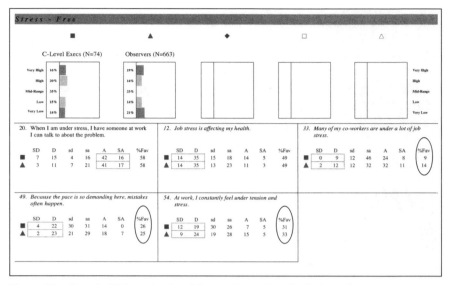

Figure 7.5 • *Campbell™ Organizational Survey* Stress-Free Scale Questions

According to Campbell and Hyne, "high scores suggest that the work environment is psychologically comfortable and that stress levels are tolerable, perhaps even stimulating [while] low scores usually indicate a level of stress that is perceived as corrosive and disruptive" (1995, 10). Standard scores in the COS Stress-Free scale were 50 for both senior executives and observers, as indicated in Figure 7.6. In the COS as a whole, scores on Stress-Free were among the lowest realized, validating what many of us have come to experience firsthand: the impact of a fast-paced, results-at-all-costs work environment. This is particularly clear in the item-level questions on coworkers' perception of job-related stress, impact on quality, and increased tension.

Summary of Data

From the data reviewed here, it seems that senior executives approach achieving balance from three vantage points: how their personality affects their approach to leisure, how their responses to work and life demands are perceived, and how they manage stress within the organizations they lead.

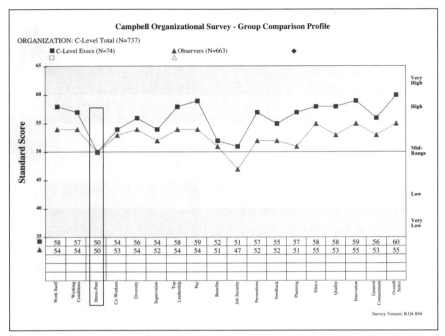

Figure 7.6 • *Campbell™ Organizational Survey* **Stress-Free Scale**

As noted earlier, psychologists believe some people are able to essentially play at work. This not only helps them achieve results but serves as motivation and inspiration for others to join in the work effort. However, it may complicate life for senior executives, who often have (or at least appear to have) an imbalance in their sphere of influence, particularly in their family lives, as they are drawn toward areas where they feel they have most impact—that is, their work. However, when senior executives do choose to engage in leisure activities, their personality type will influence their approach intellectually, educationally, socially, and physically.

Several perception gaps exist between superiors, peers, and subordinates regarding how senior executives lead others. Specifically, how senior executives are perceived in being "Forceful," "Enthusiastic," "Headstrong," and "Temperamental" differs widely between observers. This perception gap raises two questions:

- How do the power distances between senior executives' superiors, peers, and subordinates influence perceptions of the way executives approach achieving balance?

- Are senior executives aware of the perception gaps they may inadvertently create between themselves and their superiors, peers, and subordinates, and between each of these groups and the others?

Finally, with regard to how senior executives lead their organizations, stress is of major concern, appearing as one of the lowest-rating COS items. This was especially visible in areas such as stress related to quality, tension, and even employee health.

OBSERVATIONS ON EXECUTIVE BALANCE IN WORK AND LIFE

There was a time in my job when I regularly took the shuttle from North Carolina to New York. The routine was so commonplace that I'd become acquainted with many of my fellow fliers—and all of us knew our flight crew by name. There was also a ritual that many of us seemed to follow. At the end of a flight, as we touched down in New York, each and every one of us pulled out a cell phone and connected with the home office. The plane had barely come to a stop when you could overhear several conversations reviewing meeting details, sales plans, and customer issues. And scenes like this play out hundreds of times a day. A peer recently shared a similar story from her trip to Mexico. Of the hundred people waiting in the gate area before the flight, nearly half were on a computer, PDA, or cell phone. With the never-ending pace of a 24/7 world creating so much pressure, how do senior executives find needed balance in their lives?

Finding Balance

Maslach and Leiter suggest that burnout is not so much a function of a person's ability to cope with a hectic work pace as of the social work environment—how people in the workplace engage in their jobs and relate to one another (1997, 18). Work done by CCL likewise emphasizes that compelling, supportive social environments are created by enabling networks with individuals who have similar passions, experiences, and situations—and are therefore empathically supportive of one another (McCauley 2005, 5–6). It seems that self-renewing people stay connected to the world around them. They seek out friends who can and will talk about whatever needs to be talked about—the whole life experience, up and down and all around (Hudson 1991, 211).

But what does the phrase "finding balance" mean? Balance to one person may not be balance to another. Earlier I mentioned Gurvis and Patterson's definition of work-life balance as being able to find time for everything you want to do. But there is more. "Searching for the point of equilibrium among all these pursuits, however, can become all-consuming and nonproductive" (2005, 3).

In other words, the key to finding the balance in your work and personal life is to seek out those activities and connections that bring you inspiration and rejuvenation. In so doing, you can actually gain energy in your work (Gurvis and Patterson 2005, 4). While Jaffe and Scott remind us that rest and diversions are important as a means to relieve tension and pressure (1984, 165), it is important to comprehend that diversions from work do not always equate to time away from work. A diversion can be anything that breaks the normal work routine—even momentarily. This does not suggest that *rest*—that is, taking a break from work—is unnecessary. Again, Jaffe and Scott suggest the following questions (142):

- How many times a day do you laugh out loud?

- How playful are you in your personal and work relationships?

- Can you let down your guard and respond playfully to conditions around you?

O'Neil (1994, 41) reminds us that for successful people, control—or the perception of control, as suggested by Senge (1990, 290–292)—is the central point: "the place where psychological quirks and external pressures are bound to show up eventually." The desire of managers to gravitate toward areas where they can have the greatest impact parallels with the work of University of Chicago researcher Kobasa. Kobasa highlighted patterns of healthy executives who likewise placed their energies in areas where they had more impact, and in doing so achieved a greater sense of involvement while being more creative and motivated to seek out challenges and take risks (cited in Jaffe and Scott 1984, 62–63).

Connecting to Purpose

Exposing employees to new ideas and concepts via directed assignments is a key method of connecting people to the work of the organization, be it in a social initiative or a strategic frontier (Gryskiewicz 2005, 8). CCL is currently researching this concept of *connected leadership,* which "focuses on the development of leadership as an outcome of teamwork and team learning, works to enhance the connections between individuals and between groups in an organization, and attempts to facilitate the emergence of a culture that supports a recognition of inter-independence among organizational members and groups, collaborative work across organizational boundaries, the bottom-up emergence of ideas and innovation, and increased comfort with managing unpredictable outcomes" (Van Velsor 2005, 2).

Consider, for example, Project Ulysses, a PricewaterhouseCoopers (PwC) initiative in which staff take on directed work engagements intended to connect with key stakeholders associated with PwC's social initiatives. These may include leadership assignments to developing countries where employees can apply their expertise in helping nations deal with various complex social and economic challenges. Another example comes from IBM Global Services. IBM partners with the Department of Education by lending out resources and expertise to help with various educational initiatives (Pearce and Doh 2005, 34). In the case of PwC the upside benefit from this effort is renewed employee commitment, dedication, and retention (32–33). And IBM's partnership with the Department of Education provides critical strategic insight for the organization's education-related line of business.

Self-Awareness

How do you know when your stress level is rising? What feedback mechanisms do you look to or what signals help you assess how you are coping during times of increased work demands or pressures? How do you know when you simply need to get away for an extended time to recharge? Lazarus and Folkman describe psychological stress as the "relationship between the person and the environment that is appraised by the person as taxing or exceeding his or her resources and endangering his or her well-being" (McCauley 2005, 4). Work overload is more than simply stretching to meet demands; it crosses beyond the physical and mental capabilities of the person (Maslach and Leiter 1997, 10). It would appear, then, that a critical component of rest and renewal, be it on the job or in extended time off the job, is the capacity for self-awareness and self-assessment of stress. That is, "research in psychology and psychiatry has shown the extent to which mental health is bound up in a reasonably objective view of self, in accessibility of self to consciousness and in acceptance of the self" (Gartner 1963, 13).

Noted cardiologist and researcher Herbert Benson points to this important need: We must maintain a certain level of stress (needed to tune the body for high performance) as well as rest (needed to release tension) (cited in Jaffe and Scott 1984, 168). However, personal energy, involvement, and efficacy are, as Maslach and Leiter describe, "the direct opposites" of the dimensions of stress. When burnout occurs, a person's sense of engagement wanes, energy fades into exhaustion, and efficacy gives way to ineffectiveness (Maslach and Leiter 1997, 24). Here again, research has shown that human bodies react poorly during times of complex change, lost connection with people, helplessness, and over-exertion without rest (Jaffe and Scott 1984, 10–11).

It would appear that one of the most critical components of renewal is the ability to discern when stress levels are beginning to interfere with the ability to function at peak levels. O'Neil emphasizes this point: "Self-observation is essential to the process of renewal. Too often in our struggle for success we fail to probe into our deeper selves" (1994, 129). This ability to understand how you are responding to the stresses around you appears to be key to renewal, be it for the short term (catching your second wind) or the long term. Here again, O'Neil refers to this as locating the "observation point"—a specific checkpoint that provides feedback on your condition. Marathon runners typically develop several key indicators, such as time between markers, that help them understand how they are performing. But all too often stress-related observation points come long after available resources of energy have been expended (131). When this occurs, the increased anxiety and tension often leads people to an ill-considered decision or action (119). "Having stress-related symptoms is a message from your body that you are not managing the pressure and demands of your life well enough" (Jaffe and Scott 1984, 157).

CALL TO ACTION

According to *Jobs Rated Almanac*, 2001, the position of senior corporate executive is the third most stressful job, behind president of the United States and firefighter (Krantz 2000). But how harmful to health are the stresses that accompany the executive role, what are the implications for leadership performance, and what can executives do to cope with stress? It is clear, as Senge notes, that "traditional organizations undeniably foster conflict between work and family" with a carrot-and-stick approach that says, "If you want to get ahead here, you must be willing to make sacrifices" (1990, 307). Still, "nothing is more vital to the renewal of an organization than the system by which people are nurtured" (Gartner 1963, 76), and key to this nurturing are times of rest and reflection.

It is critical for us to understand individual and organizational sources of stress and the possible solutions to managing and negating these stressors if we are to enjoy healthy families and sustainable organizations. Our ability to identify and manage these stresses will not only affect organizational success but the health and well-being of our families. The following considerations may be helpful to senior executives as they balance the alignment between work and life.

Self-Assessment

Self-assessment tools, perhaps including biofeedback, along with supportive friends and families, can reveal energy levels and indicate whether the needed renewal is a short-term or long-term period of rest. Seivert suggests a simple self-assessment process for measuring stress and the need to recharge by regularly checking how you interact with those around you—family, friends, and coworkers—particularly in the way you communicate and your level of patience. This assessment should also include your physical state as evident in health or nervous patterns such as biting your nails or clenching your jaw (2001, 76). Here again, the need for self-assessment, particularly as it relates to understanding those areas where we have the greatest control, allows us to balance demands on our energy with our given capacity and thereby "protect our health, and ensure our success" (Jaffe and Scott 1984, 63). According to McCauley, "Those who experience lower stress believe that they themselves, not external forces, control their lives. They are optimistic and believe they have the ability to improve themselves. Furthermore, they are not bothered by ambiguity and uncertainty" (2005, 5).

Physical Activity and Serious Play

Physical activity can help clear the hormonal by-products of the body's response to stress (Jaffe and Scott 1984, 167), so it may prove beneficial for organizations to provide physical stress releases at work. This includes walking trails, on-site gyms, or after-hours exercise classes (McCauley 2005, 7). These options may provide effective short-term renewal as well as long-term health benefits.

Make sure you find time for serious play at work—the kind of activity that allows people to come together as a cohesive community and exercise the power of creativity and innovation (Palus and Horth 2002, 114–115; O'Neil 1994, 200–201). To this point MIT researcher Michael Schrage suggests that the qualities of play, namely "curiosity, exuberance, spontaneity, improvisation [and] a feeling of being outside of time" are instrumental for effective organizations (Palus and Horth 2002, 108).

Building Connected Networks

Continually seek out and build connected networks that provide inspiration and support for the work and passions you pursue. We all find energy and respite in understanding and acknowledging the connectedness we all share through a circle of compassion (Seivert 2001, 163), so that the "greater our social networks and the number of people available to help us, the healthier we are likely to be (Jaffe and Scott 1984, 99). Likewise, partner with other organizations to bring expertise and experience back into your own organization. Thus, challenging assignments help "employees stay alert—this alertness connects the employees to the task at hand and provides the ability to look at situations in fresh, new perspectives. Rather than becoming mired in the same old routine, employees and organizations experience a 'perpetual state of renewal'" (Gryskiewicz 2005, 103–104).

PERSONAL REFLECTION:
ON-THE-JOB RENEWAL

Recharging your batteries doesn't necessarily mean taking a break from work any more than working very hard automatically throws you into burnout. It is fascinating to me to see how a few rare individuals actually seem to draw energy from their work. Looking more closely at these individuals, I've come to understand that they've developed the ability for on-the-job renewal (OJR)—the ability to catch their second wind as long-distance runners do. The following are a few notes I've made from observing how people find OJR.

The primary key to OJR seems to be a work environment that encourages people in the workplace to compassionately engage in their jobs and relate to one another in networks of individuals who have similar passions, experiences, and situations, and therefore have the mutual empathy to support one another.

OJR thrives in organizations that have a strong commitment to developmental assignments and job rotations, which provide opportunities for both encouragement and renewal. Organizations that have a successful track record for promoting from within are able to develop the proficiencies of their workforce while concurrently providing new and reenergizing assignments.

OJR is fostered where there is a strong sense of community among peers and coworkers. This community provides a safe environment for those times when tension is released with group venting sessions as team members acknowledge shared frustrations and issues. At times a solution to a particular stress-causing issue will surface during venting sessions, but even when no solution is reached, the opportunity to simply share like experiences and frustrations is very cathartic. Key in this engagement is a wellspring of energy and renewal coming from the support and encouragement received from coworkers and teammates.

As noted earlier, OJR occurs more readily in environments that encourage and support having fun at work. It should not be unusual to hear hearty laughter and cheers coming from team meetings and gatherings. Likewise, regularly conducted team-building and retreat exercises (some of a few hours in duration and others lasting an entire day) help create a playful and vibrant work environment.

Perhaps most important is an environment where employees have a great sense of accomplishment and pride in being associated with the organization. A strong belief in the work that is performed and each person's contribution to this work is a key ingredient to OJR.

At some point employees do need to take extended time away from work for physical, emotional, and spiritual rest and renewal. However, employees can reenergize by connecting their work to a particular passion, as in a strategic initiative or social cause, and this renewal may be effective as a source of short-term OJR. Developing sources of effective short-term renewal may prove invaluable for achieving time-critical business objectives. Wilkinson highlights connecting to this energy from engaging your passion by suggesting the need to find your "sweet spot"—working at a job hard all day doing something you love—so that while you may be physically exhausted you are happy (that is, energized) to the core (2003, 84–85). The adage "Do a job you love and you'll never work a day in your life" echoes the wisdom of Solomon: "A man can find nothing better than to eat and drink and find satisfaction in his work" (Ecclesiastes 2:24; *The Holy Bible* 1996).

8

Conclusion: Balancing Your Sphere of Influence

My goal in this book has been to help executives think about balancing their spheres of influence through the defining questions for effective leadership posed at the beginning of the book. By way of review, here they are again:

- Is an effective executive's decision-making process values based or results oriented?

- Can an effective executive be grounded in day-to-day business objectives while simultaneously focusing on future opportunities?

- Can effective executive leadership be measured through hitting performance metrics? Or does performance need to encompass a greater good to be truly effective?

- And what influence does an executive really exert over an organization's effectiveness (or are executives simply along for the ride)?

Observations throughout have examined the effect of multiple influencers on executive behavior. Influencers may be unbalanced and surrounded by myth, the organizational topic of Part 1, and paradox, that of Part 2.

One discovery has been that a comparatively narrow sphere of influence forms many executives' leadership perceptions. The influences within that sphere can be limited or in conflict with one another, yet have great bearing on leadership styles and behaviors.

To help senior executives maintain balance within their individual spheres, I began by defining leadership effectiveness, which includes three goals:

- Produce desired results

- Ensure long-term sustainability

- Enhance the well-being of the workforce

Note that within changing personal and managerial goals, this definition includes compassion, encouragement, and support for the deeper aspects of the whole person. Leaders who pay attention to others' needs for emotional and spiritual expression release their teams to incorporate their whole selves into their work. This, in turn, produces a synergy that fulfills the individuals and benefits the organization as well.

Data collected over the past several years from CCL's work with C-level executives and presidents provided insights into the way senior executives lead. But while these insights are helpful, it would be dangerous to regard them as providing any absolute truths. Three thoughts are important to keep in mind:

- My observations, assertions, and calls to action are framed against the backdrop of the more frequent occurrences found in the data, that is, the data that reflect somewhat over seventy senior executives and seven hundred observers (bosses, peers, and direct reports).

- From this backdrop, generalizations help frame an understanding of how senior executives approach their leadership positions.

- Nonetheless, senior executives come in all shapes, sizes, and leadership styles.

The third observation is the most important. Just because a particular personality preference does not frequently appear in our data, or one leadership dimension or competency is more frequently observed than another, this does not suggest these attributes preclude or predispose anyone for success at a senior level. In other words, the data are directional—helpful in framing an understanding of the senior leadership style, to be sure, but no more than an indication of what seems to work most often.

This final section gives an overall view with tables of composite data about C-level executives' characteristics. All tables include information on personality preferences, personal characteristics, and organizational view, and a final category, "How This Plays Out with C-Level Executives." All tables except 8.7 (on work-life balance, p. 232) have a column on leading the organization, others, and self, and Table 8.1 (on leadership styles) and Table 8.2 (on decision making, p. 222) feature an additional column, "Relating Interpersonally." The tables provide an at-a-glance view of observations about the leadership approach of the executives in the CCL research.

SUMMARY OF MYTHS REGARDING EFFECTIVE LEADERSHIP

Part 1 focuses on myths of effective leadership: Chapter 1 on power and influence, Chapter 2 on decision making, and Chapter 3 on intuition and analytics, or "elegant reasoning."

Power, Influence, and the Myth of Effective Leadership

Although power and influence are tools for leading, how they are used colors people's perceptions regarding effective leadership. You can think of leadership as the space between power and influence. Drawing a composite view, the data in Table 8.1 reflect how senior executives engage power and influence in their leadership positions.

PERSONALITY PREFERENCES	RELATING INTERPERSONALLY	LEADING ORGANIZATION, OTHERS, SELF	PERSONAL CHARACTERISTICS	ORGANIZATIONAL VIEW	HOW THIS PLAYS OUT WITH C-LEVEL EXECS
Build on reliable, stable, and consistent performance.	Likely to focus on establishing trust relationships, exchanging personal reactions and opinions to build loyalty.	Clearly convey objectives, deadlines, and expectations.	Display enthusiasm, even passion, about their work, and their excitement and dedication are inspiring to others.	Set high standards for others' ability to get things done (executives are tough graders).	May get caught in a routine of connecting and drawing insight from only a restricted number of people (few confidants).
Respect traditional, hierarchical systems.	Less interested in fitting in and getting involved with people than satisfying their need for control.	Communicate confidence and steadiness during difficult times.	Are articulate and influential.	In general, the organization perceives it is better led than managed.	May see others who disagree with them as challenging their authority and may argue their point aggressively.
Reward those who follow the rules while getting the job done.	Are very flexible, changing the roles they play over time and across different circumstances.	Speak candidly about tough issues facing the company.	Generate public buy-in of their ideas.	Executives have higher perception for the organization's vision and mission than employees have.	May not acknowledge accomplishments of others or celebrate successes.
Act strongly and forcefully in the field of ideas.	Are more apt to engage power and influence by developing strong personal loyalties and networks.	Persevere in the face of problems and difficulties.	Achieve power through ability to convince others.	Both executives and employees have so-so perception of the effectiveness of organizational communications.	Tend to use intellect to overpower those opposed to their ideas.
Can be tough-minded with self and others.	Will expand their influence by adhering to important personal and organizational values and by showing how they serve others.	Command attention and respect.	Have strength, motivation, and passion to make things happen.		May worry about failure, competency, and performance—more so in times of uncertainty; may internalize these events as personal failures.
Relate to people based on expertise rather than position.			Appear confident, enthusiastic, full of life, and to be born leaders.		Adapt well to being in groups or alone, but this may be misinterpreted as indifference or insensitivity.
Seek to interact at an intellectual rather than an emotional level.					
Apply logic and find models for change.					
Use compelling reasons for what they want to do.					

Table 8.1 • Common Observations on Leadership Styles of Senior Executives

For executives who find their sphere of influence out of balance, the following actions may prove helpful in regaining a healthy position. (For further discussion, see Chapter 1.)

- **Find and listen to other voices.** Deliberately seek out and include in your sphere of influence people who do not share your point of view or have different perspectives, insights, or experiences from your own.

- **Engage in a stretching exercise.** Find a worthy sparring partner—someone who is comfortable taking an opposing view and can thoughtfully challenge your thinking and presumptions.

- **Enlist the power of self-awareness.** Seek out open, honest, and direct feedback on your strengths and weaknesses from your peers, bosses, and direct reports.

The Myth of Effective Decision Making

To counteract the traditional top-down executive mandates, senior executives need to create an environment that not only encourages multiple scenarios and alternative solutions but allows them to be unafraid to make a wrong decision. As noted by Daniel Gilbert, inaction tends to leave more regrets than poor action does (2006, 179). Again, the composite view of the data in Table 8.2 shows how senior executives tend to engage the decision-making process.

The following considerations (from Chapter 2) are designed to help executives manage their decision making:

- **Consider an "adaptive decision-making process."** In the context of organizational structure and strategy, this allows people to understand the actions and activities (decisions) required to achieve desired results.

- **Create an open environment.** This should be one that encourages multiple scenarios and alternative solutions, and acknowledges that the only bad decision is the one not made.

PERSONALITY PREFERENCES	RELATING INTERPERSONALLY	LEADING ORGANIZATION, OTHERS, SELF	PERSONAL CHARACTERISTICS	ORGANIZATIONAL VIEW	HOW THIS PLAYS OUT WITH C-LEVEL EXECS
Want to be thoroughly grounded in the facts, which are analyzed in a logical framework.	Approach working in a team as a dependent function: "It depends on what's at stake and what the potential rewards are."	See underlying concepts and patterns in complex situations.	Persistent achievers who get things done—hit deadlines and budgets.	Set high standards for others' ability to get things done (executives are tough graders).	May see others' disagreement as challenging their authority and may argue their point aggressively.
Want to use their internal vision for strategies, systems, and structures that they have objectively determined.	Will be more focused on actually making a decision than on the decision-making process.	Readily grasp the crux of an issue despite having ambiguous information.	Practical problem-solvers who perform as promised.	Perceive a stronger organizational commitment to quality and continuous improvement than employees do.	May be so focused on getting the task done that they look past people's feelings and their accomplishments.
Want to use their internal logic to structure problems and solutions while attending to the facts and specifics.	May be quick to set limits—bounds separating what can be considered in decision from what cannot.	Accurately differentiate between important and unimportant issues.	Planful and frugal.		Make decisions quickly and may react to unforeseen circumstances too abruptly.
Want to logically analyze and control situations based on an internal understanding of what could be.	Will engage in team decision making by leading with authority.	Persevere in the face of problems and difficulties.			May not take time to celebrate success because they're on to the next project.
					Great at killing problems but not at preventing issues from becoming troublesome.
					May cut off group dialogue too quickly or impose undue pressure to act.
					May assert that they may not know what the answer is, but they certainly know what it's not.

Table 8.2 • Common Observations on How Senior Executives Approach Decision Making

- **Develop a network of advisers.** Look for people who do not have a personal stake in the outcome and can provide a sounding board for the kinds of decisions you make.

- **Engage in decision-making postmortems.** This step helps you revisit the reasoning behind a decision to better understand why you were influenced to act or respond in a particular way.

Intuition, Analytics, and the Myth of "Elegant Reasoning"

The really compelling strategies are those that emerge through both intuitive thought (elegant reasoning) and careful analytical consideration in discerning the best path to follow. While executives and those they work with identify strategic planning as a critical leadership characteristic, bosses, direct reports, and even the executives themselves did not see strategic planning as their strong suit. As leaders approach developing strategies for their organizations, they need to be aware of how their leadership styles can enable and at times distract from thinking, planning, and leading strategically. Table 8.3 recaps the observations for how executives approach strategy.

Executives can increase the effectiveness of their strategic thinking, planning, and leadership by considering the following influencers (from Chapter 3):

- **Expand your sphere of influence.** Don't give in to the pressure to be the one who has the mystic vision for the organization. Bring in other voices and insights into your sphere of influence from various levels of your organization as well as thought leaders from outside your company.

- **Get over being perfect—embrace uncertainty and take small steps.** Develop strategies that account for uncertainties and crises—even if you're not sure what crisis may arise—by making accommodations in your strategies for the unforeseen. Also define your strategies as a series of smaller steps toward a bigger picture.

PERSONALITY PREFERENCES	LEADING ORGANIZATION, OTHERS, SELF	PERSONAL CHARACTERISTICS	ORGANIZATIONAL VIEW	HOW THIS PLAYS OUT WITH C-LEVEL EXECS
Base opinions on logical criteria, experience, and knowledge.	Strategic planning is seen as an important leadership competency albeit not a strength of senior executives.	Know their industry well and are comfortable with its technical jargon.	Executives feel strongly that the organization has a vision for the future, but employees do not agree.	May get caught in a routine of connecting and drawing insight from only a restricted number of people (a few confidants).
Are long-range planners who are independent—trusting their own perceptions and judgments.	Display strong performance relating to:	Are both forward-thinking and insightful—attentive toward the future while identifying upcoming trends.	Executives and employees are less confident in the organization's ability to establish plans that will guide future action.	May get caught up in "knowing what they know" and be unable to discover and address what they don't know.
Quickly see inconsistencies and enjoy taking apart and reworking ideas by building complex theoretical systems to explain the realities they see.	• Working a strategic plan • Balancing long-term with day-to-day concerns			May worry about failure, competency, and performance—more so in times of uncertainty.
Solvers of organizational problems, keenly aware of the intricate connections within organizations; action oriented.				

Table 8.3 • Common Observations on How Senior Executives Think, Plan, and Lead Strategically

- **Remember risk management versus risk avoidance.** An executive who is risk averse will put off setting a course of action for fear that the risk will outweigh the benefits. Develop a risk management mind-set by being careful not to get caught up in "knowing what you know" to the point where you become unable to discover and address what you don't know.

SUMMARY OF PARADOXES REGARDING EFFECTIVE LEADERSHIP

Part 2 explores the paradoxes of effective leadership: Chapter 4 on values, ethics, and performance; Chapter 5 on creativity, innovation, and operational excellence; Chapter 6 on developing the next generation of leaders; and Chapter 7 on balancing work and life.

Values, Ethics, and the Performance Paradox

The paradox confronting executives in this area is one of balancing their passion (or pressure) to achieve results (performance) while being true to their values and ethics. That is, they face two distinct ROI calculations: return on investment and risk of incarceration. Table 8.4 provides a visual overview of how senior executives often seek to balance values, ethics, and performance.

Executives can ensure that they keep the performance paradox in check by considering the following suggestions (from Chapter 4):

- **Allow those around you to hold you accountable.** You can do this by regularly examining your own values and ethics and making this known publicly. This can also be accomplished by finding a partner who is willing to tell you when you're drifting away from your values. Finally, understand that while it is important to keep up with the times, it is equally important to acknowledge that some core values remain timeless.

PERSONALITY PREFERENCES	LEADING ORGANIZATION, OTHERS, SELF	PERSONAL CHARACTERISTICS	ORGANIZATIONAL VIEW	HOW THIS PLAYS OUT WITH C-LEVEL EXECS
Seek to find a standard or principle that will apply in all similar situations.	Place ethical behavior above personal gain.	Are articulate and influential.	Have highly favorable opinion of communication channels, appraisal process, and overall dissemination of information within the workplace.	Have ability to modify their behavior based on the situation, but this may be seen as too lax (that is, situational) with regard to acceptable behavior.
Have ability to moderate their behavior based on the situation.	Act in accordance with stated values.	Have sense of drive, urgency, and an expressed desire for forward progress.		
	Are trusted to maintain confidentiality.	Make things happen and have strength, motivation, and passion to do so.		May worry about failure, competency, and performance; may assign blame to others.
	Encourage honesty throughout the organization through words and deeds.	Get things done—meeting deadlines and budgets (persistent achievers).		May be so focused on getting the task done that they may look past questionable ethical behavior.
		Perform as promised as practical problem solvers.		Possess solid communication skills and reputation for maintaining confidentiality and keeping commitments, which may be helpful in building environment of openness.

Table 8.4 • Common Observations on How Senior Executives Balance Values, Ethics, and Performance

- **Be both open and transparent.** This will help you manage the perception that your use of organizational politics is not seen as an attempt to buy favors or influence. One approach may be to regularly bring new people from the organization into your sphere of influence to watch your decision-making process. Likewise, be quick to acknowledge mistakes and use them as learning opportunities while encouraging others in the organization to do the same.

- **Keep your commitments and maintain confidences.**

Creativity, Innovation, and the Operational Excellence Paradox

For an innovative organization to thrive competitively it must build infrastructure and processes to facilitate delivery of goods and services at a compelling value. However, it is often these same operational processes that constrain the creative energies that led to the organization's success. These observations reveal another nagging paradox as senior executives attempt to balance creativity, innovation, and operational excellence. Table 8.5 summarizes these observations.

The following suggestions (from Chapter 5) may help executives harness the creative and innovative energies within their organizations while achieving the operational excellence needed to lead effectively.

- **Realize that creativity is influenced by environment, while innovation is influenced by leadership.** Do whatever you can to create an environment that produces as much creative energy as possible, but at the same time harness the organization's creative energies through effective leadership of innovative applications of those creative energies.

- **Keep in mind the importance of creativity and innovation.** While creativity can put your organization on the right path, innovation will make the journey along the path productive.

- **Understand that if your employees trust their leadership, you'll see remarkable innovative breakthroughs.** On the other hand, if

PERSONALITY PREFERENCES	LEADING ORGAINZATION, OTHERS, SELF	PERSONAL CHARACTERISTICS	ORGANIZATIONAL VIEW	HOW THIS PLAYS OUT WITH C-LEVEL EXECS
See the big picture. Focus on the relationships and connections between facts. Mentally remove themselves from the situation to examine the pros and cons objectively. Good at solving problems and making things work.	Align organizational resources to accomplish key objectives. See underlying concepts and patterns in complex situations. Develop solutions that address underlying problems effectively. Persevere in the face of problems and difficulties. Deliver on promises. Adapt to new situations and accept setbacks gracefully.	Are engaged in activities they find compelling, and their excitement and dedication are inspiring to others. Generate public acceptance of their ideas. Protect the organization's resources. Seek new opportunities and challenges rather than stagnate in place.	Seen as competent, with a readiness to take advantage of new opportunities.	May worry about failure, competency, and performance—more so in times of uncertainty. Ready to accept change but slow to effect change. Though outwardly accepting of setbacks, they may internalize these events as personal failures. So driven to produce requests they may stifle creative energies of others. May become overly dependent on a specific set or sources of data. May step in too quickly to save the day and short-circuit the team's energy. May appear too abrasive or confrontational. May see everything as a problem that needs to be solved.

Table 8.5 • Common Observations on How Senior Executives Balance Creativity, Innovation, and Operational Excellence

employees place their trust in the organization, the best outcome will be clever problem solving.

- **Be aware that the best creative outcomes are those that are inspired.** At the same time, the best innovative thinking can be facilitated with compelling incentives. So, inspire ideas and reward results!

Gifted Leadership's Paradox of Developing Future Leaders

Using the example of an all-star athlete and a winning coach, it is easy to see the paradox executives face as they both compete in the game and concurrently try to develop the next wave of all-stars. Executives who are gifted at leadership may not be able to develop leaders under them. Table 8.6 highlights several observations that play out in this paradox.

To help balance this paradox and address the challenge of developing an organization's next generation of leaders, executives can ensure the sustainability of their organizations by engaging in succession planning and talent management that develops leaders who can meet the business challenges of today and tomorrow. See Chapter 6 for more discussion on the following steps:

- **Define leadership competencies.** Define the skills and knowledge needed to meet current and future business challenges and outline the leadership resources needed to meet mission challenges within the framework of leadership behaviors, critical business objectives, and the internal systems needed to support leadership development initiatives.

- **Determine the level of mastery needed for each critical leadership competency.** Simultaneously, outline the framework needed to meet the target outcomes.

- **Develop sound criteria for success.** For example, consider the evidence that must be available to prove you indeed have a solid pipeline of leadership talent that will take the organization into the future.

PERSONALITY PREFERENCES	LEADING ORGANIZATION, OTHERS, SELF	PERSONAL CHARACTERISTICS	ORGANIZATIONAL VIEW	HOW THIS PLAYS OUT WITH C-LEVEL EXECS
Need interpersonal contact and interaction (somewhat moderately).	Delegate work that provides substantial responsibility and visibility.	See themselves as helping, encouraging, and supporting others to achieve more than they thought possible.	See themselves as effective in helping others' careers.	The isolation of the position and the predisposition of their personality prevent executives from identifying up-and-coming leaders firsthand.
Are choosy about how, when, and where they associate with others and are cautious about how they use or share authority.	Support the actions and decisions of subordinates.			May be inclined to find and groom mirror images of themselves.
				Direct reports may feel as though executives are more focused on their own careers than on helping others advance.
				Focus on results may come across as too pragmatic and insensitive—which may show up as an inability to provide helpful, encouraging feedback.
				Organizational politics and favoritism may be perceived as more important to promotions than actual performance.
				Not readily supportive of mentoring others or providing helpful feedback.

Table 8.6 • Common Observations on How Senior Executives Approach Developing Talent

The Paradox of Balance in Work and Life

The book's last paradox deals with how senior executives struggle to balance work and life demands. Executives are drawn toward the areas where they have the most visible and immediate rewards—specifically work—and tend to shy away from areas where they feel the rewards may be longer in materializing (such as family life). Table 8.7 outlines the observations that bear on this paradox.

How executives identify and respond to this paradox is critical to their families and their organizations. The following considerations (from Chapter 7) may be helpful to senior executives as they balance the alignment between work and life:

- **Develop the ability to self-assess your reaction to stress.** This will help determine your energy levels as well as signal that you need a short-term or long-term period of rest.

- **Engage in regular physical activity.** Walking trails, on-site gyms, or after-hours exercise classes can be effective methods for short-term renewal and long-term health benefits.

- **Make sure you find time to have serious play at work.** Serious play allows individuals to come together as a cohesive community, and within this community is the power of creativity and innovation.

- **Continually seek out and build connected networks.** Strong networks can provide inspiration and support for the work and passions you pursue.

A STORY OF EFFECTIVE LEADERSHIP

So how much real influence do senior executives have in their organizations? Given the embedded myths that encumber leaders with a misconception of the actions they should engage, as well as the competing paradoxes that challenge leaders to buy in to practices that inevitably fail, it's a wonder that organizations ever achieve any measure of success. And yet success does happen; in some organizations leaders seem to have

PERSONALITY PREFERENCES	PERSONAL CHARACTERISTICS	ORGANIZATIONAL VIEW	HOW THIS PLAYS OUT WITH C-LEVEL EXECS
Enjoy activities that increase self-esteem and foster pursuit of individualistic ideas.	Display enthusiasm, even passion, about their work.	Organizational level of stress may be perceived as corrosive and disruptive.	Are hearty, outgoing leaders in many activities, organizing a group of friends or their community.
Are perpetual learners of something new—perhaps through reading, independent study, school.	Are engaged in activities they find compelling, and their excitement and dedication are inspiring to others.		Often feel they cannot play until their work is finished.
Enjoy acquiring new skills and technical knowledge.	Appear strong and athletic with high endurance.		Usually enjoy parties and competitive sports.
May be less aware of their physical well-being and health.	Display passion and enthusiasm about their work—their excitement is contagious.		May be caught off guard at retirement by lack of accomplishment, identity, purpose, and worth they found in work.
Enjoy seeing patterns of ideas in films, books, arts.	Have characteristics of calmness, flexibility, optimism, and trust (along with a moderate perception of resilience).		Senior executives and observers do not perceive behaviors relating to resiliency as highly as they do behaviors relating to leadership.
Find interest in elegant logic of activities such as chess.			May demonstrate more energy than they actually feel they have.

Table 8.7 • Common Observations on How Senior Executives Approach Balancing Work and Life

benefited their organizations by productively aligning with market demands, building a sustainable business model, and ensuring the well-being of their workforce.

But another measure of success goes beyond the walls of the organization and into its community. And it is with this story of effective leadership that I'll end the journey . . . for now.

In 2004 and 2005 the Center for Creative Leadership had the privilege of working with some organizations in the Gulf Coast states. Hurricanes battered the state of Florida in 2004, but that was just a preview of what the region would see in 2005. While the 2005 storms Katrina, Rita, and Wilma had a devastating effect on many communities—some actually disappeared—the city of New Orleans received the most horrific damage from Katrina. The impact on the city's infrastructure was unimaginable.

In recovering from a disaster, restoring water and power is top priority. But if water and power form the air a community breathes, then the banking system is the community's life-blood. After basic services like power and water are restored, a community needs access to financial services to reestablish some level of normalcy.

As the city struggled to get back on its feet, only a limited number of banking offices were able to restore basic services. Meanwhile, New Orleans officials directed that no single bank would reopen until all the banks could reopen, so that no segment of the population would gain an advantage because of access to financial services not available to everyone in the city.

A meeting of senior leaders from all the New Orleans banks was held to review each bank's status for reopening. Looking beyond their individual needs, the banking leaders decided that those offices that had the infrastructure in place to reopen would carve out space to allow their competitors to come in with them. CapitalOne, in other words, would provide space in its bank branches for BankOne. And Bank of America would open space for AmSouth, and so on!

This co-location remained in place for nearly three weeks. The net effect was that New Orleans residents were able to gain access to invaluable financial services that would otherwise have remained off-line. This is truly effective leadership.

APPENDIX A

Leadership Competencies Measured by *Executive Dimensions*

The following chart lists the leadership competencies measured with the *Executive Dimensions* assessment. Beneath each competency are the specific item-level questions used to help draw out an understanding of an executive's strengths and opportunities.

SOUND JUDGMENT

- Sees underlying concepts and patterns in complex situations
- Gives appropriate weight to the concerns of key stakeholders
- Readily grasps the crux of an issue despite having ambiguous information
- Makes effective decisions in a timely manner
- Accurately differentiates between important and unimportant issues
- Develops solutions that effectively address underlying problems

STRATEGIC PLANNING

- Regularly updates plan to reflect changing circumstances
- Translates his or her vision into realistic business strategies
- Weighs concerns of relevant business functions when developing plans
- Articulates wise, long-term objectives and strategies
- Develops plans that balance long-term goals with immediate organizational needs
- Develops plans that contain contingencies for future changes
- Successfully integrates strategic and tactical planning

RESULTS ORIENTATION

- Assigns clear accountability for important objectives
- Pushes the organization to address the concerns of key stakeholders
- Clearly conveys objectives, deadlines, and expectations
- Holds self accountable for meeting commitments
- Aligns organizational resources to accomplish key objectives
- Acts with a sense of urgency

LEADING CHANGE

- Correctly judges which creative ideas will pay off
- Supports activities that position the business for the future
- Pushes the organization to adopt new initiatives
- Offers novel ideas and perspectives
- Fosters a climate of experimentation

GLOBAL AWARENESS

- Leads the organization in understanding international issues and customers
- Monitors global trends that may affect the organization
- Understands how world events might affect the organization's plans
- Seeks opportunities to learn about different cultures and customs
- Adapts behavior to fit different cultural norms

BUSINESS PERSPECTIVE

- Understands the perspectives of different functional areas in the organization
- Understands the strengths and weaknesses of major competitors
- Has a firm grasp of external conditions affecting the organization
- Stays informed about the strategic moves of major competitors
- Regularly seeks data about customer satisfaction

INSPIRING COMMITMENT

- Rallies support throughout the organization to get things done
- Publicly praises others for their performance
- Infuses the organization with a sense of purpose
- Understands what motivates other people to perform at their best
- Provides tangible rewards for significant organizational achievements

FORGING SYNERGY

- Focuses others' energy on common goals, priorities, and problems
- Helps subordinates resolve their conflicts constructively
- Seeks common ground in an effort to resolve conflicts
- Works harmoniously with key stakeholders
- Identifies and removes barriers to effective teamwork
- Maintains smooth, effective working relationships

DEVELOPING AND EMPOWERING

- Delegates work that provides substantial responsibility and visibility
- Acts as a mentor, helping others to develop and advance in their careers
- Supports the decisions and actions of subordinates
- Utilizes others' capabilities appropriately
- Develops staff through constructive feedback and encouragement
- Encourages individual initiative in determining how to achieve broad goals

LEVERAGING DIFFERENCES

- Promotes policies that are sensitive to the needs of a diverse workforce
- Works well with people who differ in race, gender, culture, or age
- Leverages the unique talents and viewpoints of others
- Hires people with a diversity of skills and backgrounds
- Respects employees regardless of their position or background

COMMUNICATING EFFECTIVELY

- Expresses ideas fluently and eloquently
- Prevents unpleasant surprises by communicating important information
- Encourages direct and open discussions about important issues
- Writes clearly and concisely
- Conveys ideas through lively examples and images
- Clearly articulates even the most complex concepts

INTERPERSONAL SAVVY

- Tailors communication based on others' needs, motivations, and agendas
- Understands own impact on situations and people
- Influences others without using formal authority
- Knows when and with whom to build alliances
- Wins concessions from others without harming relationships
- Adjusts leadership style according to the demands of the situation
- Accurately senses when to give and take when negotiating

COURAGE

- Takes the lead on unpopular though necessary actions
- Acts decisively to tackle difficult problems
- Perseveres in the face of problems and difficulties
- Confronts conflicts promptly, so problems do not escalate
- Has the courage to confront others when necessary

EXECUTIVE IMAGE

- Communicates confidence and steadiness during difficult times
- Projects confidence and poise
- Adapts readily to new situations
- Commands attention and respect
- Accepts setbacks with grace

LEARNING FROM EXPERIENCES

- Reflects on and learns from experiences
- Accepts responsibility for his or her problems
- Understands own weaknesses and how to compensate for them
- Seeks candid feedback on his or her performance
- Changes behavior in response to feedback

CREDIBILITY

- Uses ethical considerations to guide decisions
- Through words and deeds encourages honesty throughout the organization
- Speaks candidly about tough issues facing the company
- Tells the truth, not just what important constituents want to hear
- Can be trusted to maintain confidentiality
- Places ethical behavior above personal gain
- Follows through on promises
- Acts in accordance with his or her stated values

APPENDIX B

Executive Dimensions Report Out

On the following pages is an *Executive Dimensions* group profile report for C-level executives attending CCL's Leadership at the Peak program from 2000 to 2004. The group profile report represents the average of all C-level executives and others (including bosses, direct reports, and peers) responding to the assessment. "Importance Ratings" reflect the number of group raters that chose the particular scale as one of the eight most important for success, rated on a scale of 1 (least critical) to 5 (most critical). "Competence Ratings" reflect others' perceptions of C-level executives' strengths in a particular competency, rated on a scale of 1 (deficient) to 5 (exceptional).

Overall for C-Level Leadership at the Peak Participants

Competence Ratings
Self (S) *N* = 137, compared to all observers (O) *N* = 1,395

		Deficient 1	Marginally Effective 2	Effective 3	Highly Effective 4	Exceptional 5
FACTOR I	Sound Judgment				S/O	
Leading the Business	Strategic Planning				S/O	
	Leading Change				S/O	
	Results Orientation				S/O	
	Global Awareness			S/O		
	Business Perspective			S/O		
FACTOR II	Inspiring Commitment				S/O	
Leading Others	Forging Synergy				S/O	
	Developing & Empowering				S/O	
	Leveraging Differences				S/O	
	Communicating Effectively				S/O	
	Interpersonal Savvy				S/O	
FACTOR III	Courage				S/O	
Leading by Personal Example	Executive Image				S/O	
	Learning from Experience				S/O	
	Credibility				S/O	

Note: The lines running through each S and O reflect the confidence interval associated with the inherent inaccuracy that arises when rating a person's behavior. The confidence interval is derived from the dispersion of ratings around the mean rating of all senior executives and observers.

Feedback Report for C-Level Leadership at the Peak Participants

Group Report—Importance Ratings
Self (S) $N = 137$ compared to all observers (O) $N = 1,395$

Scale: 1 = Least Critical to 5 = Most Critical

Factor	Competency	Approximate position (S = Self, O = Observers)
FACTOR I — Leading the Business	Sound Judgment	O and S near 4.5 (S slightly above/right of O)
	Strategic Planning	S above O, near 4.1
	Leading Change	S/O near 4.0
	Results Orientation	S/O near 4.0
	Global Awareness	S near 2.1, O near 2.3
	Business Perspective	S near 3.7, O near 3.8
FACTOR II — Leading Others	Inspiring Commitment	O near 3.95, S near 4.05
	Forging Synergy	S/O near 3.7
	Developing & Empowering	O near 3.7, S near 3.8
	Leveraging Differences	S near 2.9, O near 3.0
	Communicating Effectively	O near 4.0, S near 4.1
	Interpersonal Savvy	S near 3.6, O near 3.7
FACTOR III — Leading by Personal Example	Courage	O near 4.0, S near 4.05
	Executive Image	S/O near 3.6
	Learning from Experience	S/O near 3.55
	Credibility	O near 4.3, S near 4.4

Feedback Report for C-Level LAP Participants

Group Report—Importance Rating
Self (S) $N = 137$ compared to subgroups $N = 1,395$

		Least Critical 1 — 2 — 3 — 4 — 5 Most Critical
FACTOR I **Leading the Business**	Sound Judgment	S, B, P, D near 4.5–4.7
	Strategic Planning	S, B, P near 4.1; D near 4.3
	Leading Change	B, S near 4.0; P near 3.8; D near 4.0
	Results Orientation	S, B, P, D near 4.3
	Global Awareness	S, B, P, D near 2.6–2.8
	Business Perspective	S, B, P, D near 3.5–3.7
FACTOR II **Leading Others**	Inspiring Commitment	B, S near 4.0; P, D near 3.7–3.8
	Forging Synergy	S, B, P, D near 3.6–3.7
	Developing & Empowering	S, B near 3.7; P, D near 3.6–3.7
	Leveraging Differences	S, P, D near 2.6–2.8; B near 3.0
	Communicating Effectively	S, B near 4.1–4.2; P, D near 4.0
	Interpersonal Savvy	S, B, P, D near 3.5–3.7
FACTOR III **Leading by Personal Example**	Courage	S, B near 4.0; P, D near 3.8–4.0
	Executive Image	S, B, P, D near 3.6–3.7
	Learning from Experience	S, B, P, D near 3.5–3.6
	Credibility	S, B near 4.1–4.2; P, D near 4.0

Bosses (B) $N = 147$ Peers (P) $N = 339$ Direct Reports (D) $N = 661$

Group Profile (by Subgroups) for C-Level LAP Participants

Competence Ratings
Self (S) N = 137 compared to all subgroups N = 1,097

		Deficient	Marginally Effective	Effective	Highly Effective	Exceptional
		1	2	3	4	5
FACTOR I	Sound Judgment			S B P D		
Leading the Business	Strategic Planning			S B P D		
	Leading Change			S B P D		
	Results Orientation			S B P D		
	Global Awareness			S B P D		
	Business Perspective			S B P D		
FACTOR II	Inspiring Commitment			S B P D		
Leading Others	Forging Synergy			S B P D		
	Developing & Empowering			S B P D		
	Leveraging Differences			S B P D		
	Communicating Effectively			S B P D		
	Interpersonal Savvy			S B P D		
FACTOR III	Courage			S B P D		
Leading by Personal Example	Executive Image			S B P D		
	Learning from Experience			S B P D		
	Credibility			S B P D		

Bosses (B) N = 147   Peers (P) N = 339   Direct Reports (D) N = 611

References

"The Art of Foresight: Preparing for a Changing World." 2004. *Futurist* 38, no. 3. Updated version available online from the World Future Society, www.wfs.org. Access date: October 26, 2006.

Baer, M., Oldham, G., and Cummings, A. 2003. "Rewarding Creativity: When Does It Really Matter?" *Leadership Quarterly* 14 (2003): 569–586.

Balanced Scorecard Collaborative. 2007. "Building a Strategy-Focused Organization." Available online: www.bscol.org/education/conferences/executive/index.cfm?id=8123D0DF-B9B3-83AC-FE60E5DD0F9636452007.

Barna, G., and Hatch, M. 2001. *Boiling Point.* Ventura, CA: Regal Books.

Basadur, M. 2004. "Leading Others to Think Innovatively Together: Creative Leadership," *Leadership Quarterly* 15: 103–121.

Behrman, J. 1988. *Essays of Ethics in Business and the Professions.* Englewood Cliffs, NJ: Prentice Hall.

Beinhocker, E. 1997. "Strategy at the Edge of Chaos." *McKinsey Quarterly* 3, no. 1:25–39.

Bennett, J., Pernsteiner, T., Kocourek, P. and Hedlund, S. 2003. "The Organization vs. the Strategy." *Strategy & Business* 21.

Bennis, W. 2004. "What Do Leaders Know?" *Executive Excellence* 21, no. 12:3–4.

Black, J., Morrison, A., and Gregersen, H. 1999. *Global Explorers.* New York: Routledge.

Blackaby, H., and Blackaby, R. 2001. *Spiritual Leadership.* Nashville: Broadman and Holman.

Booz Allen Hamilton. 2002. "When Everyone Agrees, but Nothing Changes." November. Booz Allen Hamilton. Available online: www.boozallen.com/media/file/126123.pdf.

Brandt, J. 2002. *The 50-Mile Rule: Your Guide to Infidelity and Extramarital Etiquette.* Berkeley, CA: Ten Speed Press. Available online: www.the50milerule. com/50milewelcome.html. Access date: October 27, 2006.

Breen, B. 2004. "The 6 Myths of Creativity," *Fast Company* (December), 75–78.

Brown, D. 2005. *Study Documents Ethical Problems in Youth Sports.* University of Notre Dame. November 29. Available online: http://newsinfo.nd.edu/content. cfm?topicid=14762. Access date: October 27, 2006.

Campbell, D., and Hyne, S. 1995. *COS Campbell Organizational Survey Manual.* Colorado Springs, CO: Pearson Reid London House.

Cappelli, P., and Hamori, M. 2005. "The New Road to the Top," *Harvard Business Review* 83 (January): 25–32.

CCL. 2000. *Executive Dimensions Development Planning Guide.* Greensboro, NC: Center for Creative Leadership.

———. 2004. *Campbell Leadership Index.* Greensboro, NC: Center for Creative Leadership.

Charan, R., Drotter, S., and Noel, J. 2001. *The Leadership Pipeline.* San Francisco: Jossey-Bass.

Chewning, R. 2000. "Hermeneutics and Biblical Ethics: An Illustration: God's Immutability and Human Integrity," *Journal of Biblical Integration in Business.*

Churchill, W. 1941. *Blood, Sweat and Tears.* New York: Putnam.

CLC. 2003. *Corporate Ethics: The Mission for HR.* Washington, DC: Corporate Leadership Council.

CLO Media. 2005. "IBM Report: Baby Boomers Will Leave Growth at Risk," *Chief Learning Officer.* Available online: www.clomedia.com/common/newscenter/newsdisplay.cfm?id=3887. Access date: October 27, 2006.

Collins, J. 2005. "Level 5 Leadership: The Triumph of Humility and Fierce Resolve," *Harvard Business Review* (July–August): 136–139.

Conger, J., and Nadler, D. 2004. "When CEOs Step Up to Fail," *MIT Sloan Management Review* 45, no. 3:50–56.

Conley, J., and Wagner-Marsh, F., eds. 1998. *The Integration of Business Ethics and Spirituality in the Workplace.* New York: Wiley.

Conley, L. 2004. "Innovation Scorecard," *Fast Company* (December): 65–67.

CPP, Inc. 2005. *FIRO-B® and MBTI® Form K Modal Profiles.* Mountain View, CA: CPP, Inc.

Daft, R. 2004. *Organization Theory and Design,* 8th ed. Mason, OH: Thomson South-Western.

Donaldson, G., and Lorsch, J. 1983. *Decision Making at the Top.* New York: Basic Books.

Drath, W. H. 2003. "Leading Together: Complex Challenges Require a New Approach," *Leadership in Action* (March–April).

Engstrom, P. "21st Century Leadership Challenges." 2005. Talk recorded May 17. SAIC, Greensboro, NC.

Gadiesh, O., and Gilbert, J. 2001."Transform Corner-Office Strategy into Frontline Action," *Harvard Business Review on Advances in Strategy* 79, no. 5 (May): 72–79.

Galbraith, J. 2000. *Designing the Global Corporation.* San Francisco: Jossey-Bass.

———. 2002. *Designing Organizations.* San Francisco: Jossey-Bass.

Gandossy, R., and Kao, T. 2004. *Channels to Anywhere: The Supply Chain for Global Talent.* Lincolnshire, IL: Hewitt Associates.

Gartner, J. 1963. *Self-Renewal.* New York: Harper and Row.

Gelb, M. 1998. *How to Think Like Leonardo Da Vinci.* New York: Dell.

Gilbert, D. 2006. *Stumbling on Happiness.* New York: Knopf.

Greenleaf, R. 1998.*The Power of Servant Leadership.* San Francisco: Berrett-Koehler.

———. 2002. *Servant Leadership.* New York: Paulist Press.

Gryskiewicz, S. 2005. "Leading Renewal: The Value of Positive Turbulence," *Leadership in Action* 25, no. 1:8–12.

GuideStar. 2007. Salvation Army National Corp. Available online: http://partners.guidestar.org/controller/searchResults.gs?action_gsReport=1&partner=networkforgood&ein=22-2406433.

Gurvis, J., and Patterson, G. 2005. "Balancing Act—Finding Equilibrium Between Work and Life," *Leadership in Action* 24, no. 6:3–8.

Hackman, M., and Johnson, C. 2000. *Leadership, a Communication Perspective,* 3rd ed. Prospect Heights, IL: Waveland Press.

Hammett, P. 2005a. "Entremanures Kill Innovations," *Sales and Service Excellence* 5, no. 5:16.

———. 2005b. "Leadership Anthropology," *Chief Learning Officer* (July). Available online: www.clomedia.com/content/templates/clo_article.asp?articleid= 1018& zoneid=29. Access date: October 24, 2006.

———. 2005c. "There Are No Points for Original Thought." *Leadership Advance Online* (spring). Available online: www.regent.edu/acad/global/publications/lao/issue_5/there_are_hammett.htm.

Hargadon, A. 2005. "Technology Brokering and Innovation: Linking Strategy, Practice and People." *Strategy & Leadership* 33, no. 1:32–36.

Hartman, A., Sifonis, J., and Kador, J. 2000. "Executive Summary: Net-Ready Strategies for Success in the E-Conomy." Cisco Systems. Available online: www.cisco.com/warp/public/779/ibs/netreadiness/netready_es3.pdf.

Hay Group. 2003. *Designing the Accountable Organization.* N.p.: Hay Group.

Henry, M. 1996. *Mathew Henry's Commentary of the Whole Bible.* Montville, CT: Hendrickson.

Hirsh, S., and Kummerow, J. 1998. *Introduction to Type® in Organizations,* 3rd ed. Mountain View, CA: CPP, Inc.

Hitchens, C. 2004. *Powell Valediction.* Available online: www.foreignpolicy.com. Access date: October 14, 2005.

Hofstede, G. 2001. *Culture's Consequence.* Thousand Oaks, CA: Sage.

The Holy Bible: New International Version. 1996. Grand Rapids, IA: Zondervan.

Howe, N., and Strauss, B. 1991. "The Cycle of Generations," *American Demographics* 13, no. 4:24–52.

———. 1992. "The New Generation Gap," *Atlantic* 270, no. 6:67–83.

Hudson, F. 1991. *The Adult Years.* San Francisco: Jossey-Bass.

Hughes, R., and Beatty, K. 2005. *Becoming a Strategic Leader.* San Francisco: Jossey-Bass.

Isachsen, O., and Berebs, L. 1991. *Working Together: A Personality-Centered Approach to Management.* Coronado, CA: Neworld Management Press.

Jaffe, D., and Scott, C. 1984. *From Burnout to Balance.* New York: McGraw-Hill.

Joas, H. 2000. *The Genesis of Values.* Chicago: Chicago Press.

Johnston, R., and Bate, D. 2003. *The Power of Strategy Innovation.* New York: AMACOM.

Josephson Institute. 2006. Josephson Institute Report Card on the Ethics of American Youth. Part 1: Integrity Summary of Data. Available online: www.josephsoninstitute.org/reportcard/.

Kahtamaki, M., Kekale, T., and Viitala, R. 2004. "Trust and Innovation: From Spin-Off Idea to Stock Exchange," *Creativity and Innovation Management* 13, no. 2: 75–78.

Kaplan, R., and Norton, D. 2000. "Having Trouble with Your Strategy? Then Map It." *Harvard Business Review* 78, no. 5 (September–October): 167–176.

———. 2001. *The Strategy-Focused Organization.* Boston: Harvard Business School Press.

Kaplan, R., Draft, W., and Kofodimos, J. 1991. *Beyond Ambition.* San Francisco: Jossey-Bass.

Kotter, J. 1985. *Power and Influence: Beyond Formal Authority.* New York: Free Press.

Kramer, R., and Neale, M., eds. 1998. *Power and Influence in Organizations.* Thousand Oaks, CA: Sage.

Krantz, L. 2000. *Jobs Rated Almanac, 2001: The Best and Worst Jobs—250 in All— Ranked by More Than a Dozen Vital Factors Including Salary, Stress, Benefits, and More,* 5th ed. New York: St. Martin's Press.

Krause, D. 2004. "Influence-Based Leadership as a Determinant of the Inclination to Innovate and of Innovation-Related Behaviors: An Empirical Investigation," *Leadership Quarterly* 15, no. 1 (February): 79–103.

Lee, C., and Pinney, A. 2002. *So What! Now What?* Cascade, CO.: Catalyst Consulting.

Leonard, D., and Rayport, J. 1997. "Spark Innovation Through Empathic Design." *Harvard Business Review* 75, no. 6:102–113.

Levesque, L. 2001. *Breakthrough Creativity.* Mountain View, CA: Davies-Black Publishing.

Lombardo, M., and Eichinger, R. 2000. *FYI—For Your Improvement.* Minneapolis: Lominger Limited.

Lopinot, J. 2005. "UMSL Researchers Examine Ethics in Youth Sports." University of Missouri, November 28. Available online: www.umsl.edu/services/ur/media/newsrel/nov28ethics.htm. Access date: December 1, 2005.

Luporter, C. 2000a. "Communicating with Generation Y." *Workforce Management*.

———. 2000b."What Gen Y-ers Are Looking For in Their First Job," *Workforce Management*.

Malina, M., and Selto, F. 2002. "Communicating and Controlling Strategy: An Empirical Study of the Effectiveness of the Balanced Scorecard." May 16. Available online: www.bettermanagement.com/library/library.aspx?l=635. Access date: October 28, 2006.

Marsh, N., and McAllum, M. 2002. *Strategic Foresight: The Power of Standing in the Future*. Melbourne, Australia: Crown Content.

Martin, A. 2005. *The Changing Nature of Leadership*. Greensboro, NC: Center for Creative Leadership.

Martineau, J., and Hannum, K. 2004. *Leadership Development Business Case*. Greensboro, NC: Center for Creative Leadership.

Maslach, C., and Leiter, M. 1997. *The Truth About Burnout*. San Francisco: Jossey-Bass.

McCall, M., and Kaplan, R. 1990. *Whatever It Takes: The Realities of Managerial Decision Making*. Englewood Cliffs, NJ: Prentice Hall.

McCauley, C. 2005. "Stress and the Eye of the Beholder," *Leadership in Action* 25, no. 1:3–7.

———. 2006. *Developmental Assignments: Creating Learning Experiences Without Changing Jobs*. Greensboro, NC: CCL Press.

McCauley, C., and Van Velsor, E., eds. 2003. *The Center for Creative Leadership Handbook of Leadership Development*, 2nd ed. San Francisco: Jossey-Bass.

McDowell-Larsen, S. 2002. "Stress Takes a Toll on Leaders," *Leadership in Action* 22, no. 2:18–19.

McSwain, L. 1995. "Christian Ethics and the Business Ethos." In *On Moral Business*, edited by M. L. Stackhouse, D. P. McCann, S. Roels, and P. N. Williams, Grand Rapids, MI: Eerdmans.

Merriam-Webster. 2005. "Merriam-Webster Online." Available online: www.m-w.com. Access date: October 27, 2006.

Meyer, A., Tsui, A., and Hinings, C. 1993. "Configurational Approaches to Organizational Analysis," *Academy of Management Journal* 36, no. 6:1175–1195.

Michalko, M. 2001. *Cracking Creativity*. Berkeley, CA: Ten Speed Press.

Mintzberg, H. 1994. *The Rise and Fall of Strategic Planning*. New York: Free Press.

———. 1996. "Musings on Management." *Harvard Business Review* 74, no. 4 (July–August): 61–67.

Mintzberg, H., Ahlstrand, B., and Lampel, J. 1998. *Strategy Safari*. New York: Free Press.

"Moral Relativism—Neutral Thinking?" 2003. *All About God*. September 15. Available online: www.moral-relativism.com. Access date: October 26, 2006.

Myers, I. 1998. *Introduction to Type®*, 6th ed. Mountain View, CA: CPP, Inc.

Nadler, D. 2005. "Confessions of a Trusted Adviser," *Harvard Business Review* (September): 67–69.

NASA. 1986. *Shuttle Mission Archive.* Available online: www-pao.ksc.nasa.gov/kscpao/shuttle/missions/51-l/mission-51-l.html.

Neilson, G., Pasternack, B., and Mendes, D. 2003. "The Four Bases of Organizational DNA," *Strategy & Business,* no. 23:1–10.

Nilsen, D., and Campbell, D. 1998. *Development Planning Guide for the CLI Campbell Leadership Index.* Colorado Springs, CO: Pearson Reid London House.

Norris, M. 2005. "When the Great Ones Turn to Coaching." *All Things Considered,* August 8. Audio segment. Available online: www.npr.org/templates/story/story.php?storyId=4791079. Access date: October 27, 2006.

O'Neil, J. 1994. *The Paradox of Success.* New York: Putnam.

Palus, C., and Horth, D. 2002. *The Leader's Edge.* San Francisco: Jossey-Bass.

Patton, M. 1990. *Qualitative Evaluation and Research Methods.* Newbury Park, CA: Sage.

Pearce, J., and Doh, J. 2005. "The High Impact of Collaborative Social Initiatives." *Sloan Management Review* 46, no. 3.

Pearson. 2005a. *Campbell Leadership Index.* Minneapolis, MN: NCS Pearson.

———. 2005b. *Campbell Organization Survey.* Minneapolis, MN: NCS Pearson.

"President Truman Did Not Understand." 1960. Interview with Leo Szilard. *U.S. News & World Report.* August 15. Available online: www.peak.org/~danneng/decision/usnews.html. Access date: October 27, 2006.

Price, T. 2006. *Understanding Ethical Failures in Leadership.* New York: Cambridge University Press.

Provost, J. 1990. *Work, Play, and Type: Achieving Balance in Your Life.* Mountain View, CA: Davies-Black Publishing.

Rogers, M. S. 2005. *The Capability Within: The Role of HR in a Growth Economy.* IBM. Available online: www.general-hosting.com/leaderic/IBM2005GlobalHumanCapitalStudy.pdf

Rokeach, M. 1979. *Understanding Human Values.* New York: Free Press.

Rothwell, W. J. 2001. *Effective Succession Planning.* New York: AMACOM.

The Ryrie Study Bible. 1976. Chicago: Moody Press.

Sanders, I. 1998. *Strategic Thinking and the New Science.* New York: Free Press.

Savage, G., Nix, T., Whitehead, C., and Blair, J. 1991. "Strategies for Assessing and Managing Organizational Stakeholders," *Academy of Management Executive* 5, no. 2:61–75.

Schnell, E., and Hammer, A. 1993. *Introduction to the FIRO-B® in Organizations.* Mountain View, CA: CPP, Inc.

Schultz, W. 1995. "Futures Fluency: Explorations in Leadership, Vision, and Creativity." Unpublished PhD dissertation, University of Hawaii.

Schwartz, P. 1991. *The Art of the Long View.* New York: Doubleday Currency.

Seabrook, A. 2005. "Scandals Raise Questions over Congressional Ethics." *Talk of the Nation.* National Public Radio. December 27. Available online: www.npr.org/templates/story/story.php?storyId=5070998.

Seivert, S. 2001. *The Balancing Act.* Rochester, NY: Part Street Press.

Select Bipartisan Committee to Investigate the Preparation for and Response to Hurricane Katrina. 2005. *A Failure of Initiative.* Washington, DC: U.S. House of Representatives.

Senge, P. 1990. *The Fifth Discipline.* New York: Doubleday Currency.

Senge, P., and Joni, S. 2005. "Outside Insight: Balancing Private and Public Inquiry," *Reflections* 6, no. 1. Available online by subscription only: www.reflections.solonline.org.

Shalley, C., and Gilson, L. 2004. "What Leaders Need to Know: A Review of Social and Contextual Factors That Can Foster or Hinder Creativity." *Leadership Quarterly* 15: 33–53.

Shavinina, L., ed. 2003. *The International Handbook on Innovation.* Oxford, England: Pergamon.

Shaw, G., Brown, R., and Bromiley, P. 2002. "Strategic Stories: How 3M Is Rewriting Business Planning." In *Harvard Business Review on Advances in Strategy,* 51–70.

Shields, D., Bredemeier, L., LaVoi, N., and Power, F. 2005. "The Sport Behavior of Youth, Parents, and Coaches: The Good, the Bad, and the Ugly." *Journal of Research in Character Education* 3, no. 1 (December): 43–59.

Silzer, R., ed. 2002. *The 21st Century Executive.* San Francisco: Jossey-Bass.

Slaughter, R. 1995. *The Foresight Principle.* Westport, CT: Praeger.

Stackhouse, M., McCann, D., Roels, S., and Williams, P., eds. 1995. *On Moral Business.* Grand Rapids, MI: Eerdmans.

Sternberg, R., ed. 1999. *Handbook of Creativity.* New York: Cambridge University Press.

Sternberg, R., Kaufman, J., and Pertz, J. 2004. "A Propulsion Model of Creative Leadership," *Leadership Quarterly* 14, no. 415:455–474.

Swenson, R. *Margin.* 1992. Colorado Springs, CO: NavPress.

Taylor, J., and Wacker, W. 2000. *The Visionary's Handbook.* New York: Harper Business.

Taylor, S. 2005. "The Leadership Gap: The Present State of Leadership and Strategies for Preparing Leaders." June 8. American Society for Training and Development.

Truman, H. 1945. Diary, July 25. Available online: www.dannen.com/decision/hst-jl25.html. Access date: October 27, 2006.

Tucker, E., Kao, T., and Verma, N. 2005. *Next-Generation Talent Management: Insights on How Workforce Trends Are Changing the Face of Talent Management.* Lincolnshire, IL: Hewitt Associates.

Tushman, M., and O'Reilly, C. 1997. *Winning Through Innovation.* Boston: Harvard Business School Press.

Van Velsor, E. 2005. *Using Action Learning Teams to Enhance Organizational Capacity for Leadership.* Greensboro, NC: Center for Creative Leadership.

VandeHei, J. 2005. "Bush Orders Staff to Attend Ethics Briefings," *Washington Post.*

Waterman, J., and Rogers, J. 2004. *Introduction to the FIRO-B® Instrument.* Mountain View, CA: CPP, Inc.

Weiss, D., and Molinaro, V. 2005. *The Leadership Gap.* Mississauga, Ontario: Wiley Canada.

Wilkinson, B. 2003. *The Dream Giver.* Sisters, OR: Multnomah.

Wren, D. A. 1994. *The Evolution of Management Thought.* New York: Wiley.

Yukl, G. 2002. *Leadership in Organizations.* Upper Saddle River, NJ: Prentice Hall.

Index